A Practical Guide to Small Claims

Jeanne Cox

Whilst every care has been taken to ensure the accuracy of the contents of this work, no responsibility for loss occasioned to any person acting or refraining from action as a result of any statement in it can be accepted by any of the authors or the publishers.

First published 1994

Second edition December 1999
Third edition October 2002

A Practical Guide to Small Claims

Third Edition

by Alan Simons LLB
District Judge at Swindon County Court

and Caroline Harmer
Barrister, Legal Training Consultant

Original text by
George Applebey LLB, MCL, ACI Arb
Faculty of Law, The University of Birmingham

Members of the LexisNexis Group worldwide

United Kingdom	LexisNexis Butterworths Tolley, a Division of Reed Elsevier (UK) Ltd, Halsbury House, 35 Chancery Lane, LONDON, WC2A 1EL
Argentina	LexisNexis Argentina, BUENOS AIRES
Australia	LexisNexis Butterworths, CHATSWOOD, New South Wales
Austria	LexisNexis Verlag ARD Orac GmbH & Co KG, VIENNA
Canada	LexisNexis Butterworths, MARKHAM, Ontario
Chile	LexisNexis Chile Ltda, SANTIAGO DE CHILE
Czech Republic	Nakladatelství Orac sro, PRAGUE
France	Editions du Juris-Classeur SA, PARIS
Hong Kong	LexisNexis Butterworths, HONG KONG
Hungary	HVG-Orac, BUDAPEST
India	LexisNexis Butterworths, NEW DELHI
Ireland	Butterworths (Ireland) Ltd, DUBLIN
Italy	Giurè Editore, MILAN
Malaysia	Malayan Law Journal Sdn Bhd, KUALA LUMPUR
New Zealand	LexisNexis Butterworths, WELLINGTON
Poland	Wydawnictwo Prawnicze LexisNexis, WARSAW
Singapore	LexisNexis Butterworths, SINGAPORE
South Africa	Butterworths SA, DURBAN
Switzerland	Stämpfli Verlag AG, BERNE
USA	LexisNexis, DAYTON, Ohio

© George Applebey 2002

All rights reserved. No part of this publication may be reproduced in any material form (including photocopying or storing it in any medium by electronic means and whether or not transiently or incidentally to some other use of this publication) without the written permission of the copyright owner except in accordance with the provisions of the Copyright, Designs and Patents Act 1988 or under the terms of a licence issued by the Copyright Licensing Agency Ltd, 90 Tottenham Court Road, London, England W1T 4LP. Applications for the copyright owner's written permission to reproduce any part of this publication should be addressed to the publisher.

Warning: The doing of an unauthorised act in relation to a copyright work may result in both a civil claim for damages and criminal prosecution.

Crown copyright material is reproduced with the permission of the Controller of HMSO and the Queen's Printer for Scotland.

A CIP Catalogue record for this book is available from the British Library.

ISBN 0 7545 1760 8

Typeset in Great Britain by YHT Ltd, London
Printed and bound in Great Britain by Hobbs the Printers Ltd, Totton, Hampshire

Visit Butterworths LexisNexis *direct* at www.butterworths.com

Preface to the first edition (extract)

The aim of this little volume is to provide a readable description of the procedure and practice of small claims in the network of county courts throughout England and Wales. It also gives a brief account of arbitration schemes available to consumers as an alternative to going to court. I have tried to deal with the subject so as to be of use not only to the average small business or private individual who may become involved with their own small claim or recovery of a debt, but also to the legal practitioner or other professional who requires a concise guide to this area of law, and as a handbook for the many advisers, both unpaid and professional, who help small litigants and who are now given a statutory right to appear in court, on others behalf. Research has shown that businesses both large and small continue to avail themselves of the advantages of the streamlined small claims process, often on a recurring basis, for the recovery of debts. The small claims court is also a forum for consumer complaints. This book can be used either from a plaintiffs or defendants point of view, and whether the person suing is in business or not. It also includes a chapter on the final (and often most difficult part) of the procedure, namely enforcement of judgment.

Trying to appeal to such a wide readership is not, of course, easy. The free booklet which used to be available from the county courts was described by one commentator as an attempt to reconcile the irreconcilable – in trying to describe how to sue or defend without a lawyer in a system designed for and developed by solicitors. The system itself is changing, however, and the recent reforms described in this book should provide better access to justice for litigants in person as well as improvements in court efficiency.

In 1973, an American, Douglas Matthews, wrote a small claims book entitled *Sue the B*st*rds*. Subtitled The Victims Handbook, it explained how to get even with a host of oppressors. The purpose of the book was to make the reader armed and dangerous. That is far from the intention here. Legal action should normally be treated with caution. When embarked upon, it has to be done with a clear view of the difficulties involved. Having said this, the small claims procedure is designed for the ordinary person to use on his or her own and when the occasion arises

Preface to the first edition (extract)

they should do so with confidence. Many thousands have already done so successfully. It is hoped that this book will help others in the future.
The law as stated applies only to England and Wales, not to Northern Ireland, nor sadly (writing as a Glaswegian) does it apply to Scotland, since both of the latter have their own small claims procedure as befits their status as distinct legal systems.

1994
George Applebey
Faculty of Law
The University of Birmingham

Preface to the third edition

Having been concerned with the second updating of this book, I have been asked to write the preface to the third edition and I have felt it appropriate to include a lengthy extract from the preface George Applebey wrote, in the summer of 1994, to the very successful first edition. It not only details the 'target' audience at which the book was and remains aimed, but it also shows that George Applebey's view of litigation sits comfortably with the Civil Procedure Rules 1998 with their accompanying Practice Directions and Protocols. It has not been necessary to alter the thrust of the first edition, but the book has been updated and rewritten where necessary to properly reflect the CPR and the 28 amendments made to them.

I am extremely hopeful that the third edition of this book will prove invaluable to its target audience and additionally will assist those advocates, legal executives, solicitors or barristers attracted to the small claims track by reason of the increase in jurisdiction and the more complex disputes litigated. The arguments over 'credit hire', litigated to the House of Lords, are complex but have mainly been argued on the small claims track. This book should enable such advocates to acclimatise more easily to the different rules and methods employed on this track. The needs of the lay litigant and the litigation friend have, nevertheless, been fully met in this edition as they were in the previous editions.

The first three chapters and Chapter 14 of the book have been updated and enhanced by Caroline Harmer and I have updated and where necessary rewritten the remaining chapters. New forms have been reproduced and precedents introduced. The new enforcement provisions which came into force this year are fully dealt with. The contact addresses and telephone numbers have been updated.

It remains for me to acknowledge that this book relies very much on George Applebey's original research and application, and to thank my wife, Yvonne, and friends at Butterworths Tolley for their help throughout my work on this third edition. This book is generally up to date to 31 August 2002 and by dealing with the pilot scheme 'Money Claim Online' and the pilot scheme running at Lincoln, Wandsworth and Wigan until 7 October 2002 dispensing with allocation questionnaires on

Preface to the third edition

the small claims track, I have tried to prepare readers for future possible changes.

2002
Alan Simons
District Judge
Swindon County Court

A note on using this book

Those who have purchased this book as a practical guide to pursuing or defending their own small claim can be spared going through each chapter in numerical order if they adopt these simple directions.
If you are a claimant:

(a) A consumer claim. Read Chapters 1, 2, 3, 4 and *then* Chapter 14, before deciding whether and how to proceed. Thereafter Chapters 5–13.

(b) A business pursuing debts or other action. Read Chapters 1 and 4 and then 5–13. You may proceed quite swiftly – Chapter 8 (Judgment in default) and Chapter 13 (Enforcing judgment) should prove most useful.

If you are a defendant, begin at Chapter 8, then read Chapter 5 onwards.

Contents

	page
The main steps in the procedure up to judgment in the county court	xv
Glossary of terms contained in the Civil Procedure Rules	xvi
Glossary of other legal terms	xix

Chapter 1:	**Introduction**	1
	1. Actions for debt	2
	2. Breach of contract and consumer claims	2
	(a) Defective goods	3
	(b) Stop Now Orders (EC Directive) Regulations 2001	4
	(c) Unfair contract terms	5
	(d) Defective services	6
	(e) Consumer Protection (Distance Selling) Regulations 2000	6
	(f) E-commerce Directive	7
	(g) The existence of a contract	7
	(h) Advice and information	7
Chapter 2:	**What are small claims?**	9
	1. Type of claim covered by small claims procedure	9
	2. Some points to note about small claims	10
	3. What are not small claims?	13
	4. Examples of small claims	13
	(a) Holiday nightmare	13
	(b) The faulty PC	13
	(c) New house in the wilderness	14
	(d) The tables turned	14
	(e) Crushed finger	14
	5. Points of law	15
Chapter 3:	**Complaining**	16
	1. Small consumer disputes	16
	(a) Stages in complaining	16
	(b) Defective goods	16

Contents

	(c) Bad workmanship	18
	(d) Building contractors	19
	(e) Other complaints	20
	2. Seeking recovery of a debt	20
	(a) Before commencing legal proceedings	21
	(b) Negotiating a settlement	21

Chapter 4: **Getting advice** 22
1. Advice centres 22
   (a) Consumer advice 22
   (b) Legal advice centres 23
2. Citizens Advice Bureaux (CABx) 23
3. Solicitors 24
   (a) Free or cheap legal advice 25
   (b) Insurance policies 25
   (c) Web sites 25
4. The county courts 25
5. Which? Legal Service 26
6. Trade unions 28
7. Money advice or debt counselling centres 28
8. Negotiating a settlement 29
   (a) 'Without prejudice' 29
9. Letters before action 30

Chapter 5: **The county courts** 32
1. The personnel of the courts 33
   (a) Judges 33
   (b) Administrative staff 33
   (c) Bailiffs 34
2. Small claims procedure 34
   (a) The sources of small claims rules 35
   (b) A word of warning 36
   (c) Practice directions 36
   (d) Forms 36
   (e) The implementation of Lord Woolf's two reports on Access to Justice by the Civil Procedure Rules 36
3. The Courts Charter 37

Chapter 6: **Who to sue?** 39
1. Claims for debt or breach of contract 39
2. Actions in negligence 40
   (a) Motor accidents 41
   (b) Medical negligence claims 41
   (c) Employers' liability 41
   (d) Dangerous premises 42
   (e) Defective products 42
   (f) Other tort actions 42

		3. Special parties	42
		(a) Companies and other corporate bodies	43
		(b) Partnerships	44
		(c) Persons under disability – children and patients	44
		(d) Death of one of the parties	45
		(e) Bankruptcy	45
		(f) Vexatious litigants	46
		4. Doubts over who to sue	46
		5. Time limits for bringing actions	46
Chapter 7:		**Starting legal action**	48
		1. Which court?	49
		(a) Which court to commence proceedings?	49
		(b) In which court will the hearing take place?	50
		2. The claim form – CPR Part 7	50
		(a) Filling in the claim form	51
		(b) Value	57
		(c) Multiple claims	60
		(d) Money claims online	60
		3. Service	62
		(a) By post	62
		(b) By court bailiff	62
		(c) Personal service	63
		(d) Service by alternative method	63
		(e) Service on special parties	63
		(f) How do you know on what date the person receives the claim form?	66
		(g) What happens if the defendant does not receive the claim form?	66
Chapter 8:		**Judgment in default; admitting or defending a claim; summary judgment**	67
		1. What to do when you receive a claim form	67
		2. Judgment in default	70
		(a) Calculation of time	70
		(b) If the defendant ignores the claim form	71
		(c) Entering judgment	71
		3. Admitting the claim	72
		(a) The defendant	72
		(b) The claimant	72
		(c) Reviewing the decision of the court staff – CPR r 14.13	73
		(d) The appointment	74
		(e) Admitting part of the claim	74
		4. Payment of money claimed	75
		5. Defending the claim	75
		6. Counterclaims – CPR Part 20	77
		7. Setting aside judgment	78
		(a) Grounds for setting aside judgment	78

Contents

	8. Defended actions: which court? – CPR r 26.2	78
	(a) Transfer to another court	79
	(b) Possible grounds for arguing for change of court	79
	9. Summary judgment	79
	10. Forms	81
	(a) Form N205A – notice of issue (specified amount)	81
	(b) Form N205B – notice of issue (unspecified amount)	82
	(c) Form N225 – request for judgment and reply to admission (specified amount)	83
Chapter 9:	**Before the hearing**	84
	1. Should the claim be discontinued?	84
	2. Allocation to track	85
	3. Small claims track or fast or multi-track	86
	4. Completing the allocation questionnaire	89
	4A. The small claims pilot scheme – CPR 27 Practice Direction 27B	90
	5. Directions and preliminary hearings	90
	(a) Directions	90
	(b) A preliminary hearing? – CPR r 27.6	91
	(c) Non-appearance at preliminary hearing	93
	(d) Disposal without a hearing	93
	(e) Changing the hearing date	93
	6. Dropping the action or settling	93
	7. Amending the claim or defence – CPR Part 17	94
	8. Counterclaims and defences to counterclaims – CPR Part 20	95
	9. Indemnity or contribution – CPR Part 20	95
	10. Preparing your case for the hearing	95
	(a) Exclusion of rules of civil procedure	95
	(b) Proper evidence	96
	11. Small claims on site	99
	12. Forms and directions	100
	(a) Form N150 – allocation questionnaire	100
	(b) Appendix A to the CPR Part 27 Practice Direction	105
Chapter 10:	**The hearing**	110
	1. To appear on your own or with a representative?	110
	2. Lay representatives	111
	(a) Companies in court	111
	(b) The Lay Representatives (Rights of Audience) Order 1999	111
	(c) The fees of a lay representative	113
	3. Lawyers – a barrister, solicitor or legal executive employed by a solicitor	113

4. Attendance at court		114
5. The judge		115
6. The hearing		115
(a) Documents only?		116
(b) Hearings in Wales		116
(c) Non-English speakers		117
(d) Putting parties or witnesses on oath		117
(e) Presenting your case		117
(f) The importance of evidence		118
(g) Experts		119
(h) Non-attendance by the parties		119
(i) Setting aside judgment – CPR r 27.11		120
7. The judgment		120
8. Appeals		121
(a) Permission required		121
(b) The appellant's appeal notice		121
(c) Grounds to be established to obtain permission		122
(d) Documents to be filed with the appeal notice		122
(e) Respondent's notice		122
(f) Hearing of the appeal		123
(g) The order appealed against		123
(h) Costs		123
9. Small claims for more than £5,000		124
10. Judgment of the court		124

Chapter 11: **No costs** 125
    1. When costs can be claimed 125
    2. Unreasonable behaviour 127
    3. Inflating a claim to recover costs 128
    4. The question of costs considered 128
    5. The fees or charges of a lay representative 128
    6. Litigants in Person (Costs and Expenses) Act 1975 128
    7. Costs in small personal injury claims 129
    8. Costs of an appeal – CPR r 27.14(2)(c) 129

Chapter 12: **Small personal injury claims** 130
    1. The difficulties with personal injury claims 132
    2. Seeking advice about personal injuries 133
    3. Pre-action protocol for personal injury claims 134
    4. Issue of claim 134
    5. Allocation of claim 134
    6. Valuing a small personal injury claim 134
    7. Pre-action protocol for personal injury claims 136

Chapter 13: **Enforcing judgment** 150
    1. Introduction 150

Contents

2. The court order	151
3. Payment of a judgment debt	151
(a) Immediate payment or instalment orders?	151
(b) Variation of orders	152
4. Registration of county court judgments	152
(a) Credit repair companies	154
5. The effect of judgment	155
6. Orders to obtain information from the judgment debtor – CPR 71	155
(a) Attending the examination hearing	156
(b) The questions	156
(c) Conclusion of the examination	157
Methods of enforcement	157
7. Warrant of execution – seizure and sale of goods	157
(a) Procedure	158
(b) Disputes as to ownership – retained County Court Rules, Order 33	158
(c) Effect of insolvency	159
(d) Other creditors	159
(e) What if the goods are elsewhere?	159
(f) Withdrawal or suspension of execution process	159
(g) Fees	160
(h) County court bailiffs	160
(i) The levy procedure	161
(j) Enforcement in the High Court	162
8. Third party debt orders – Part 72 CPR	162
(a) Making and serving the application	162
(b) Further consideration of the interim order	163
(c) Hearing of the application for a final third party debt order	163
(d) Hardship payment orders	163
9. Attachment of earnings order	163
(a) Obtaining information from the employer	164
(b) The amount of the order	165
10. Charging order – CPR Part 73	165
11. Insolvency or bankruptcy	166
12. Costs of enforcing judgment	167
Chapter 14: Alternatives to the county court	168
Mediation and conciliation	168
Arbitration	169
1. Arbitration clauses in contracts	169
2. Arbitration Act 1996, ss 89–91	170
3. Trade association arbitration schemes	170
(a) A better alternative?	171
(b) Court or arbitration? Factors to consider	171
(c) The Chartered Institute of Arbitrators	172
(d) How to use the schemes	173

	(e) Codes of practice – the main schemes approved by the OFT	174
	(f) The Chartered Institute of Arbitrators	174
	(g) Dispute Resolution Services of the Chartered Institute of Arbitrators	175
Appendices:	Contents	179
Appendix 1:	Some current county court fees	180
Appendix 2:	Principles of allocation – CPR Part 26.5–26.10 and Practice Direction to Part 26 paragraphs 7 and 8	183
Appendix 3:	Conduct of hearings on the small claims track – CPR Part 27 and associated Practice Direction	189
Appendix 4:	Practice Direction – pilot scheme for small claims	193
Appendix 5:	Appendix A to Practice Direction to Part 71 Orders to obtain information – Record of examination	195
Appendix 6:	List of relevant civil court forms – CPR Part 4	207
Appendix 7:	Addresses of county courts of England and Wales	210
Appendix 8:	HM Land Registry, District Land Registries and Land Charges Department	231
Appendix 9:	Trade association voluntary codes of practice supported by the OFT	235
Index		237

The main steps in the procedure up to judgment in the county court

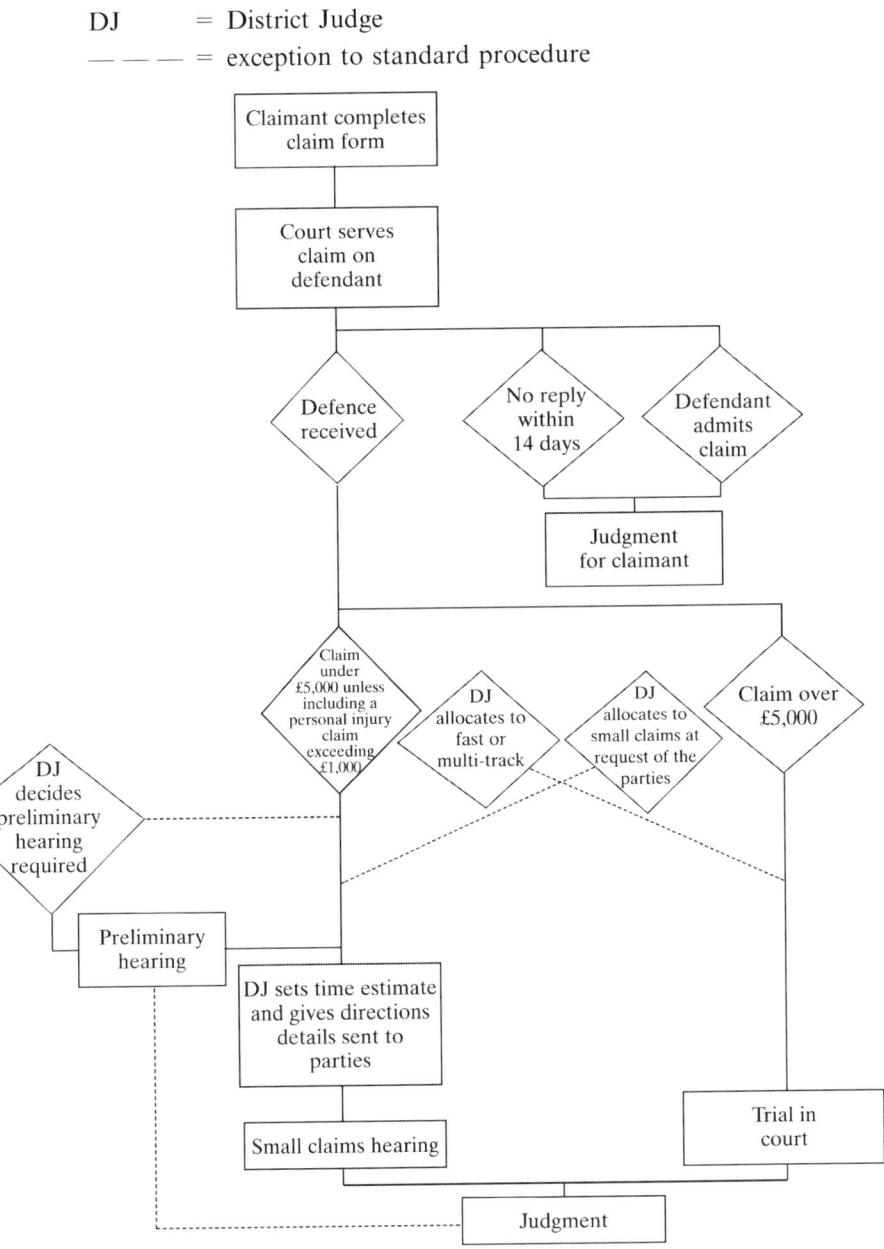

Glossary of terms contained in the Civil Procedure Rules

Affidavit	A written, sworn statement of evidence.
Alternative dispute resolution	Collective description of methods of resolving disputes otherwise than through the normal trial process.
Base rate	The interest rate set by the Bank of England which is used as the basis for other banks' rates.
Contribution	A right of someone to recover from a third person all or part of the amount which he himself is liable to pay.
Counterclaim	A claim brought by a defendant in response to the claimant's claim, which is included in the same proceedings as the claimant's claim.
Cross-examination (and see 'evidence in chief')	Questioning of a witness by a party other than the party who called the witness.
Damages	A sum of money awarded by the court as compensation to the claimant.
• aggravated damages	Additional damages which the court may award as compensation for the defendant's objectionable behaviour.
• exemplary damages	Damages which go beyond compensating for actual loss and are awarded to show the court's disapproval of the defendant's behaviour.
Defence of tender before claim	A defence that, before the claimant started proceedings, the defendant unconditionally offered to the claimant the amount due or, if no specified amount is claimed, an amount sufficient to satisfy the claim.
Evidence in chief (and see 'cross-examination')	The evidence given by a witness for the party who called him.
Indemnity	A right of someone to recover from a third party the whole amount which he himself is liable to pay.

Glossary of terms contained in the Civil Procedure Rules

Injunction	A court order prohibiting a person from doing something or requiring a person to do something.
Joint liability (and see 'several liability')	Parties who are jointly liable share a single liability and each party can be held liable for the whole of it.
Limitation period	The period within which a person who has a right to claim against another person must start court proceedings to establish that right. The expiry of the period may be a defence to the claim.
List	Cases are allocated to different lists depending on the subject matter of the case. The lists are used for administrative purposes and may also have their own procedures and judges.
Official copy	A copy of an official document, supplied and marked as such by the office which issued the original.
Practice form	Form to be used for a particular purpose in proceedings, the form and purpose being specified by a practice direction.
Pre-action protocol	Statements of understanding between legal practitioners and others about pre-action practice and which are approved by a relevant practice direction.
Privilege	The right of a party to refuse to disclose a document or produce a document or to refuse to answer questions on the ground of some special interest recognised by law.
Seal	A seal is a mark which the court puts on a document to indicate that the document has been issued by the court.
Service	Steps required by rules of court to bring documents used in court proceedings to a person's attention.
Set aside	Cancelling a judgment or order or a step taken by a party in the proceedings.
Several liability (and see 'joint liability')	A person who is severally liable with others may remain liable for the whole claim even where judgment has been obtained against the others.

Glossary of terms contained in the Civil Procedure Rules

Stay	A stay imposes a halt on proceedings, apart from taking any steps allowed by the Rules or the terms of the stay. Proceedings can be continued if a stay is lifted.
Strike out	Striking out means the court ordering written material to be deleted so that it may no longer be relied upon.
Without prejudice	Negotiations with a view to a settlement are usually conducted 'without prejudice', which means that the circumstances in which the content of those negotiations may be revealed to the court are very restricted.

Glossary of other legal terms

'Accident line'	Legal advice and assistance service started in June 1994 for personal injury victims.
Adjournment	Postponement of hearing or attendance at court to another date.
Adjudication	Trial before a judge using ordinary rules of civil procedure and evidence. In this context, an alternative to the informal procedure governing small claims.
ADR	Alternative Dispute Resolution. Any alternative to formal litigation, usually mediation but also often out of court arbitration and various other techniques.
Affidavit	A statement in writing and on oath, sworn before someone who has the authority to administer it.
Appellant/Respondent	Parties to an appeal (rare in small claims).
Arbitration	Covers a wide spectrum of less formal methods of judging disputes. Hearings are before any third party whom parties may agree to arbitrate on their dispute. Found in small consumer matters and also widely used in the commercial world.
Attachment of earnings	Method of enforcement of judgment (see Chapter 13).
Battle of the forms	Dispute over whose set of terms and conditions govern a particular contract.
Bailiff	County court officer, appointed mainly to carry out enforcement of judgments.
CA	Consumers' Association.
CAB	Citizens Advice Bureau.

Glossary of other legal terms

Case law — A Source of legal rules established by previous decisions of the higher courts used to establish a point of law. A very fluid technique in the hands of lawyers. Probably best avoided by non-lawyers. Case law is not really necessary for most small claimants, although the judge must decide the case in accordance with law. Cases are cited with the names of the parties, e.g. *Smith v Applebey* [1994] 1 All ER 200. The 'v' is pronounced *and* by English lawyers. The first number in square brackets refers to the year, then follows the volume number of the series of reports, e.g. All England Law Reports, and finally the page. Textbooks on law are not technically legal authority, though frequently they may be a very useful source of knowledge.

Chambers — Judges' private rooms – alternative to open court. The public may attend. Almost all small claims hearings are in chambers.

Child — A person under 18.

CI Arb — Chartered Institute of Arbitrators.

Court Manager — Principal official of each county court. It is to him or her that correspondence should be addressed.

Claimant/Defendant — Parties to legal action.

Claim form — Process initiating civil action.

CLS — Community Legal Service which has replaced the Legal Aid Scheme.

Common law — Name for English type of legal system, based on the precedent of judges – more narrowly, the expression can also mean actions in contact and tort, and description for certain criminal offences. Traditionally distinguished from equity, which emanated from the Court of Chancery, and statute law made by Parliament.

Contract — With only a few exceptions, such as acquiring an interest in land (including buildings), contracts can be made orally; there is no requirement of writing. However, the terms still need to be proved. Usually created by offer and acceptance, it must also contain something of value

Glossary of other legal terms

	given by both parties. This is called consideration. Mutual promises to do something in the future are sufficient.
County courts	Lower civil courts where small claims procedure is based. It is correct to use capital letters before the name of a particular court, e.g. Little Snoring County Court, but not where speaking generally, e.g. the county courts of London. (See Chapter 5.)
Court of Appeal	Court which deals with small claims appeals although a rare occurrence. Presided over by the Master of the Rolls. From the Court of Appeal there may be a limited right of appeal to the House of Lords.
CPR	The Civil Procedure Rules 1998.
Damages	Action for sum of money which requires to be assessed by a judge. Usually for compensation, and most commonly found in personal injury actions, or damage to property.
De minimis	*De minimis non curat lex* means the law is not concerned with matters of trivial importance.
Discontinuance	Abandoning of legal action.
Disclosure	Process of seeking to obtain information about opponent's case. Usually used to refer to disclosure of documents.
District judge	Lower ranking judge of county courts. Lawyers of at least seven years' experience – judges who hear small claims and other arbitrations without limits – but also other cases in court up to £15,000; addressed in court as 'Sir' or 'Madam'.
Enforcement of judgment	Methods of recovering money after obtaining a court judgment. (See Chapter 13.)
Evidence	The way in which the facts of cases are established. The rules are relaxed for small claims.
Ex tempore	Judgment delivered at end of hearing.
Green Book	Lawyers' name for the two green coloured volumes which comprise *The Civil Court Practice*. It contains and provides gui-

Glossary of other legal terms

	dance on the court rules and procedure as well as statutes and forms for lawyers and judges. Published annually by Butterworths.
Injunction	Legal remedy asking court to order someone to do, cease or refrain from doing some act. Found in relation to trespass, private nuisance, or domestic violence, for example.
Injury	Widely used by lawyers as any wrong suffered by a person, unlawfully. Not restricted to physical harm, can include, for instance, reputation.
Judgment	Decision of the court; also the reasons for the decision.
Letter before action	Final letter threatening to take other party to court, prior to commencing proceedings.
Litigant in person	Acting on own in legal proceedings, without a lawyer.
Litigation friend	A person who, in accordance with the Civil Procedure Rules, conducts litigation on behalf of a 'child' (see *ante*) or a patient (see below).
LJ	Lord Justice – Judge in the Court of Appeal. Addressed as 'My Lord'. In April 1994 the Lord Chancellor announced that for the first time female Lord Justices could be addressed as 'My Lady'. One may also say 'your Lordship' or 'your Ladyship'.
NCC	National Consumer Council.
Nisi	Literally 'unless'; provisional order until after formality, it becomes 'absolute'. Now, mostly replaced by 'interim' and 'final'.
OFT	Office of Fair Trading.
Patient	A person who by reason of mental disorder is incapable of managing and administering his own affairs.
Precedent	Another name for process of applying previous case law to future case.

Glossary of other legal terms

Proper officer	Normally the court manager of the court – includes court officials empowered to carry out various administrative tasks of the court. Used at various stages in small claims.
Res ipsa loquitur	Literally 'the thing speaks for itself'. Eases the burden of proof on plaintiffs in negligence actions.
Remedy	This has a special legal meaning. The relief sought or outcome of legal action, e.g. damages, specific performance etc.
Reserved judgment	Given after a period of consideration. Common in higher courts, exceptional in small claims.
Service	Process of delivering a claim form etc. to another party to commence legal proceedings.
Small claims track	Track for straightforward claims within the prescribed financial limits – generally at present £5,000.
Specified claim	Claim for a fixed sum of money rather than damages.
Statutory Instrument	Form of delegated legislation used for making rules and regulations.
Third party debt order	Method of enforcing judgment (see Chapter 13).
Tort	Any common law action not a breach of contract. For instance, negligence, but also covers a wide range of matters from defamation to false imprisonment and trespass, to land, goods or person. There are also economic torts.
Ultra vires	Literally 'beyond the powers', means exceeding jurisdiction or power granted by law.
Unspecified claim	Claim for damages not specified in amount.
Vexatious litigant	One who is barred for frequent misuse of legal procedures.
Warrant of execution	A method of enforcing judgment (see Chapter 13).

Chapter 1

Introduction

The basic principle of English small claims since October 1973 has been to help non-legally qualified persons make or defend claims for less than a certain amount without having to use a lawyer. The current limit is £5,000 and was introduced in April 1999. There is a lower level (currently £1,000) for personal injury claims and certain housing disputes (see Chapter 2). The reasons for this are simple. The cost of legal services is usually too high in proportion to the value of the sums involved, and there is a natural desire to avoid the lengthy delays and expense associated with courts of law. The solution is to encourage people to appear in small claims courts themselves, in other words, to act as litigants in person. Private individuals without legal experience should expect to have their case heard in an informal atmosphere and without the risk of having to pay the full legal costs of their opponent should they lose – the objectives being that the system should be cheap, quick and easy to use for the average person. The evidence since the system was first introduced is that, generally speaking, this is true. As we shall see, there are still pitfalls, although there have been changes over the last few years aimed at reducing these, particularly for the individual user of the courts.

Who are these potential small claimants and defendants? Practically every one of us, at some time or another, it seems. Those who have been disappointed with something which they have bought which was defective, or broke down soon after purchase. Those who have had cause to complain about a service provided by someone, a builder for example, or had a dispute with a neighbour. Those who have not received payment of – or paid – a bill. Victims of a road accident or of a minor injury at work, perhaps, or of a holiday which turned out to be a disaster. Every year thousands of people fall into one or other of these categories. The subject-matter of small claims is myriad: from a small firm of office cleaners suing for unlawful termination of their contract, to a university student suing her ex-landlord for return of a deposit, who is in turn suing her for unpaid rent. Even a bride bringing an action for a specially made dress which did not fit her properly and split on her wedding day causing her to arrive late at church, as well as distress and embarrassment. The main types of small claims are described later in Chapter 2. However, two

Introduction

important groups stand out and merit particular attention, before we begin.

1. Actions for debt

The county courts were originally introduced to help the less well off, but the greatest benefits from the start were conferred on small tradesmen for the recovery of debts, which multiplied in the middle of the nineteenth century due to a growth of credit. Times have not changed. Today it is still the case that an important part of the business of the county court is its debt procedures. Of around two million proceedings commenced in the county courts annually, the great majority are brought by firms or companies for the recovery of money owed. The county courts operate a streamlined system for dealing with debts. These are mostly small and owed by businesses and shops as well as individuals. If there is a dispute over the money owed and it is for less than £5,000, then the small claims procedure will apply. The main arguments will usually be about the facts and also about the law of contract. In fact most claims go through by default, in other words without a defence. Very often both parties are in business – tradesmen or professionals suing for a fee. The image of small claims as a 'consumers only' court is therefore deceptive. Actions for debt or for a 'specified' sum, i.e. a quantifiable sum of money, predominate, and the overwhelming majority of defendants are private individuals or small businesses. Numerically the biggest users of the debt procedures are banks, credit/storecard issuers, mail order catalogues and utilities such as water and electricity companies. In 2000 they issued 942,674 claims for non-payment of bills. This was 48 per cent of all county court claims and made this group the country's biggest litigants. A special procedure exists for bulk users in this way, which is described later. Usually small claims are 'one off', however, and the small claims rules are designed for the first-time litigant, either claimant or defendant. Sometimes the reason for non-payment is that it is claimed that the goods are, or work done is, defective. The claim for non-payment will then be met by a defence that the money is not owed. A consumer law issue may sometimes therefore arise 'in reverse'. More often than not, however, there is no defence. The procedure for these claims is described in Chapter 8.

2. Breach of contract and consumer claims

Each year, the Office of Fair Trading (OFT) reports on complaints and enquiries about faulty goods and services recorded by Citizens Advice Bureaux and trading standards officers. In 2000, for instance, there were 842,720 complaints reported to trading standards departments. The largest category of complaint was house fittings and appliances, followed by personal goods and services, transport (including purchase and repair of cars) and leisure (including package holidays). Even this is regarded as less than a true picture of the problem, as not everyone with a grievance actually made a complaint. However, a large number do take up their complaint with their suppliers. Not surprisingly the percentage taking action tends to rise as the price of the goods increases. Many complainants achieved a satisfactory outcome. Success rates for complaints were much lower against suppliers of services. Dissatisfaction was greatest with regard to grievances about double glazing, building work, holidays and professional services. Only a small number of those with complaints, use further redress mechanisms. The small claims court is the main forum for such actions as indeed it is for the many thousands of small businesses who sue each year for breach of contract.

In most cases disputes are resolved by mutual agreement. Sadly, however, many complaints are rejected immediately or ignored. It is at this point that this book seeks to be of assistance. First, how to seek redress without court proceedings, and when this fails, how to sue on your own behalf in the county courts. In 2000 there were 55,836 cases dealt with by the small claims procedure. There are of course many more cases settled without a hearing. It is worth noting that the present £5,000 limit acts only as the maximum for the 'no costs' rule (see Chapter 11), and that in practice claims for up to any amount may be heard in the small claims track before a district judge, if both parties agree or one party applies and the district judge so orders. As a result of the no costs rule, you might think that solicitors are an extinct species as far as small claims are concerned. Far from it. The figures show a widespread use of legal professionals despite the disincentive of the no costs rule.

(a) Defective goods

Although the law of contract is not the subject of this book, a brief outline will be relevant for many readers, as so many cases ultimately hinge upon it. Towards the end of the nineteenth century an effort was made to codify (i.e. put in statutory form) a number of important commercial areas of the English common law. The Sale of Goods Act 1893 was such a code. This governed business contracts for the sale and purchase of goods, and with amendments and re-enactment in various Acts still forms the basis of civil liability of traders and retailers to their customers. The Sale of Goods Act reversed the original common law rule of *caveat emptor* (let the buyer beware) and replaced it with various implied terms in contracts of sale. Both businesses and private individuals as buyers of goods are protected by the Sale of Goods Act 1979. The following criteria must be applied when goods are sold in the *course of a business*:

- as regards defects which ought to have been revealed by an examination, goods must be 'of satisfactory quality'. There is no liability if defects were brought to the buyer's attention or if the buyer did examine the goods;
- goods must be 'reasonably fit for their purpose';
- goods must correspond with their contractual 'description';

Introduction

- the seller must have title to sell (this normally means that he or she must be the owner):
- where goods are sold by sample, the bulk must correspond with the sample.

If the seller is a private individual, for example selling you her second-hand car, then the full provisions of the Act do not apply: the goods do not have to be fit for their purpose or of satisfactory quality. So you have to be careful.

If the goods are not of satisfactory quality, the buyer may bring a claim for damages for breach of contract for the reduction in value of the goods and for any necessary expenditure to put them right.

In deciding whether goods are of satisfactory quality the Act provides (section 14(2)) that the test to be applied is whether they are of a standard that a reasonable person would regard as satisfactory, taking account of any description, the price and all relevant circumstances. In looking at the quality of the goods, their state and condition, fitness for all common purposes, appearance and finish, freedom from minor defects, safety and durability will be taken into account.

If goods are not satisfactory the buyer has a right to reject them, i.e. return them and get his or her money back. However, this right is lost after, for example, a lapse of a reasonable time or if the buyer acts in a way which is inconsistent with ownership (see section 11 (4)).

(b) 'Stop Now' Orders (EC Directive) Regulations 2001

The Stop Now Orders (EC Directive) Regulations 2001 (SI 2001 No 1422) came into effect in June 2001. The Directive upon which these Regulations are based aims to harmonise the level of consumer protection throughout the European Union. The Regulations go over much of the same ground as can be found in the Sale of Goods Act. However, there are some new matters to be found in them, for example, the goods must be delivered in 'conformity with the contract of sale' which is somewhat like the phrase 'satisfactory quality' but is defined to include in addition the reasonable expectation of consumers. Goods which have to be installed by the seller or under his responsibility, e.g. a washing machine or a part in a car, are covered by the Regulations. Thus, if faulty installation occurs so that the goods do not come up to the consumer's reasonable expectation in the circumstances, then the buyer will have the same rights against the seller as if the goods were delivered in a faulty state. The same applies if the buyer is meant to install the product with the help of instructions and the instructions are faulty.

The Regulations apply to second hand goods sold in the course of a business as well and continue to apply where the lack of conformity with them becomes apparent within a minimum of two years from the date of delivery. The goods will be assumed not to conform to the Regulations if the defect shows up within six months of delivery. Second-hand goods, however, will not be expected to be of the same standard as new goods. It is important to note that the Regulations only apply where the seller is selling in the course of a business. If an individual puts an advert in the 'small ads' section of a newspaper, or takes goods to a car boot sale to sell, he or she is neither bound by the Regulations nor by the Sale of Goods Act.

(c) Unfair contract terms

Very often you may find yourself in a dispute where it appears that your rights have been taken away by small print in a contract. Until the 1970s these rights could be excluded by such a disclaimer or clause, or by a notice in a shop or elsewhere. Such exclusions are now dealt with by the Unfair Contract Terms Act 1977. In the case of consumer sales such exclusion clauses are now void. If the buyer is purchasing as a business, the exclusion is subject to a test of 'reasonableness'. There are similar requirements in contracts for services if one party is a consumer. Such rights cannot be altered by contract. Since the 1977 Act it has not been possible to exclude or restrict liability for personal injuries, though many notices seem to say otherwise. Misleading signs in shops and elsewhere can be reported to the local trading standards department and in some cases these constitute a criminal offence.

Where exclusion clauses or disclaimers are void, they are simply of no effect and may be ignored if you wish to pursue legal action. Where 'reasonableness' is the test, however, you may have to argue this point in court. Guidance is given by statute and by the courts. The factors to be taken into account include:

- Equality or inequality of bargaining power between the parties.
- Was one party a consumer? If so, an exclusion clause is less likely to be reasonable. If two businesses are contracting, exclusions are regarded as fairer and therefore more likely to be binding.
- Had there been a number of previous transactions? If so, the clause is more likely to be enforceable.
- Knowledge of the terms and conditions.
- Was either party insured?
- The price and any special terms in the contract.
- Was the contract 'all or nothing'? – i.e. take these terms or have no contract.

It is for the party relying on the clause, not for the consumer, to prove that it is reasonable. The decision is at the discretion of the judge based on the facts of each case. As these are infinitely variable, no particular case sets a precedent.

What is 'a consumer sale'? For the purposes of invalidating an exclusion clause in a contract the definition of 'dealing as a consumer' is very wide. It includes:

- a transaction of any type ordinarily supplied for private use or consumption;

Introduction

- most cases where the transaction is a one-off, i.e. not part of a regular course of business;
- any transaction which is not integral to the purposes of the business, for example having the office carpet cleaned. (See *R and B Customs Brokers v UDT* [1988] 1 All ER 847 and *Rasbora v JCL Marine* [1977] *1 Lloyds Reports* 645.)

What this means is that a large number of business contracts will fall into this category. It is for your opponent to prove that you did *not* deal as a consumer. If you buy at an auction, you are treated as dealing as a business and any disclaimers are therefore subject to a reasonableness test (Unfair Contract Terms Act 1977, s 12(2)). The 1977 Act is badly named, however, as it applies only to exclusion or limitation clauses, not to all unfair terms in contracts. In 1993, however, the European Union issued a directive on unfair terms in consumer contracts generally, and this widens the scope for challenge against such conditions. This was implemented by the Unfair Terms in Consumer Contracts Regulations 1994 which were replaced by a new set of regulations on 1 October 1999.

The Unfair Terms in Consumer Contracts Regulations 1999 (SI 1999 No 2083) provide that a contractual term 'which has not been individually negotiated shall be regarded as unfair if ... it causes a significant imbalance in the parties' rights and obligations arising under the contract, to the detriment of the consumer'. If the terms have been drafted in advance, or if it is a pre-formulated standard contract it will not be individually negotiated. The Act provides a list of terms which may be regarded as unfair.

Contracts must be written in plain, intelligible language. Unfair terms will not be binding on the consumer. The Director General of Fair Trading may take steps to apply for an injunction against any seller who appears to be using an unfair term in a consumer contract.

(d) Defective services

Customers also have rights against those who provide services, such as plumbers, roofing contractors and estate agents. Under the Supply of Goods and Services Act 1982 the service must be performed:

- with reasonable skill and care;
- within a reasonable time: and

the customer must pay a reasonable charge.

(e) Consumer Protection (Distance Selling) Regulations 2000

These apply to businesses selling goods on-line, as well as by telephone, fax or e-mail but they do not apply to financial services which have their own sets of rules.

The Regulations provide that the seller must give the consumer full information as to their identity, the goods or services being bought and the price. Information must be confirmed in writing – e-mail is likely to be accepted in this respect. The consumer has the right to withdraw from the contract within seven days without penalty and without giving reasons and the consumer must be told of this right. If the seller has not given all the information required by the Regulations, then the right to cancel lasts for three months. The goods or services must be supplied within 30 days unless otherwise agreed.

(f) E-commerce Directive

The European Commission has implemented the E-commerce Directive which should have been incorporated into English law. However, at the time of writing the government has still not done so.

When it is part of English law it will apply to those who use their website to advertise their business, whether they sell goods or services, and if they provide a means of contracting (buying) on-line or placing an order on-line.

The Directive requires certain information to be available on the website including, for example, the name and address of the business, accurate and unequivocal information about costs, how to conclude the contract, a means of correcting inputting errors, etc.

If the Directive is not complied with the buyer will then have redress against the seller.

(g) The existence of a contract

Sale of goods and supply of services are both examples of contracts. There is no need for any written document in order to make a contract – a spoken agreement is sufficient. However, you still have to prove that the words were said, if they are challenged in court. This merely emphasises the importance of having good evidence if you wish to claim. The initial stage of a contract is vital. There has to be both offer and acceptance, by word or conduct, and the terms should be certain. If you sign a document, even without reading it, you are generally bound by its terms, unless there has been fraud or misrepresentation or mistake. However, this rule has been modified by the Unfair Contract Terms Act 1977 and the 1999 Regulations. Contractual terms are also to be found on tickets or even notices in the places where contracts are entered into, such as cloakrooms – 'reasonable steps' must be taken to bring them to your attention.

(h) Advice and information

In Chapter 4 there is a discussion of where to go for advice on the law relating to a potential claim, a sensible step before embarking on any legal action, so as to avoid wasting time on fruitless proceedings. A number of good introductions to consumer law and the law of contract are available, and reference to these should be made accordingly.

Introduction

A good starting point is the web site of a useful organisation, for example:

(a) www.oft.gov.uk
 Click on 'publications' and then 'consumer leaflets'. You will find such leaflets as 'Buying by post'; 'Buying a service' and 'Buying a used car'.
(b) www.which.net
 As a member you will be able to access many leaflets and guides, for example 'faulty goods' (February 2001). You can also join *Which? Legal Service.*

Chapter 2

What are small claims?

A small claim is any dispute which gives a right of legal action for less than £5,000 so long as it suitable for the small claims track. If your claim is not too complicated, and can be expressed as a sum of money it is usually suitable for such track. It is permissible to reduce your claim in order to be within the ceiling for the small claims procedures. Claims for more than £5,000 can be allocated to the small claims track only with the agreement of both parties, but the loser risks having to pay the costs of the action. If a claim for more than £5,000 turns out to have been exaggerated and transpires to be actually within the small claims limit, the claimant may lose entitlement to costs even if he or she wins. The £5,000 limit is therefore an important yardstick. Most small claims are for the recovery of a debt or a specific sum of money. The likelihood is that the claim will be about a debt owed to you or about the quality of goods or services.

Note that wherever the figure £5,000 is mentioned it is not relevant for personal injury or certain housing claims where the limit is £1,000.

1. Type of claim covered by small claims procedure

Overwhelmingly the main types of claim which are suitable for the small claims procedure are claims in contract or tort of which the following are the most common:

1. Claims for payment of debts, whether for goods sold, work done, or money lent. Most of these are essentially for breach of contract, and are between two businesses, or between a business and an individual.
2. Claims arising out of the sale of goods, including the repair of damaged goods, failure to supply goods ordered or supplying the wrong article or a defective one.
3. Claims against people providing services, such as garages, dry cleaners, repairers of electrical and other goods in respect of faulty workmanship or failure to do the work that was agreed.
4. Claims for repayment of a loan.

What are small claims?

5. Claims for arrears of rent, return of deposits or other disputes between landlord and tenant.
6. Claims for damage to property caused by negligence, such as a claim arising out of a road accident. Usually these are covered by insurance, but where the amount is less than the excess on a policy or the insured has only third party cover or does not want to risk his 'No claims bonus' he may wish to sue the other driver. However, if damage is substantial or there are serious personal injuries then these normally go for trial, and it is advisable to see a solicitor.
7. Small personal injury claims where the amount claimed for the injury (excluding claims for financial losses) does not exceed £1,000 and the total claim does not exceed £5,000. These most commonly occur on the roads, at work, or as a result of defective premises or products. Small personal injury claims can now proceed as small claims but this is still a controversial area (see Chapter 12).
8. Claims in private nuisance, against a neighbour for instance, if damages are sought.
9. Claims by a tenant requiring the landlord to carry out repairs of not more than £1,000.

This list is not exhaustive and almost any claim for less than £5,000 will be subject to the small claims procedure, unless the court considers that it should be dealt with in the fast track.

It is wise to seek advice in advance about the nature of your claim, and whether it is likely to be treated by way of the small claims procedure without the risk of costs. Almost any claim for a definite sum of money can be dealt with in this way. Certain claims will not be dealt with under the small claims procedure, e.g. claims against a landlord for unlawful eviction or harassment. Under the old rules injunctions could not be granted under the small claims procedure; now they may be. It remains to be seen whether the district judge will allocate such cases to the small claims track. If you wish to stop your neighbour's dog barking at night as it is preventing you from sleeping soundly, you can seek an injunction to stop a private nuisance. Newspaper readers may recall the case of Corky, the noisy cockerel which was forbidden to crow between midnight and 7.00 am. The case was heard by a judge in Taunton County Court. On the other hand, if your neighbour's dog bites you on the leg, you may sue the neighbour for damages, for pain and suffering and any other loss such as loss of earnings, and so long as the claim for the pain and suffering is for £1,000 or less it should be treated as a small claim.

2. Some points to note about small claims

- The majority of claims are relatively simple.
- They do not involve complex points of law.

What are small claims?

- They are mostly disputes about establishing the facts of the case. Facts can be notoriously hard to prove. You will be in a much stronger position if you can provide evidence other than your own word, such as witnesses, documents or photographs.
- It is for the person bringing the action to prove his or her case on the *balance of probabilities* (known as the burden of proof). This means that the judge has to be more satisfied than not that your version of events is likely to be true. This is a lower burden of proof than exists in criminal law where the prosecution must establish a case beyond a reasonable doubt.
- Cases in dispute are argued on facts or law, or a combination of both. Small claims are mostly about the facts. In other words one side says something happened while the other says it happened otherwise. Usually in the county court witnesses are examined by their own lawyer, and cross-examined by their opponent's lawyer. However, this *adversarial* approach is not encouraged in small claims where the district judge is more likely to adopt an *interventionist* role, that is to ask questions of the parties themselves directly. The judge may also require that questions from one side to the other should be directed through himself; this is meant to cut down the need for legal skills which would make the procedure more daunting for non-lawyers to use.
- Although you should be clear that you have at least an arguable point of law in support of your claim, you do not need to go fully armed with legal argument. However, you should ensure that you understand your legal case and have the documents or evidence ready to support it. The district judge will decide the *law* to be applied in the case if you present the *facts* on which you rely. Legal argument centres on the law to be applied once the facts have been established. Law is found in statutes or Acts of Parliament, plus volumes of statutory instruments or regulations, and case law – based on the decisions of courts – published in law reports. Textbooks on law, however authoritative, are not sources of law, though they do of course provide invaluable assistance. Normally if your claim is simple, as most small claims are, then in legal terms you can proceed without trepidation. However, if you feel or are advised (see Chapter 4) that your claim may involve difficult points of law, then you may have to decide on whether it is worth being represented by a solicitor or seeking to go to trial in court. Alternatively you may take a lay representative with you, to act as an advocate on your behalf.
- It is impossible to say that some particular types of claims are always better handled on your own, whilst others are best suited for a solicitor. Most consumer cases are quite manageable for litigants in person. If your claim arises from a personal injury, you may need to seek legal advice. It may be that the best solution is to seek the advice and assistance of a solicitor or advice centre but to appear in person at the hearing itself.

What are small claims?

- Your complaint must be one with which the law can deal, and also one where you have at least a fair chance of winning. There is no point in pursuing a claim which cannot succeed in law. You will simply be wasting your own and other people's time. No matter how morally righteous you feel about the dispute or how convinced that justice must be on your side, you still have to make a legal case which the judge will accept. Nor is there much to be gained from taking legal action simply to make the point that the law as it stands is wrong and should be reformed. This might make sense in the High Court but not in small claims. The best way to do this is to write to your MP or one of the consumers' organisations, such as the Consumer's Association (CA) or National Consumer Council (NCC).

- If you are not certain whether you have a legally enforceable claim you ought to seek advice. Normally there will be no real difficulty. But often the law does not correspond with what one might imagine it to be. If your claim is concerned with goods that were on display in a shop window, for instance, and the shopkeeper refused to sell them or insisted upon a higher price, then your claim would fail because no contract had been formed. There was only an 'invitation to treat'. There might be a breach of the Trade Descriptions Act, but this is a criminal matter.

- Try to stand back and look at your case from a different point of view. You may be sure that you are right but the case may well be coming to a hearing because the other party is equally sure that he is right. The most valuable help that a lawyer gives is not knowledge of law or procedure but the ability to look at the case from an objective point of view, and to advise whether it is a good case and what evidence may be required. Although it is difficult for a litigant in person, he should attempt to stand back and look at his case, taking into account what his opponent has said in claim or defence, and try to see the case as the arbitrator will see it. It can even be helpful to let a friend look at the papers and comment on the case. Much is common sense but it is the objective view that is so important.

- Having stressed the need for advice, one should also emphasise that the small claims procedure is designed to be as easy as possible for litigants and relatively cheap if you get something wrong. It will, however, cost you the court fees, your time and effort and expenses such as postage and travelling to court. If you have a reasonable case then it is worth the risk and you should not be put off. The references to legal advice in this book are there for those cases in which technical difficulties arise, and not for the more usual cases which can be handled successfully on your own.

- Finally it is worth considering the financial resources of the person you intend to sue. In some cases it may not be worth bringing legal action. Difficulties of enforcing judgments are discussed in Chapter 13.

3. What are not small claims?

- Claims for unfair dismissal. Most of these are dealt with by employment tribunals. However, claims for breach of contract of employment and wages due may be small claims and dealt with by the county court.
- Housing possession actions. These are dealt with in the county courts but not within the small claims procedure. Actions for repair of property can be treated as small claims.
- Personal injury claims where the injuries are sufficiently serious to merit more than £1,000 in general damages.
- Very complicated tort or contract actions.
- Claims for arrears of council tax. These go to the magistrates' courts.

4. Examples of small claims

Real life examples of those who have taken action over small claims appear in the *Which? Legal Service* brochure and on the back page of *Which?* magazine, under the heading 'Brief Cases'. (The service itself is described in Chapter 4.) Illustrations (a)–(d) below are taken from these publications. Some examples can also be seen on www.which.net/legal/case.html.

(a) Holiday nightmare

Mr and Mrs R booked two weeks at Unijet's Club Antigua Hotel for their honeymoon. The total cost was £2,586. When they arrived they found that their honeymoon suite had twin beds and not the double bed that they had been promised in the brochure. They found the general attitude of the hotel staff to be sloppy and the Unijet representative seemed unconcerned and unhelpful.

Mr R complained to Unijet, which offered £200, then £300. Mr R rejected both offers and sought further guidance from *Which? Legal Service*.

Which? Legal Service wrote to Unijet on their behalf claiming breach of contract and highlighting the resulting loss of enjoyment and the distress and inconvenience caused.

Unijet still only offered £400 so proceedings were issued in the small claims court. Unijet doubled its offer but Mr and Mrs R stood firm.

The court awarded them £1,000 plus £80 court issue fee, and £60 each for earnings they had lost in attending the hearing.

(b) The faulty PC

Mr S ordered a PC from T Computers in August 1995. As he was going on holiday at the end of August and then into hospital, he asked for the computer to be delivered on 21st August.

What are small claims?

The PC arrived only an hour and a half before Mr S was due to leave. He was, therefore, unable to set it up and inspect it until the end of September when he found a few problems including faulty software. After several frustrating weeks he made contact with T's technical support line in November. T agreed to replace the processor.

When the PC was returned at the end of December, it still had many of the same problems. In January 1996 Mr S wrote to T asking for a full refund. They refused saying he had had the PC too long.

Mr S asked *Which? Legal Service* lawyers for their help. They explained that, considering the delays he'd experienced he had rejected the computer within a reasonable time. They drafted letters for him to send to T, asking for his money back. T still refused to pay.

Which? Legal Service lawyers then wrote directly to T and after further correspondence one of the *Which? Legal Service* lawyers visited the company. Eventually, in July 1997, T agreed to a full refund which Mr S accepted.

(c) New house in the wilderness

When Mr R bought a newly built house the specification said the front garden would be grassed, and the back garden rotavated. In the event the front grassing was very poorly done, and the back garden was left covered with builders' rubbish and rubble. The builders refused to do anything about it, so Mr R employed his own contractors. The builders refused to reimburse him, so *Which? Personal Service* (now *Which? Legal Service*) helped Mr R to issue a summons and advised him how to proceed. Mr R won, and was complimented by the judge on the able presentation of his case.

(d) The tables turned

Mr P bought a table which was sold as being an 'oak farmhouse table, circa 1800' for £550. He was on the verge of moving house at the time, and so the table was put straight into store for six months, without being examined. When it was brought out there were splits in the table top, and the wood seemed rather pale for a piece of furniture supposedly nearly 200 years old. A member of the Antique Dealers' Association, called in for an opinion, thought it was not an antique and probably not worth more than £200. *Which? Personal Service* advised Mr P that the table did not meet its description as required by the Sale of Goods Act, and he should reject it. Mr P followed this advice and got a full refund.

(e) Crushed finger

Entwistle v Furness and White (Foundries) Ltd, 15 April 1999, unreported:

Mr E, a welder, was injured at work when one of the metal castings in a pallet shifted position and dropped onto his hand, crushing his little

What are small claims?

finger. He was discouraged from taking time off work. First aid was not administered at the time of the accident, but an X-ray taken two days later revealed that he had a fractured little finger. He was prescribed antibiotics but the wound became infected and Mr E's nail had to be removed. He was in extreme pain for nine days and was unable to pursue his hobbies – cycling and attending the gym – for four weeks after the accident.

His case was taken to court by his solicitors and he was awarded £1,000 in general damages.

* * *

The examples described perhaps show a rather higher success rate for individuals than may be typical. They are also all consumer claims or actions by individuals acting in a private capacity. As already noted, this is far from the norm in small claims (see Chapter 1). Businesses are just as likely to sue customers for non-payment of debts, or to sue other businesses. Broadly speaking, however, the principles are the same and ultimately depend on the law of contract or tort.

5. Points of law

- The general rule is that you should keep to a minimum any financial loss you incur as a result of faulty work. This usually means giving the original contractor a chance to put work right. If repairs are not carried out within a reasonable time or they are not satisfactory, you are entitled to ask another contractor to do the work, and claim reasonable costs from the first contractor.
- If someone damages your property, you can claim compensation from them provided that you can prove that they were negligent. You are entitled to claim the current value of whatever is damaged, based on its age and condition. Alternatively you can claim for the cost of having the damaged item repaired if this is possible.
- If you win a case you may still have difficulty in getting your opponents to pay up. If they go into liquidation, or go bankrupt, you should let the liquidators know what you are owed. However, sadly, you will be at the back of the queue, behind preferential creditors such as banks and the Inland Revenue, and may not get anything.

Chapter 3
Complaining

1. Small consumer disputes

Whatever the nature of your claim, it is important to try to resolve it first before taking legal action. This is only prudent as it may save both you and everyone else involved a good deal of time and effort in pursuing an action which could have been avoided. In debt recovery cases the preliminaries (which should always be observed) – allowing time to pay – are generally far more straightforward than the attempts which a consumer or other type of claimant has to make, as the issues and facts are usually more complex in the latter. Before complaining, it may be wise to seek advice (this is dealt with in Chapter 4). However, as often as not, you can make a complaint on your own without requiring the assistance of a third party. The majority of small consumer disputes are resolved without going to court. If you are firm and determined enough you can usually make your point with more reputable businesses.

(a) Stages in complaining

- go directly to the other party;
- try to get a satisfactory settlement;
- contact their trade association, if there is one. They may offer conciliation, mediation or arbitration (see Chapter 14);
- if you get no satisfaction it may be wise to seek advice, particularly from a solicitor, the Citizens Advice Bureau (CAB) or another local advice centre;
- write a letter warning of legal action, if the claim is not dealt with in, say, 14 days.

(b) Defective goods

- Take the item back to the shop promptly and ask for the manager or someone in charge. If they cannot deal with you straight away, offer to wait or make an appointment to see them later. If you cannot go back to the shop soon after you discover the fault,

Complaining

telephone and tell the manager about the item and arrange a convenient time when you can bring it in. Take a note of the conversation and the name of the person you talked to.
- Ask the shop for your money back or say whether you are willing to consider a repair or replacement. If you do agree to a repair, you may lose your right to reject the goods. If the shop does not accept the fault and wants to examine or test the item, ask for a new receipt for the item and give the shop a copy of your old receipt if you still have it, keeping the original yourself.
- If the manager refuses to give you a refund, find out the name and address of their head office and write to them or to the customer relations department (if the firm has one).
- If you paid by cash, get a receipt and keep it. A cheque stub or bank statement which shows evidence of payment can also be used. Many people reduce their chances of winning by not asking for details in writing or throwing away or losing receipts, letters or other bits of paper dealing with the transaction. Although legally there is no requirement to produce a receipt, you have to have proof of purchase. When the case comes to court the seller or business are likely to have all their records in front of them which gives them a great advantage. Whatever the merits of the case, it is difficult for a court to prefer someone's rather vague memory of what happened to clear and precise statements and documents. Therefore you stand a much better change of winning if you too can produce copies of written agreements, letters, invoices, receipts etc.
- Keep a copy of any advertisement which you read before you made the purchase, if this is relevant, and any guarantee or warranty that comes with the article.
- Make of note of any phone calls or visits you make to the shop to complain about the article, and record the date each time.
- Keep a copy of all letters you send or receive.
- If you buy on hire-purchase, keep all the documents you get from the finance company. Remember that this contract is with the finance company, not with the trader who sold you the goods.
- Stop using the item and take it back to the shop (if you can) as soon as possible. This is to avoid the legal conclusion that you have 'accepted' the goods. If you have accepted goods, you lose your right to reject them or to rescind the contract, and you may then only claim damages.
- You do not have a right of replacement. If the goods are defective in terms of quality, you have right to reject the goods and demand a refund.
- If you do not receive a satisfactory reply write to the shop again saying that you intend to take it to court to claim either a refund or compensation unless your claim is dealt with within, say, 28 days. This is called a letter before action.

Complaining

- If after 14 days you still have not received a reply or offer which satisfies you, pursue your claim in the county court.

(c) Bad workmanship
- Whenever possible get a written estimate beforehand, listing the work to be done and the estimated cost.
- Get the details of the work actually done on your receipt, and keep it.
- Make a note of the hours spend on the job and the number of workmen.
- Seek a second opinion, preferably from an expert, about the quality of the work, if this can be done without excessive cost.
- In the case of contracts for services it is advantageous to retain at least a part of the price, if not all of it, until assured that the work is properly completed.
- Point out any badly done work as soon as you notice it, preferably while the tradesmen are still there. In many cases it is useful to have photographs of bad workmanship.
- If the work done is unsatisfactory, refuse to pay the bill or pay only what you think is reasonable. Put this in writing to the firm and send the letter recorded delivery.
- Where a firm employs the tradesman responsible, write to the owner or managing director complaining about the job. Give the firm a chance to put it right. If the firm disputes that the job was badly done, get an independent expert in (perhaps from a trade association) for confirmation.
- If you still do not get satisfaction, write to the firm giving it 14 days to put the work right, stating that otherwise you will take it to court under the Sale and Supply of Goods Act 1994, or at common law. If you can afford it, you might get a solicitor to write for you. A trading standards officer or CAB worker may help as well. Trading standards departments cannot prosecute a tradesman for bad workmanship, but they can prosecute if he provided a written account of what he has done which does not accord with reality. Therefore when you write to the firm, ask for a description of the work done as justification for the bill, then show this to the trading standards officer.
- If all this fails, send a letter before action (i.e. warning of legal action if the claim is not dealt within, say, 28 days), and then begin legal proceedings two weeks later. In more complex cases you might wish to seek advice.
- Alternatively, you can contact any trade association the firm may belong to and use their arbitration scheme if there is one. If the firm is not a member (and it is a good idea to choose a firm which does belong to a recognised association before you agree a job), the association can put you in touch with one of its members who

Complaining

can do an independent assessment of the work done, and then you can use this in court. They may offer to examine the work or check the product for you. There may be a charge for this. Other expert advice can be expensive.

- Finally, if you have not paid the bill because the work was badly done, do not be dismayed by any court action that the firm might threaten or use against you to get its money. It is extremely important, however, to respond to a county court claim form within the time limit. Failure to do so will lead to a judgment against you. You should acknowledge service saying you intend to defend or put in a defence straight away (see Chapter 8). The firm will have to take a civil action against you. You can counterclaim against the firm for compensation for any loss caused by its bad workmanship. However, it will be wise to find out the cost of putting right the bad workmanship as you will have to pay the firm any money due to them after taking into account the cost of the additional work.

(d) Building contractors

Specifically in relation to building contractors the Office of Fair Trading (OFT) recommends the following procedure:

- Decide what you want done before asking a builder in, and check if the job needs planning permission from your local council.
- Shop around for at least two quotes and find out about the firms you are thinking of using. Ask them what other work they have done and get references.
- Agree a contract with them, in writing if you can, specifying the work needed, the cost, the materials to be used, cancellation rights and guarantees, the time the job will take and if they will clear up the mess.
- Be careful about deposits. Do not pay for all the work in advance, and try and pay only for work once it has been done and you approve the quality. It is, however, reasonable to pay for materials before any work is done.
- Make it clear to the builders that they must get your agreement before taking on any new work that they discover might need doing – and agree the cost.
- If you ask them to do anything extra or change the work agreed, check the cost of doing this and make sure it is recorded in writing.
- Draw attention to any defects in the work as soon as you spot them. Take photographs.
- If you are still dissatisfied with the work, contact the firm and then your local trading standards department.

It may well be worth checking if the firm is a member of the Building Employers Confederation or another trade association. Some trade associations offer insurance against their members going bankrupt and others a warranty system guaranteeing work. They also offer a code of practice with an arbitration scheme attached (see Chapter 14).

(e) Other complaints

The response you receive to your complaint depends of course on the complaint and the firm. Marks & Spencer, for example, are justifiably famous for their policy on handling consumer complaints, and so are many other firms. However, you may not be lucky. Good businesses know that making an effort to handle individual complaints and then analysing and learning from them can have a significant role in increasing profits and improving products. Studies by the Office of Fair Trading (OFT) and the Technical Assistance Research Programmes Institute (TARP) showed that most firms investigated complaints to establish whether the product was faulty and, so long as the consumer had obeyed the rules, would recompense them – though this would be confined to the article or service with no allowance for other losses despite the fact that many complainants were entitled to an allowance for consequential loss. The survey also showed that dissatisfied complainants were more likely to tell others of their experience and very much less likely to buy again. Loyalty was higher among satisfied complainants than among customers who had no problem. One effect of the small claims system is that it has encouraged many of the larger shops and suppliers to set up their own procedures for dealing with complaints. Most of these now have a customer relations department and their own internal complaints procedure. Often it may be best to write directly to the customer relations officer with the complaint. This may then lead to an acceptable outcome.

If satisfaction is still not obtained, and you believe you have a good case which you wish to pursue, you should write a letter setting out your complaint and explaining that you will pursue you claim through to the small claims court if necessary.

2. Seeking recovery of a debt

If a bill has not been paid, you should send a reminder or statement as soon as the debt is overdue. If you do not receive a reply, contact the other party by letter or telephone. Explain that the money should be paid, or ask for reasons why it has not been. It is important to be polite and explain the facts. Make clear the address and to whom the cheque is payable. You should then give the other party a chance to settle the claim. Finally you should send a letter before action saying you will issue a claim form if they do not pay. A specimen letter can be found at the end of Chapter 4. Allow a reasonable time of, say, a fortnight before taking any legal action.

(a) Before commencing legal proceedings

- Consider whether the person you are suing has the resources to meet any claim. You might also check the register of county court judgments to see if the other party has any judgments against them. Judgments for the past six years are kept at a central register which anyone can search. (See Chapter 13 for more details). You should receive a quick response which will tell you whether the person has had any judgments against them and whether they have been paid. If the person has unpaid judgment debts, it may not be worth suing them.
- If you are in business it may be worth subscribing to a credit reference agency. This will give you easy access to the credit worthiness of individuals and businesses.
- Check that you have the correct details of the other party before initiating legal action. This includes their name or business name and their proper address for service of summons.
- Consider whether it is advisable to hand recovery of the debt over to a debt collection firm.

(b) Negotiating a settlement

For all the other miscellaneous types of small claim it is wise to discuss a settlement with your opponent. This is dealt with more fully at the end of the next chapter.

Chapter 4

Getting advice

If complaining gets you nowhere, the time has come for you to look for some help and advice. This can usually be obtained locally at a Citizens Advice Bureau, from a solicitor, or a nearby legal advice or consumer advice centre. Finding one of these should be reasonably easy. You may find their addresses in the telephone directory, or by asking at your local council offices or library. The adviser will ask you all the details of the case and then may write to or phone the other party to check the facts. Because someone else is taking an interest in the problem, the two sides often reach agreement more easily, and the matter can be resolved at this point. Of course, all too often it is not, and then legal procedures have to begin.

The main sources of small claims advice

1. Consumer or legal advice centres.
2. Citizens Advice Bureaux, located throughout the country.
3. Solicitors.
4. The county courts.
5. *Which? Legal Service* run by the Consumers' Association.
6. Trade unions – if you are a member. These are particularly helpful with personal injury claims.
7. Money advice or debt counselling centres.

1. Advice centres

(a) Consumer advice

Many towns and cities throughout the country have advice centres, usually run by trading standards or consumer services departments of the local authority. These are often called consumer advice centres or some similar name. Consumers with a problem can call a free helpline which will connect them to one of these advice centres. An interview with staff can often be obtained simply by walking into one of their offices. They will consider the merits of the problem and, if of the view that the claim is

Getting advice

worth pursuing, they will approach the other party, negotiate on behalf of the claimant and, if the claim is not settled, give advice on using the small claims procedure. It is important to remember that the main purpose of trading standards officers is to enforce the law and to prosecute:

- if goods or services have been misleadingly described;
- if the price of something bought was wrong or not displayed;
- where there were certain problems with credit, for example if the wrong interest rate was advertised;
- if goods were sent which were not ordered;
- if goods bought were unsafe;
- in cases involving a short weight or measure.

Trading standards officers can also give you advice about your rights when you think you have been cheated but no criminal law has been broken. It is best to ring them first – the number will be under your local council in the telephone directory. They may also test goods for you or put you in touch with a technical expert. Your local consumer advisers should certainly give you assistance in letting you know whether your claim has merits which are worth pursuing, and may also assist you by trying to reach a satisfactory settlement.

The Office of Fair Trading (OFT) can provide you with details of any relevant trade association to which you can send your claim.

Telling a shop or provider of services that you did or will report them to the trading standards department can be a useful weapon. Local authorities have power to prosecute offenders and they do keep a list of those against whom there have been persistent complaints.

(b) Legal advice centres

There are a variety of legal advice (or law) centres around the country, often staffed by a qualified lawyer, by part-time volunteers, or even law students. This will depend on the area in which you live. The funding for such centres is likely to come from the Legal Services Commission and a grant from the local council.

The centre may, typically, be a registered charity and a member of the Law Centres Federation. It will offer free specialist advice on certain areas of the law and may in some cases offer legal representation or help at court.

You will not be charged but you may be asked about details of your income and asked to sign a Legal Help form. This is to enable the centre to claim its funding from the Legal Services Commission.

2. Citizens Advice Bureaux (CABx)

The first Citizens Advice Bureau was set up in September 1939 as an emergency service during the Second World War. Since then they have

Getting advice

grown enormously. The National Association of Citizens Advice Bureaux (NACAB) now consists of more than 1,750 outlets, which includes over 700 main bureaux, plus numerous other extension bureaux and other places of advice. A large proportion of the people who work in the CAB service are volunteers. CABx have no law enforcement powers. The aims of the CABx are to:

- ensure that individuals do not suffer through ignorance of their rights and responsibilities or of the services available, or through an inability to express their needs effectively;
- exercise a responsible influence on the development of social policies and services both locally and nationally.

The CABx receive a vast number of enquiries and requests for advice, currently running at around six million a year. The range of advice covers the full extent of social problems from immigration to social security. Consumer and debt problems constitute the second largest category with over 20 per cent of the total. The CABx can give advice, information referral, action and advocacy. They will attempt to negotiate a settlement for you, and, if this fails, will give advice on how to proceed with a claim in the county courts. They will also help with filling in forms and other aspects of the case, including giving advice on how good a case the client has. The CABx are also an invaluable source of help if you are being sued or are in debt. Much of the advice given by CABx is by unpaid volunteers who have a wide range of problems to deal with, other than consumer complaints, and they do not profess to be legal experts. The larger offices, however, may have their own lawyer, and legal advice can usually be readily obtained. Increasingly, many have legal help, under the Community Legal Service (CLS), available for advice and representation regarding social security, housing and debt problems.

If you are lacking in confidence or have some other difficulty, such as a language problem, a CAB may occasionally agree to represent you at a hearing, but resources and time are scarce and you may well be advised that you should appear on your own if possible. CABx with paid, specialist advisers can represent you in the fields of law mentioned above and are a good place to obtain the name of a local solicitor if you need one.

3. Solicitors

It is of course an option to use the services of a solicitor for advice or representation or both. Though the possibility of excluding lawyers from small claims hearings has been regularly canvassed, this has not happened, and lawyers appear quite frequently in small claims, particularly on behalf of businesses or traders. This is a factor which every litigant in person should bear in mind. Even if a lawyer is used, a party cannot recover his costs from an opponent if the claim is for more than the small claims limit (see 'No costs', Chapter 11). Nothing prevents a party using and paying for his own solicitor – litigants may well decide that a legal representative is worth retaining even if they have to pay for this service out of their own pocket.

Getting advice

Legal help, funded by the Legal Services Commission, is not normally available for small claims.

(a) Free or cheap legal advice

However, legal advice is available quite widely on a free or cheap initial interview basis, which is probably all you need. The small claims procedure is designed to work without resort to solicitors, but at the preliminary stage proper legal advice can be very useful. The first question is where to find a solicitor who will help you. Large commercial firms are usually not interested in this type of work, so it is best to look for smaller 'High Street' firms for advice. If you do not already know a local solicitor, then you can:

- ask your local CAB or other advice agency to recommend one;
- look in the *Yellow Pages* under the entry for solicitors;
- ask your local county court for a list of solicitors;
- look in your local newspaper for solicitors advertising a free initial interview or holding a free weekly clinic;
- if you have been injured a free initial consultation can be obtained under the Accident Line scheme endorsed by the Law Society: tel 0800 19 29 39.

(b) Insurance policies

Many people have insurance policies covering legal costs and many house, contents, motor and personal accident insurance policies include cover for legal expenses. It is very worthwhile if you have such insurance to check whether it covers legal expenses and, if so, in what circumstances.

(c) Web sites

There are a number of web sites (e.g. the Court Service web site – see below) providing information and advice on procedure.

4. The county courts

The staff of the court are expected to offer useful advice on the procedure, forms and practical steps to be taken in pursuing a claim. However, they are under strict instructions not to discuss the legal merits of a case, i.e. whether or not a person is likely to win, and are not allowed to give legal advice. They will provide you with all the necessary and appropriate forms, and should give some instruction as to how these must be filled in. Questions such as 'do I have a good claim?', 'whom should I sue?', 'how much should I claim by way of damages?' should be addressed either to someone at an advice centre or to a solicitor.

Getting advice

- **Leaflets**

There is now a series of explanatory leaflets provided by the Lord Chancellor's Department free of charge and available at all county courts. As well as being useful these are clear and concise and of course are the official guidance on the steps required at each stage of the procedure.

- **Court Service web site**

Procedural guidance can be obtained from this web site: www.courtservice.gov.uk

5. Which? Legal Service

The Consumer's Association (CA), publishers of *Which?* magazine, runs an advisory service for subscribers with a consumer complaint. On paying a joining fee by direct debit (£9.75 a quarter; the price for non-*Which?* members is £12.75) members can have the assistance of the Consumer's Association's lawyers who give telephone advice on the merits of the case, and explain how to claim compensation.

The terms and conditions of *Which? Legal Service* are:

1. Your membership will allow you and your partner access to our telephone legal advice and case fee service (see section 5) during Which? Legal Service opening hours (Mon-Fri, 9–5). You are also entitled to a free quarterly newsletter and free factsheets.

2. If you would like us to look through documents or provide you with written advice, and we agree to take your case on, we will give you a fixed fee quotation. If you agree to this fee we will:
   - advise you on your legal position throughout your case;
   - draft letters for you to send to other parties;
   - in small claims proceedings: draft court documents, advise on procedure, and explain what you need to do at a hearing;
   - advise on other ways of sorting out your problem;
   - at our discretion and with your agreement, contact other parties directly.

   This is subject to your continued subscription to Which? Legal Service for the duration of the case.

3. Which? Legal Service helps you with Small Claims Court matters, and at our discretion we will help negotiate on larger disputes. In some cases you may have to get a lawyer to represent you in court. We do not provide this sort of service, but will help you to find organisations that do.

4. We aim to provide the following levels of service:
   - if you telephone – respond to your call within 3 working hours of receipt;
   - if you write – a response within 10 working days of receipt.

Getting advice

5   Which? Legal Service are consumer specialists and offer legal advice if something goes wrong with goods or services you have bought in the UK. However we are unable to help you with certain types of legal problems including:
- Neighbours/boundary disputes
- Landlord and tenant problems
- Problems which concern you in a business, not a personal context
- Wills and probate
- Land law/Conveyancing
- Planning law
- Timeshare covering foreign jurisdictions

We reserve the right to not provide advice/or to charge a premium for advice on pre-existing problems.

6   We have a complaints procedure. If you are not happy with any aspect of the service we provide, please write to the Manager of Which? Legal Service at Gascoyne Way, Hertford X, SG14 1LH. Our aim is to respond fairly and speedily. If your complaint cannot be resolved, you will be told how to make a formal complaint and what to do if you are not happy with the outcome.

The experience from this work is ploughed back for the benefit of consumers at large in two ways. Cases from *Which? Legal Service* provide the regular 'Brief Cases' feature on the back page and are also found in the *Which? Legal Service* brochure (see Chapter 2) and, where the law proves inadequate to protect consumers, pressure is brought to bear for changes in the law. CA has brought about many important changes in the law affecting consumers. *Which? Legal Service* can be joined by obtaining an application form by telephoning 0800 252100.

Which? Legal Service produced a useful checklist to help ascertain the nature and likely success of any complaint, and the following list could be sensibly borrowed by other advisers.

1. **What is the name of the item purchased, or the nature of the service?**
    Name and address of manufacturer.
    Instructions for use
    Receipts/bills/invoices.
2. **What is the name and address of the supplier?**
3. **How and when did you make your order?**
    By letter?
    By telephone?
    In person? If so where – in the shop?
    Estimates/quotes.
4. **If by mail order, please let us have copies of the advertisement or catalogue**.
5. **What was the quoted price/the price charged?**

Getting advice

6. **How did you pay?**
   Account.
   Cash.
   Cheque.
   Credit Card.
   HP etc. – please enclose details.
7. **Were there any conditions of sale, booking conditions or other small print?**
8. **Was there a service contract?**
9. **When was the item/service supplied?**
10. **Was there a special offer?**
11. **Was it secondhand?**
12. **Who paid/is paying?**
13. **What is wrong with the item/service?**
14. **Have you enclosed the relevant documents – insurance policy, contract, holiday brochure etc?**
15. **Have you taken any steps to sort out the problem?**
    Please give brief history (with dates) and enclose copies of the relevant correspondence.
16. **Have you been offered any money back or free repairs?**
17. **How much are you out of pocket?**
    Have you had to: pay for repairs; hire a car; hire a builder?
18. **What redress are you seeking?**

6. Trade unions

Many unions specialise in pursuing personal injury claims for their members and have considerable expertise in this area. If the case is basically an employment law matter, it may go to the employment tribunal rather than the county court. Your union should assist you by providing the services of their own legal department or by finding a solicitor who handles personal injury claims. Small debt and consumer actions are generally outside the scope of usual legal advice for members. However, the unions and the Law Society now have a joint scheme to cover matters in this area.

7. Money advice or debt counselling centres

These are spread throughout the country, but a lack of funding has caused many closures. They will help if you are in financial difficulties, being sued or need practical advice.

Very many defendants in the county court will be people who are unemployed, on income support or have financial worries, and in these circumstances it is sensible to contact a money advice centre if there is one

Getting advice

near you. They will usually offer free confidential and independent advice to people with money problems. They can usually help and advise on:

- how to maximise your income;
- your entitlement to benefits;
- county count procedure and summonses;
- negotiating payments to creditors;
- dealing with bailiffs and warrants of execution, for which emergency procedures exist;
- filling in court forms;
- if resources permit, representation in court.

Where such a centre is not available help should be sought from CABx.

8. Negotiating a settlement

Before beginning any legal action it is sensible to try to reach a settlement with the other party if you can. This can take place at any time right up to the hearing itself. In civil litigation many cases are settled on the very day of the trial – before the parties go into court – at the doors of the court. The district judge may ask you if you have attempted to reach an acceptable settlement of your dispute, before you begin your hearing. Although settling is obviously desirable for all concerned, do not accept an unfair settlement. The small claims procedure is there for you to pursue your rights to a just conclusion.

(a) 'Without prejudice'

Where solicitors conduct negotiations by letter in order to achieve a settlement, it is normal to place the words 'without prejudice' at the top of any correspondence. Nothing said or done will then be admissible in evidence should the matter come to trial unless the party writing the letter consents. This is an important protection for litigants. Neither side could negotiate freely if to do so risked damaging the presentation of its case. The fact that a party made, replied to, or indeed ignored, a 'without prejudice' offer of compromise, cannot be used as an admission prejudicial to his case. The protection applies only to negotiations made in an attempt to settle a dispute. This device may also be used by litigants in person in small claims to support an application for costs because the other party has behaved unreasonably; see Chapter 11 para 2 page 127.

'Without prejudice' correspondence is admissible in evidence:

- if both parties consent; or
- if parties actually make a compromise; or
- solely on the issue of costs after other issues have been resolved. Such correspondence is known as a 'Calderbank' letter, and should be marked 'without prejudice save as to costs'.

Getting advice

9. Letters before action

Assuming that your complaint has not been dealt with to your satisfaction, or indeed not at all, then you should put your complaint in a written letter to your opponent. It is always customary to do this before proceeding to legal action. This is what solicitors call a letter before action, i.e. a formal notification of claim. It does not need to be particularly formal, but it may be something you wish a solicitor to write as this can often have a greater impact. A non-lawyer can write such a letter so long as certain points are borne in mind.

- The pre-action protocols should be observed even though they are not 'aimed' at the small claims track.
- Set out the main facts at issue, presenting points to support your claim, and be polite.
- Explain the steps that you have already taken to try to resolve the dispute.
- Bear in mind that this letter may later be looked at in court.
- Try not to be aggressive as this is likely to be counter-productive.
- Hesitate about making an offer of a settlement for less than the full amount which you would accept. This could later be used against you at the hearing if you continue to press for your claim in full. As we have seen, solicitors who wish to make an offer, that later will not be disclosed, write 'without prejudice' at the top to prevent its being produced. A separate 'without prejudice' letter may be written.
- Make it clear that unless you receive a satisfactory reply you will immediately start legal proceedings in the county court.
- In debt cases, where demands have already been sent, the usual practice is merely to send a short clear letter containing the threat of legal action.

Specimen letter: debt action

Dear Madam/Sir,
  Further to my letter of (*date*) to which I have not received a reply, I should like to inform you that unless I receive satisfactory proposals from you for the payment of my outstanding claim within 14 days of the receipt of this letter, I intend to issue a claim in the county court.

Yours faithfully,

....

Getting advice

Specimen letter: small consumer claim

Dear Madam/Sir,

The [washing machine][video recorder][burglar alarm system] (specify) which I purchased from you on (*date*) has [broken down][failed to work properly]. I have already notified you of this problem by [letter of (*date*)] [telephone on (*date*)] but have failed to receive a satisfactory reply to my complaint. Unless you agree to take back the goods and [return the price paid] [provide me with a replacement to my satisfaction] within 14 days of today's date, I shall have no alternative but to begin legal proceedings against you in the county court.

Yours faithfully,

....

Action for damages for personal injuries

This letter is likely to be more detailed than either of the other two examples. It is sensible to get a solicitor to draft it for you. Remember that if you do not send such a letter, the court may disallow some of your costs even if you win. The letter should be sent to the defendant in person. If the defendant is likely to be insured in respect of the claim, take the opportunity to inquire about this and ask that the letter be posted on to their insurers. In most cases, e.g. motor accidents, injuries at work, it is the insurers who conduct the defence of the action. If you know who the insurers are, send a copy of the letter to them direct. If you know that the defendant already has a solicitor acting for him, the letter before action should be addressed to his solicitor. It is improper for one solicitor to contact the opposing solicitor's client directly. The letter should set out the general nature of the allegations against the defendant and a summary of the damage that has been sustained.

Great care should be taken to make sure that you are accurate and do not make any admissions which might damage your case, as these might be used against you in any subsequent hearing or other proceedings.

You should have regard to the pre-action protocol on personal injury claims whatever track you are on (see pages 136–149 below).

Chapter 5

The county courts

There is no small claims court as such. Small claims are heard in the county courts. The courts of England and Wales are divided into a structure of four, two civil and two criminal. The county courts and High Court deal with civil matters, the magistrates' courts and Crown Courts with criminal trials. Most civil proceedings, including all small claims, take place in the county courts. The county court is essentially a local court – there is one for each district in England and Wales – and its procedures are governed by the Civil Procedure Rules 1998 (CPR) Generally cases are heard in the court of the district where the facts happened or where the defendant carries on business or resides (see Chapter 7). Small claims have always been within the county court system. The expression 'small claims court', though prevalent, is wrong, as small claims are merely a special, though distinct, procedure within the county court.

County courts have nothing to do with the old counties. Even when they were founded by an Act of Parliament in 1846 the word 'county' was a misnomer, and their numbers grew at such a rate as to outstrip any county boundaries. They now have no connection at all with local administrative divisions. There are 220 county courts spread throughout England and Wales making them one of the most dispersed and therefore readily accessible civil courts anywhere in the world. Their number, however, is slowly being reduced as courts are merged or closed down.

The Courts and Legal Services Act 1990 and the Civil Procedure Rules 1998 have effected the most radical changes since the county courts were created in 1846. This has led to a huge increase in workload for the courts, particularly the court staff. Doubts as to whether the system could cope adequately with the extra workload, not matched by an equivalent increase in personnel, were expressed in the period leading to the implementation of the Woolf Reforms by the Civil Procedure Rules 1998. The Rules were brought into effect on 26 April 1999 and it is apparent that, despite the increase in the use of technology, the staff are fully stretched and delays are very apparent. Litigants therefore have to be patient.

Each county court has a court office, sometimes more than one, and is generally assigned a Circuit judge, a district judge (formerly known as

The county courts

county court registrar), as well as court staff and bailiffs. The large county courts have more than one Circuit judge and more than one district judge. Similarly, a small county court may have no Circuit judge or a Circuit judge on certain days only and may have a district judge only on specified days. Each court is given a district which is determined in accordance with directions given by the Lord Chancellor. The boundary of each county court district may be varied by changing circumstances. Some county court districts are small, densely populated areas of cities; others cover large areas of countryside. The district is very important for purposes of starting proceedings, venue and administration (see Chapter 7). Directories are published which show each county court district. In cases of doubt, enquiry should be made at the nearest county court before an action is commenced. The towns and places included in the district of each court are listed in two official publications, the *County Court – Index of Place Names* and the *London County Courts' Directory*.

1. The personnel of the courts

(a) Judges

The principal judges of the county courts are called Circuit judges. Circuit judges can hear cases in both the county courts and also the Crown Court. They rarely deal with small claims which can only be listed for hearing before a Circuit judge with his consent. Almost all small claims work is done by district judges. District judges were created by the Courts and Legal Services Act 1990: section 71 and Schedule 10. Until recently they had always been practising solicitors, but now they can be solicitors or barristers of at least seven years' 'general qualification'. As part of their varied workload, district judges also deal with matters leading up to the hearing itself. The powers and duties of a district judge may be exercised by a part-time deputy district judge, or by an assistant district judge who has similar powers and who may also conduct small claims hearings. District judges should be addressed as 'Sir' or 'Madam', and written to as 'Dear Judge'. They do not wear wigs or gowns in small claims hearings. District judges have powers to punish for contempt of court.

(b) Administrative staff

Most tasks of a formal or administrative nature, such as issuing claim forms, service of process, listing of hearings and supervising execution of judgment, are carried out by court staff responsible to a court manager. The staff are a body of officers in the service of the court. They are civil servants employed by the Lord Chancellor. The court manager is the head official of each court. Where the rules require or permit the court to perform an act of a formal or administrative nature that act may be performed by a 'court officer'. A court officer is defined as a member of the court staff. Thus many stages of the procedure, such as questioning

The county courts

judgment debtors to obtain information, are in fact carried out by officials of the courts.

Court staff are of particular relevance with regard to small claims and litigants in person, for the provision of advice and assistance in the preparation of a case, or completing initial forms or claim forms, is vital to the success of any action. Only advice on procedure but not on law can be given. When corresponding with the courts, even if it is a matter for a district judge, your letter should be addressed to the court manager of the relevant county court.

(c) Bailiffs

Every court employs full-time bailiffs with particular legal powers and duties, mainly in relation to the enforcement of judgments and in relation to the service of certain court documents. These are employed by the Lord Chancellor's Department. However, there are also private bailiffs, but these do not carry out county court work (see further Chapter 13).

The court is open to the public from 10 am to 4 pm but if a litigant wishes to speak to a bailiff the best time to telephone is at about 9 am as the bailiff's work takes him out of the court office for most of the day.

2. Small claims procedure

Small claims procedure is dealt with in Part 27 of the Civil Procedure Rules 1998 and the Practice Direction that supplements it, and small claims are designed to be manageable by the average person. Although small claims have had their own procedure for 25 years, the procedure remains firmly bedded in the county court. This means that avenues still remain open for a claim that has been allocated to the small claims track to be re-allocated to either the fast track or the multi-track. If this happens then the costs limitations on small claims under CPR r 27.14 will cease to apply from the date of re-allocation. Where such developments occur in the course of an action, the individual litigant in person may find that he or she has to seek legal advice (see Chapter 4). However, the purpose of the small claims procedure remains one of encouraging individuals to pursue and defend on their own behalf or with the help of an adviser, and the system has been designed to ensure that delays and complexities are kept to a minimum.

- Litigants should note that at every stage of the action there are prescribed forms or practice forms which, though sometimes time-consuming, are intended to be simple to use.
- Some excellent free leaflets are readily available to all litigants when they arrive at court offices. They should be kept to hand as they are well written and can prove invaluable.
- Most steps in the action are arranged by the court.
- Parties usually only have to attend on dates fixed for a hearing, or other appointments.

The county courts

Almost all your business with the court can be conducted by post. This is a significant aspect of county court procedure, and is a great advantage for many people.

When dealing with matters in this way:

- use pre-paid post;
- address your correspondence or form to the 'Court Manager' of the court in question;
- quote your case number – failure to do so may result in the document being incorrectly filed;
- do *not* write to the judge – letters to the judge are not opened by the court staff, and if the judge is away the letter may not be opened for some time;
- enclose all the necessary documents which you could be required to produce if attending in person;
- enclose any court fees or remittances required (cheques should be made payable to HM Paymaster General);
- enclose a self-addressed envelope.

(a) The sources of small claims rules

The general jurisdiction of the county courts is derived from the County Courts Act 1984, and special jurisdiction from a variety of statutes and statutory instruments (i.e. delegated by Parliament to another rule-making body). Procedure is governed by the Civil Procedure Rules 1998, which came into force in April 1999. These rules are made by a rule committee under powers granted by Parliament. Its statutory authority is limited to matters of procedure. *The Civil Court Practice* ('the Green Book') is a book published annually which contains the text of many relevant Acts and also of the Civil Procedure Rules. This comprises two volumes and is not for the uninitiated. Specific provisions of the Civil Procedure Rules are cited by reference to their Part and rule (r) numbers, for example Part 27 r 27.6. Most of the rules on small claims are contained in Part 27 – this runs to seven pages of text with an accompanying Practice Direction of eleven pages. However, in order to keep this book as straightforward as possible, references to Part and rule numbers have been kept to a minimum. As the first part of the rule number is the same as the Part number, the Part number has been omitted from references throughout this book.

In addition to the Civil Procedure Rules and the Practice Directions to those Rules, various pre-action protocols, covering types of claim including those for clinical negligence and personal injury, have been introduced. The personal injury protocol is intended mainly for claims on the fast track, but is relevant to small claims including a personal injury claim and it must be borne in mind that all litigation should be conducted with due regard to the principles set out in the protocols.

The county courts

(b) A word of warning

We have already made note of the fact that official information and guides on procedural steps are available at the courts – these have been designed to explain the procedure without recourse to primary sources of rules by the individual claimant. Indeed, it is very unlikely that individuals using the small claims procedure will ever need to familiarise themselves with these primary sources.

Many of the so-called 'rules' can be waived by judges. They do not have to be uniformly applied in every case. This can be a considerable source of disappointment and annoyance to litigants, and can also lead to a wide divergence and lack of uniformity, but the rules relating to small claims specifically state that the hearings may be informal and the strict rules of evidence do not apply.

The small claim, however, is decided in accordance with the law in the same way as a claim on the fast track or multi-track.

(c) Practice directions

The Practice Directions that supplement the Civil Procedure Rules 1998 are made by the Vice-Chancellor with the assistance of a working group. Additional directions will be made and the existing directions amended from time to time.

(d) Forms

Finally, there are a wide variety of official forms and notices to be used, each specific to various stages in the procedure. These forms are referred to in the text. (See Appendix 6 for a list.) They are prefixed with the letter 'N' and are available free of charge at county court offices – you can also find them in *The Civil Court Practice*. Some forms have to be used – these are known as 'prescribed forms'. Those which are there in order to assist litigants and solicitors, but are not compulsory, are called 'practice forms'.

(e) The implementation of Lord Woolf's two reports on Access to Justice by the Civil Procedure Rules

The essence of the reforms is contained in Part 1 which provides that the Civil Procedure Rules 1998 are a new procedural code with the overriding objective of enabling the court to deal with cases justly. This includes so far as is practicable:

- ensuring that the parties are on an equal footing;
- saving expense;
- dealing with the case proportionately to the money involved, its importance, its complexity and the financial position of the parties;
- ensuring the case is dealt with expeditiously and fairly; and

- allotting to the case a fair share of the court's resources.

The Rules impose on the parties a duty to help the court further the overriding objective.

The court has a duty to manage cases which includes encouraging the parties to use alternative dispute resolution where the court considers that appropriate, and helping the parties settle the case. The thrust of the Rules is that legal action should be the last resort.

3. The Courts Charter

The Citizens' Charter was launched in July 1991 as 'a programme for a decade' aimed at improving standards in the public and privatised sectors of the economy, and describing consumers' rights as the 'central theme of the 1990s'. The 'Courts Charter' (a part of this programme) has applied from 4 January 1993, and was designed to set the standard of service to be expected of court staff, explain what happens when individuals attend court and what to do if something goes wrong. It is 'intended to explain what is being done to improve the service in the courts and steps being taken to make it easier to carry out business there'. The Charter covers all county courts. There are three Courts' Charter leaflets entitled 'County Court and District Registry Users', 'Legal Professionals' and 'Witnesses in the Civil Courts'.

Introducing the Charter, the then Lord Chancellor, Lord MacKay, described it as breaking new ground in guaranteeing certain levels of service and making courts more 'user-friendly'. However, the Courts Charter applies only to administrative matters – decisions by judges are not covered. On a practical level, persons attending courts should be entitled to such things as maps and details of public transport and car parks showing where courts are located and how to find them. Dates of hearings and information relating to opening hours and facilities – such as canteens, vending machines, and arrangements (if any) for child care and for the disabled, as well as the name and telephone number of a person at court to contact for information – should also be sent to court users.

On attending the court, lawyers and litigants should expect to find court staff available 30 minutes before the first scheduled hearing, wearing name badges and providing 'courteous and prompt service'. A maximum queuing time target will be displayed and also averages for quiet and busy periods of the particular court. Those telephoning should expect clear and helpful assistance from the court, and a reply or acknowledgment of correspondence within ten working days.

Courts should issue claim forms to the defendant usually within five but not later than ten working days of receiving the request for issue and fee. Greater use is now made of the Production Centre which will issue and send claim forms to defendants within 48 hours. Claimants with large quantities of cases need use only the County Court Bulk Centre at Northampton.

The county courts

Judgments will be sent within ten working days, if the court orders the debt to be paid, and enforcement proceedings will also be issued within this same time span, on receipt of the claimant's request and fee. Bailiffs will make a first visit within fifteen working days of issue of a warrant of execution, and any money received will be sent to the claimant within ten working days of receipt or clearance of any cheques.

The small claims procedure in the county courts has been simplified. A series of explanatory leaflets, published and available free of charge from the courts, set out clearly the various stages in the claim. Court staff can also explain the procedure to litigants and their representatives. Each county court will offer a hearing date within its own standards of waiting time, which should be displayed in the public area of the court building.

As with other areas of the Citizens' Charter there is no direct legal mechanism for claiming financial compensation against those who fail to achieve the standards set out in the document. Courts have to display the name of their court manager and the procedure for dealing with complaints. This will usually involve sending a letter to the court manager with the further possibility of taking complaints on to the court administrators. If the complaint is found justifiable, payments may then be made. Solicitors now commonly claim where mistakes such as giving the wrong date have occurred which resulted in their wasting time at the court premises. The Charter states that if a mistake has been made, the complainant will receive an apology, and will be told what went wrong and how the service is being put right. Court users are also urged to write to the courts with suggestions for improvements.

Chapter 6

Who to sue?

Having failed to achieve a satisfactory answer to your claim, the time has arrived to begin legal action. For the first-time user of the courts this can be a daunting moment. Unfortunately you cannot go straight to a court hearing. There are necessary delays and formalities to be gone through, though the aim of the small claims procedure is to reduce these as much as possible. Furthermore the choices which have to be made at the initial stage are vital to a successful outcome of your case. To the uninitiated the answers to some of these points may seem clear, but in practice they demand a degree of knowledge and careful attention to detail. In this chapter we deal with the question: who to sue?

Clearly you must have a right of action against the person you are suing. Most small claims are for debt, breach of contract or, less commonly, in tort. (A tort is a civil wrong such as negligence or nuisance.) Often it will be obvious which person should be sued, but sometimes the claimant does have a choice, and it may be essential to choose correctly.

However, it is important to note that you can sue more than one person with regard to the same matter if there is a cause of action against each of them. This should be done when you prepare your claim form.

1. Claims for debt or breach of contract

To sue successfully in contract you must have entered into a legally binding agreement or the debt must have been properly assigned to you. In a case involving the sale of goods you must have bought the item or have made a contract with the party whom you wish to sue. Contracts need not be in writing – they can be entirely by word of mouth. In some situations, such as booking a family holiday, one person can be regarded as agent for the others, but normally only the person who made the contract can bring an action. For instance, you cannot sue in contract for a defect in an item which was purchased by someone else, even if that person is your husband, wife or a friend. This point proved crucial for the development of the law of negligence, and also consumers' rights, in *Donoghue v Stevenson* – a famous decision of the House of Lords in 1932. The bottle of ginger beer which it was claimed contained a snail had been

Who to sue?

purchased not by the person who drank the contents but by a friend. The claimant, or pursuer as she is called in Scotland, therefore had to sue in negligence against the manufacturer, not against the seller in contract. Mrs May Donoghue was successful, and the principle of liability of manufacturers to the ultimate consumer of products was established throughout the United Kingdom. The case also gave rise to the chief tenet of negligence, the 'neighbour principle'.

You should also decide what type of contract you have made. In most cases this will be either:

- *sale of goods* whereby ownership of the goods (not land) passes or will pass. You therefore sue the person who sold the goods to you. The relevant law is contained in the Sale of Goods Act 1979 and its associated subsequent legislation and case law. You bring your action against the retailer or business, not against the shop assistant or agent; or
- *contract for work and materials, or for services*. Again you sue the firm in the firm's name, not that of the individual who actually carried out the work if they are merely employees. Contracts for services cover everything from having your television repaired to having your clothes dry-cleaned. The work has to be carried out with reasonable care and skill. The action here may be either in contract or tort.

Note If goods are being bought by *hire purchase or consumer credit agreement*, then they will have been sold to a finance company with whom the consumer has a contract rather than the trader. Legal action should be brought against the finance company. The Consumer Credit Act 1974 gives you rights in this respect. You may, however, still have rights against the trader for misrepresentation or breach of an oral warranty.

2. Actions in negligence

These cover everything from road accidents to defective products. You have to have suffered some personal injury to yourself or damage to property other than the goods themselves. Damages for pure economic loss, i.e. *only* financial loss or to the item itself, are not normally available in negligence, but only in contract. If you bought the goods, you may choose to sue the manufacturer in negligence – but you have to show that injury was reasonably foreseeable and that the producer was at fault. Sometimes the choice will be dictated by events, for example if either seller or producer goes bankrupt, or resides overseas. As far as faulty goods are concerned it is preferable to sue the retailer under the contract of sale since liability is strict, i.e. it does not depend on proving fault. So even if the seller could not have done anything about it because the goods were in a container of some kind, he or she is probably still liable. The point is illustrated by *Daniels v R White & Sons and Tabard* [1938] 4 All ER 258. Mr Daniels purchased a bottle of lemonade from Mrs Tabard, a

Who to sue?

publican at the Falcon Arms, in Battersea. It had been manufactured by R White & Sons Ltd and contained a quantity of carbolic acid. Mr and Mrs Daniels both became ill as a result of drinking it. As between the buyer, Mr Daniels, and the seller, Mrs Tabard, it was found that there had been a breach of the implied condition of merchantable quality, Mr Daniels was able to recover damages from Mrs Tabard for personal injuries without proving that she had been negligent. Mrs Daniels could not sue Mrs Tabard, but could only sue the manufacturers, R White & Sons, in the tort of negligence. On the facts she failed to prove the necessary breach of their duty of care, though in this respect the decision would probably not be followed today. Mr Daniels could also have sued the manufacturers in tort had negligence been provable but he could only recover one award of damages.

(a) Motor accidents

Commonly known as 'running down' cases, these are often small claims and are normally allocated to the small claims track. The question may arise as to whether to sue the other motorist or his insurers. When a tort is committed by an insured person, the victim has no right at common law to sue the insurer directly since he is not party to the contract of insurance. However, you should note that:

- the insurer usually has the right, by contract with the defendant, to conduct any defence on his behalf;
- in an action against a motorist the claimant usually has a statutory right to enforce against the insurer any judgment he obtains against the defendant;
- if an insurance company pays out on an insurance policy, it may then proceed against another person who may be legally liable for the injury, based on the principle of *subrogation*. Where the motorist causing the injury is uninsured, you should contact the Motor Insurers' Bureau.

(b) Medical negligence claims

If these relate to treatment within the National Health Service, your action should be against the relevant health authority. Now that many hospitals have taken out Trust status, the issue is more complex. The same is true of private hospitals. There are special rules governing the status at law of doctors and other medical professionals. Such actions are usually beyond the small claims limit and are almost invariably too complex for the small claims track. You should seek legal advice (see Chapter 4).

(c) Employers' liability

If your claim arises out of an accident or illness caused by your work, you must bring your action against your employer or any other employer who

Who to sue?

caused your injury. If an accident was caused by another employee, that person, called the tortfeasor, is named as a defendant, but his employer has to take responsibility for his acts, under the doctrine of vicarious liability. There is compulsory insurance of all employers for this type of liability (see the Employers' Liability (Compulsory Insurance) Act 1969). Many more such actions are now brought within the small claims regime (see Chapter 12).

(d) Dangerous premises

If you are injured due to the state of buildings or on ground owned by someone else, you can sue the occupier of the land – you should use the Occupiers' Liability Act 1984 in relation to such claims. The occupier is normally the owner, but can be any person who is in control of the land or building. It has become increasingly commonplace for citizens to sue their local authority for injuries caused by tripping on pavements.

(e) Defective products

Such actions can be brought against the manufacturer in negligence or against the supplier for breach of contract (see pages 40–41 above).

(f) Other tort actions

Other tort actions, such as nuisance or trespass to land, are usually against the owner or occupier of the land, or against a tenant who caused the injury. This is an area where you should seek advice, as there are many distinctive legal rules to such actions. Often different legal remedies are being sought here, such as injunctions. An injunction is a court order restraining a person from doing a particular act. These actions have to go to court. Small claims are usually for money damage suffered, but on occasions there will be an additional claim for another remedy, such as an injunction.

3. Special parties

You may need to decide whom you should sue if the defendant is not a private individual. Legal personality is not restricted to human beings. The word 'person' in law can also apply to businesses and many organisations and authorities as well as a wide range of other entities. Therefore it is important to be clear about the legal status of the person whom one wishes to sue. This can also become a problem during the course of an action due to changes in status, such as bankruptcy or death. We will now go on to consider the following:

- companies and other corporate bodies;
- partners and business names;

- persons under 18 or persons with a mental disability;
- death of one of the parties;
- bankruptcy or insolvency;
- vexatious litigants.

(a) Companies and other corporate bodies

Corporations and companies are legal 'persons' and therefore can sue or be sued in their own names. Public companies with large share capital have 'public limited company' or 'plc' after their names. The Welsh equivalent is 'cwmni cyfyngedig cyhoeddus' or 'ccc'. Other companies normally have 'Limited' or 'Ltd' after their names. This means that the companies' liability is limited. Companies often trade under names other than their own, i.e. they can drop the 'Ltd' and use a variety of other titles. For example, 'Applebey and Co Ltd' could trade as 'Applebey and Co', 'Applebeys' or the 'Applebey Group' or indeed some other name.

Limited companies must have a registered office. The head office is not necessarily the registered office, and a company search may be necessary. This is done by writing to the Companies Registration Office in Cardiff, or getting a Companies agent to do the task for you. You should write to Companies House, Crown Way, Cardiff CF14 3UZ, or call 0870 3333636. You can also visit the office personally. Where a company resides can be very relevant to where the action will be heard. A company or corporation resides where it carries on business, and it can reside in more than one place (*Davies v British Geon Ltd* [1956] 3 All ER 389). It is worth stressing that you should sue a limited company at some premises such as a shop or office which have a real connection with the cause of action.

You may also have to distinguish between a defendant firm (or partnership), a single person trading under a business name, and a defendant limited company. There are many debt claims brought against a director or a shareholder of a company whose defence is that the debt is due from the company and not him personally. In such cases the court will look carefully at any documents which might help answer this question, such as invoices and cheques.

Display of business names

A limited company must display its name on the outside of every shop or other place where it carries out business (Companies Act 1985, s 348). However, it does not have to display the address of its head office or its registered office. A limited company does not have to display the name of any parent company. Individuals and partnerships do not have to display their names on the outside of a shop or place of business.

An individual, partnership or limited company can trade under a different name, known as a 'business name'. Where a business name is used, a notice must be displayed in each place of business giving the name of the individual, each partner (unless there are more than 20) or the company, as the case may be. The notice does not have to show the names of company directors. However, it must give an address for service of legal documents to the individual, each partner or company – of course, this can be the same address as the business premises (the notice does not have to give a home address). Customers of the firm have a right to demand this information and must then be given it (Business Names Act 1985, s 4).

The Business Names Act 1985 provides that a person carrying on business in another name must give an address for service of legal documents on all of the following: all business letters, written orders for goods or services to be supplied to the business, invoices and receipts and demands for payments of debts. This is not always complied with, however. A sole trader carrying on business in a name other than his own can be sued in that name or style as if it were a firm name. This is done by adding the words 'a trading name' to the business name. Alternatively she may be sued in her own name, followed by 'trading as' abbreviated to t/a (e.g. Anne Williams t/a Northgate Beauty Salon). Unlike partners, sole traders are not allowed to sue in their business name.

(b) Partnerships

Partnerships are not legal persons. However, if partners carry on business in England and Wales they may sue or be sued in the name of their firm. Where partners sue or are sued in a firm name, the partners must – if requested in writing by any other party – deliver and file a statement of the names and places of residence of all the persons who were partners when the action arose (CCR Ord 5 r 9(2) retained by CPR).

The Limited Liability Partnerships Act 2000 creates a new form of legal entity, 'the limited liability partnership' distinct from its members. It is unlikely that the defendant will be such an entity.

(c) Persons under disability – children and patients

- Persons under 18
- Persons who by reason of mental disorder within the meaning of the Mental Health Act 1983 are incapable of managing their affairs

These persons may become involved in litigation, either suing or defending. However, there have to be safeguards in the interests of the persons themselves, and for those with whom they do business. The procedure is contained in Part 21 of the Civil Procedure Rules. A child must bring or defend proceedings by a litigation friend unless the court has made an order permitting the child to do so on his own behalf. A patient must bring or defend proceedings by a litigation friend. The name of the litigation friend is added to the title of the action, so that it reads:

Between:
JANE SMITH (a child by GEORGE SMITH
her litigation friend) <u>Claimant</u>
and
PETER JONES (by GILLIAN JONES
his litigation friend) <u>Defendant</u>

A person authorised under Part VII of the Mental Health Act 1983 to conduct legal proceedings in the name of his patient or on his behalf is entitled to be the litigation friend of the patient in any proceedings to which his authority extends (CPR r 21.4) and must file an official copy of the order giving his authorisation to act.

If nobody has been appointed by the court or, in the case of a patient, been authorised under Part VII of the Mental Health Act 1983, 'a person may act as a litigation friend if he–

(a) can fairly and competently conduct the proceedings;
(b) has no adverse interest; and
(c) where the child or patient is a claimant, undertakes to be responsible for any costs the child or patient is ordered to pay' (CPR r 21.4(3)).

(d) Death of one of the parties

Actions do not necessarily end with the death of either of the litigants. Indeed, the basic principle is that they continue, the estate being represented by the deceased's personal representative (executor or administrator) who should be joined in the proceedings, and who will be treated as substituted for the deceased. This is similar to the rule for bankruptcy or for actions brought by or against the holder of an office, if the person goes out of office. Rules exist for dealing with actions where no personal representative has been appointed, but one should consult a solicitor where this happens.

(e) Bankruptcy

The bankruptcy of the claimant in an action does not cause the action to come to an end if, within such reasonable time as the court orders, a trustee elects to continue the action and to give security. Where a defendant has a bankruptcy order made against him, or being a limited company is subject to a winding-up order, the claimant in a simple money claim should consider whether it is not best for the action to be adjourned generally and lodge a proof of debt. It would be wise to seek legal advice if this occurs. A trustee in bankruptcy should sue or be sued as 'Trustee of the Estate of AB a bankrupt' without adding his own name.

Who to sue?

(f) Vexatious litigants

Finally from the defendant's point of view, you may discover that the person bringing the action against you has already been a claimant in a number of previous actions and the claims have been dismissed as lacking in substance or as being frivolous. Sadly there are people who have a propensity to sue others without good reason. Such a person is called a vexatious litigant. A 'vexatious litigant' is one who 'habitually and persistently and without any reasonable grounds institutes legal proceedings or applications'. The usual minimum number is four or five. If you wish to make an issue of this you should really seek legal advice. The claimant will have to go before a High Court judge and, if the judge agrees that he is a vexatious litigant, the person will be required to seek leave of the High Court before bringing any more actions. Effectively this bars any further such claims. A copy of such an order is printed in the *London Gazette* and noted by all the county courts in England and Wales. One well-known vexatious litigant sought to avoid such an order by arguing before the High Court judge that the previous actions had all been brought not by himself but by an earlier incarnation of his present self. Sadly the judge did not accept his plea.

4. Doubts over who to sue

If you have doubts over the correct person to sue, for example whether your claim is against X or Y, you can sue both at the same time or you can apply to join Y in the proceedings as a defendant and let the court decide which of them is liable. Often the defendant will claim that someone else is responsible. If done in the defence, that person should be joined in the action. The defendant may also apply at a later date to have another person included in the action. This is called joinder and is done by making a Part 20 claim (see Chapter 9). There are some risks in suing more than one defendant in that additional costs may be incurred which might be claimed by the party who turns out not to be liable (but see Chapter 11).

5. Time limits for bringing actions

The law requires that proceedings should be brought within a limited time. Compared with, say, making a social security claim, the time limits for civil actions are long – but nevertheless they must be kept in mind. If time has run out, the action is said to be statute barred.

The main time limits are:

- *Contract*: six years from the breach of contract complained of.
- *Tort*: six years from the date when the injury occurred.
- *Personal injury cases*: three years, but this can be extended. This runs from the date of the cause of action or knowledge.
- *Consumer Protection Act 1987*: three years.

Proceedings are started when the court issues a claim form at the request of the claimant (CPR r 7.2), but where the claim form as issued was received in the court office on a date earlier than the date on which it was issued by the court, the claim is 'brought' for the purposes of the Limitation Act 1980 and any other relevant statute on that earlier date.

If proceedings are being started near the expiry of the limitation period you should attend at court to issue the claim – do not risk posting the claim to the court, it may contain an error that will cause it to be returned un-issued.

Chapter 7

Starting legal action

This is the point at which your work will begin. There are a number of important questions which you now have to face. Fortunately in most cases these matters are reasonably simple.

- Where to commence proceedings?
- How to begin legal action?
- How to fill in the necessary forms?
- How much money should you claim?
- How much do you have to pay in court fees?

There is also one matter which, though usually straightforward, can become frustrating:

- How to serve the claim form on the defendant?

Small claims procedure is designed to be far less formal than ordinary civil procedure. Forms are used throughout and normally need not be expressed in legal language. All stages of initiating proceedings can be done by post. By and large, most errors in procedure can be cured. Nevertheless, the first step of commencing proceedings is perhaps the most vital of all. The leaflets produced by the Lord Chancellor's Department for litigants in person are invaluable at this stage and are available free of charge at the court and also at Citizens Advice Bureaux (CABx) and consumer advice centres. You should obtain and keep these for reference.

What do you need to do?

- find your local county court;
- tell the court official what it is you are claiming;
- obtain the relevant claim form;
- fill in the claim form with the appropriate number of copies;
- pay the court fees;
- get the court to arrange for service on the defendant;

Starting legal action

- allow 14 days from date of service to see whether the other party admits or defends your claim.

1. Which court?

Finding your local court should be relatively easy. The county courts of England and Wales are listed at the back of this book, along with their addresses and telephone numbers. If in doubt ask at your nearest advice centre. Each county court is open five days a week from 10 am to 4 pm for the purpose of initiating proceedings. The county court offices are closed:

(a) Saturdays and Sundays;
(b) the day before Good Friday from noon onwards and Good Friday;
(c) the Tuesday after the Spring Holiday;
(d) Christmas Eve, or if that is a Saturday, then 23 December, or if that is a Sunday or Tuesday, 27 December;
(e) Christmas Day, unless it is a Saturday or Sunday – in which case 28 December;
(f) bank holidays.

Since there are county courts all over the country it is helpful to bear in mind which one is appropriate to deal with your claim:

- in which court should you start proceedings?
- in which court will the hearing take place?

(a) Which court to commence proceedings?

You can issue proceedings in any county court, subject to exceptions that are not likely to be relevant to a small claim. However, if there is a defence, the case is automatically transferred to the county court nearest the defendant's home or place of business provided the claim is for a specified sum of money and the defendant is an individual (CPR r 26.2). This can be a nuisance to the claimant, of course, and may even discourage some people from proceeding with a claim. If the case has been transferred, you can apply to the new court giving the reasons for the case to be re-transferred to a more convenient court. Unfortunately this can cause delay; see Chapter 8, paragraph 8(a), at page 79.

If a claim is likely to be defended and therefore subject to automatic transfer, it may well be sensible to issue the claim in the defendant's home court. This will avoid delay.

County courts are listed under 'Courts' in the telephone directory, usually with the sub-heading 'county court'. County courts should not be confused with magistrates' courts which have a largely criminal jurisdiction. Most county courts have their own building or premises, some of which in smaller towns may be quite unprepossessing – others are housed in

Starting legal action

larger courts complexes called 'Law Courts' or similar. The administration and offices of the county courts are likely to be separate from other courts even though some facilities such as court rooms may be shared. The court offices may also be in a different building from the courthouse and judges' rooms.

The official list of courts and their districts is contained in two publications, the *County Court – Index of Place Names* and the *London County Courts Directory*. Their addresses are also to be found in Appendix 7. The area covered by each court can be established by checking one of the directories at any county court, and court staff can assist you with this. Most proceedings can be commenced in any county court so you need only look for the most convenient county court for you. The CAB or other advice centre will help you, or you could enquire of a local solicitor.

(b) In which court will the hearing take place?

The proper court to hear most cases is generally the defendant's home court unless the claim is not for a specified sum or the defendant is not an individual. This means the court for the district where the defendant resides or carries on business. It is important to note that nearly all small claims were automatically transferred to the defendant's court where the hearing would take place. However, as a result of the Civil Procedure Rules 1998 (CPR) the many consumer claims and holiday claims that are issued against firms or limited companies will remain in the claimant's court and are most likely to be tried in the claimant's court.

Where there are two or more defendants, automatic transfer will be to the home court of the defendant who is first to file his defence provided he is an individual. The automatic transfer does not take place when the claimant makes a claim for an unspecified amount.

These rules will determine the venue or court where the hearing will take place. If you do not like the venue of the hearing, you can ask for a transfer (see Chapter 8). There are certain classes of claim (for example, claims for the possession of a dwelling house) that have to be issued in a specific county court (in the example given, the county court for the district where the land is situated), but these are unlikely to be small claims.

2. The claim form – CPR Part 7

Once you have discovered the location of your nearest county court you will probably wish to make your first visit to the court offices, if you have not already done so, in order to begin the necessary paperwork. However, it is not absolutely essential as this can be done by mail. Some offices are actually some distance from the court itself, though most are conveniently adjacent.

Proceedings are started when the court issues a claim form at the request of the claimant. A claimant must use practice form N1 or practice form

Starting legal action

N208. Form N208 is only appropriate for a claim brought under Part 8 of the Civil Procedure Rules 1998, that is where there is unlikely to be a substantial dispute of fact or where a rule or practice direction requires or permits the Part 8 procedure. Form N1 will almost invariably be appropriate for small claims.

When the court starts the proceedings on the filing of the completed claim form and payment of the issue fee, it will hand or send to the claimant a completed form N205A – Notice of Issue (Specified Amount) and Request for Judgment – or a completed form N205B – Notice of Issue (Unspecified Amount) and Request for Judgment. Both these forms show the date by which the defendant has to reply and if he does not, the Request for Judgment part of the form can be detached, completed and lodged at the court to obtain judgment without any hearing. If the sum claimed was specified it will be awarded for that amount, or if unspecified it will be for such sum as the court shall determine after a hearing. That hearing will only be to determine the amount, as the defendant's liability to pay will have been established by the entry of judgment.

Claim forms can also be obtained at many advice centres, and advisers may help you fill them in, or you could ask one of the court staff for assistance or seek help from a solicitor at this stage. Normally you will fill in the claim form at home in your own time and using your own language. You should do so slowly and carefully. The claim form itself contains clearly written instructions. It is the most important (indeed often the only) document that you are likely to encounter in this type of action, and it is imperative that you get it right. The form of the claim form – N1 – is reproduced on pages 52–53 below.

You need three copies of the form – one for yourself, one for the court, and one for the court to send to the person you are suing. If you are suing more than one person, you need additional copies for each of them. You need not fill out each form individually, photocopies will do, so you may wish to take the form away with you.

If photocopies are necessary it is best to make them yourself as the court charges a fee for photocopies.

(a) Filling in the claim form

Forms are only available in English (and Welsh in courts in Wales), and if there are difficulties or you have problems with reading you should tell the court staff or seek help from a friend or at an advice centre. When filling in the form, bear the following in mind.

Claimant

- You are called the 'claimant'. Write your full name, whether Mr, Mrs, Ms or other (e.g. Dr), and residential address (including postcode) and telephone number.
- If you are **a firm**, write the name followed by the words 'a firm' and the address of the firm.

Starting legal action

Form N1 – Claim form

Claim Form	In the
	Claim No.
	Issue date

for court use only

Claimant

SEAL

Defendant(s)

Brief details of claim

Value

Defendant's name and address		£
	Amount claimed	
	Court fee	
	Solicitor's costs	
	Total amount	

The court office at
is open between 10 am and 4 pm Monday to Friday. When corresponding with the court, please address forms or letters to the Court Manager and quote the claim number.
N1 Claim form (CPR Part 7) (01.02)

© Crown copyright

(Cont'd)

Starting legal action

	Claim No.	

Does, or will, your claim include any issues under the Human Rights Act 1998?   ☐ Yes   ☐ No

Particulars of Claim (attached)(to follow)

Statement of Truth
*(I believe)(The Claimant believes) that the facts stated in these particulars of claim are true.
* I am duly authorised by the claimant to sign this statement

Full name _____

Name of claimant's solicitor's firm _____

signed _____ position or office held _____
*(Claimant)(Litigation friend)(Claimant's solicitor)   (if signing on behalf of firm or company)
*delete as appropriate

Claimant's or claimant's solicitor's address to which documents or payments should be sent if different from overleaf including (if appropriate) details of DX, fax or e-mail.

© Crown copyright

Starting legal action

Example – showing how to fill out a N1 Claim form

Claim Form

In the
[(Specify name of county court)
County Court]

for court use only

Claim No.

Issue date

SEAL

Claimant   *[Both for yourself (or yourselves) as claimant and for the defendant set out:*
All forename(s) and surname and whether Mr, Mrs, Miss or Ms
Full residential address, including postcode
Telephone number
** If **trading under another name** state that this is so* – '*Alan Simons trading as No 13*'

Defendant(s)   ** If **a firm** - 'Small claim (a firm)' - specify either the residential address of one of the partners or the firm's principal or last known place of business*
** If a **limited company** registered in England and Wales - specify the precise name of the company and the address of the registered office or a place of business having a real connection with the claim*
If you do not know the defendant's forename(s) include his/her initials]

Brief details of claim
[For example:
*In a claim relating to **defective goods**-*
 '*supply of goods not reasonably fit for the purpose for which they were supplied and not of satisfactory quality' and interest*
*In a claim for the **price of goods sold and delivered**-*
 '*purchase price of bicycle sold and delivered by the claimant to the defendant' and interest*
*In a claim for **unpaid cheques**-*
 '£   *being the amount of a cheque drawn by the defendant in favour of the claimant which was dishonoured when presented' and interest]*

Value
['I do not expect to recover more than £5,000 and claim £   and £   interest to the date of issue
Total £   '
Or
'I cannot say how much I expect to recover but I do not expect to recover more than £5,000; I also claim interest']

Defendant's name and address

[Normally the same information as given above as to the defendant]

£

Amount claimed	*[Specify amount or state 'limited to £5,000']*
Court fee	
Solicitor's costs	
Total amount	

The court office at
[The court will complete this section]
is open between 10 am and 4 pm Monday to Friday. When corresponding with the court, please address forms or letters to the Court Manager and quote the claim number.
N1 Claim form (CPR Part 7) (01.02)

© Crown copyright

(Cont'd)

Starting legal action

	Claim No.	

Does, or will, your claim include any issues under the Human Rights Act 1998? ☐ Yes ☐ No
[Tick appropriate box - almost certainly 'no' in small claims]
Particulars of Claim (attached)(to follow)

[For example:
*Claim in respect of **defective goods**:*
'1 The defendant sold and delivered to me a bicycle on (specify date) for (specify price) for which a copy of the receipt is attached
2 It was an implied condition that the bicycle would be reasonably fit for the purpose for which it was supplied and that it would be of satisfactory quality
3 It was not. The bicycle had the following defects:
(list defects)
4 The defendant refused to take the bicycle back when I rejected it and refused to repay £ (specify price)
5 Alternatively, as a result of the breach of the agreement I have suffered damage because the bicycle in its present condition is virtually worthless
6 I claim either repayment of the price £ (specify price) or alternatively damages for breach of contract
7 I also claim interest at 8% pa under section 69 of the County Courts Act 1984 on the said sum of £ (specify price) being a daily rate of (specify) and up to issue totalling (specify) and continuing at the daily rate until judgment'
*Claim for **unpaid price of goods delivered**:*
'1 I sold and delivered a bicycle (describe it) to the defendant on (specify date) at a price of £ (specify) which he has not paid despite demands
2 I claim £ (specify) and interest' (continue in the same manner as in clause 7 above)
*Claim on **dishonoured cheque**:*
'1 The defendant drew a cheque (copy attached) on XY Bank for £ (specify amount) in my favour
2 On presentation the cheque was dishonoured and notice of dishonour was given to the defendant by letter dated (specify) a copy of which is attached
3 I claim £ (specify amount) and interest' (continue as in clause 7 above)]

Statement of Truth
*(I believe)(The Claimant believes) that the facts stated in these particulars of claim are true.
* I am duly authorised by the claimant to sign this statement

Full name _____
Name of claimant's solicitor's firm _____

signed _____ position or office held _____
*(Claimant)(Litigation friend)(Claimant's solicitor) (if signing on behalf of firm or company)
delete as appropriate

[Specify]	Claimant's or claimant's solicitor's address to which documents or payments should be sent if different from overleaf including (if appropriate) details of DX, fax or e-mail.

© Crown copyright

Starting legal action

- If you are **a person trading under another name**, write your own name followed by the words 'trading as' and your trading name.
- If you are **a limited company**, write the name of the company and an address where the company trades that has a real connection with the claim, or the address of its registered office.
- If you are **under 18 years of age**, you cannot make a claim yourself. Ask the court for form N235 and get someone over 18 to make the claim for you, for example one of your parents.

Defendant

The person you are claiming from is called the 'defendant'.
Write the name and address of the defendant who is to receive the form (one claim form for each defendant).

- **If you do not know their full name**, write their initials before their surname and 'Mr', 'Mrs', 'Ms' or 'Miss'.
- **If they are under 18**, write 'a child' after their name.
- **If they are a firm, a person trading under another name or a limited company** see advice given under Claimant, above.

Address for service (and payment)

- Only fill in this box if you want court papers and payments sent to you at a different address from the one written by the claimant.

Brief details of claim

You should write something like 'Goods sold'; 'Defective Workmanship'; 'Breach of Contract'; 'Money lent'. You should also set out the remedy you are seeking, for example:

- payment of money;
- return of goods;
- an order forbidding a person from doing some act (an injunction);
- damages for personal injuries.

See example claim form at page 54.

Particulars of claim

These are the details of why the defendant owes the money you are claiming, or, from the other point of view, are the particulars of the claimant's claim against you. They may be provided in the space allocated on the claim form or in a separate document headed 'Particulars of Claim' and showing case number and the parties. Separate particulars of claim may be served with the claim form or within 14 days of its service. They should include:

- a concise statement of the facts on which you rely;
- if you are claiming **interest**, a statement to that effect and the required details (see below under (b));
- if you are claiming aggravated damages or exemplary damages (this is unlikely), a statement to that effect;

Starting legal action

- details required by any practice direction for the type of claim being made. The practice direction to Part 16 contains specific provisions for the contents of the particulars of claim in a number of types of claim. Those relevant to small claims are:
  (i) personal injury claims;
  (ii) hire purchase claims.

You should then sign the statement of truth underneath the particulars of claim.

In small claims actions the particulars of claim are normally written on the claim form or attached to it. They should set out paragraph by paragraph the main facts of your case, followed by the legal basis for the claim, and the amount claimed. Most people should be able to do this themselves, though getting a solicitor or friend to do so might be an advantage in some cases. Advice centres may do this for you. They should be signed by the claimant, or by a solicitor acting for the claimant, giving an address for service.

A party in his particulars of claim may:

- refer to any point of law on which he relies;
- give the name of any witness he proposes to call;
- attach copies of any documents on which he relies (including any expert's report).

See form N1 at pages 52–53 and the example completed N1 incorporating particulars of claim at pages 54–55.

(b) Value

You must decide how much you are claiming. Obviously the claim has to be within the £5,000 limit to be considered a small claim. The following will be disregarded in assessing the value: amounts not in dispute, interest (unless due under a contract) and costs.

- You should make an honest effort to value your claim fairly. Legal advice can often be necessary to estimate for how much a claim can be made.
- What if you over-value your claim to put it beyond the limit? It will probably not be allocated to the small claims track, but if the claim turns out to be for far less you will probably lose your entitlement to costs and may be liable for the costs of the other party.
- If part of the claim is for damages for personal injuries of which the financial value of the pain, suffering and loss of amenity is more than £1,000, it will normally be allocated outside the small claims track.
- If the claim is by a tenant of residential premises and includes a request for an order that the landlord carry out repairs or other works estimated to cost more than £1,000, it will normally be allocated outside the small claims track.

Starting legal action

- If there is a counterclaim against the claimant the court will regard the larger of the two claims (the claim and the counterclaim) as determining the value.

The amount of your claim

Actions may be for a debt or for damages either for a specified or unspecified sum. Damages are normal in personal injury actions but also for consequential loss in breach of contract actions.

A claim for damages or harassment or unlawful eviction, relating to residential premises, cannot in any circumstances be allocated to the small claims track.

Most small claims are for a specified sum or debt. As a claimant it is simpler for you if this is so. You should complete the space opposite the word 'value' on the first page of form N1:

> 'The claimant expects to recover not more than £5,000 and claims £ [specify total claimed] inclusive of £ [specify interest claimed] interest to the date of issue.'

Damages

A default judgment for damages of an unspecified amount will initially be for 'an amount to be decided by the court'. After the entry of the judgment there still has to be a hearing to quantify the damages, and the defendant has the right to attend and take part in the hearing. These are more common in personal injury claims. The calculation of damages and how much to claim under the various headings such as loss of earnings, loss of future earnings, pain and suffering and loss of amenity, may call for the advice of a solicitor.

Where a small claim includes a claim for personal injuries regard must be had to the personal injuries protocol (see Chapter 12).

Further the particulars of claim in such situations actions must contain:

- the claimant's date of birth; and
- brief details of the claimant's personal injuries.

The claimant must attach to the particulars of claim a schedule of details of any past and future expenses and losses which he claims.

Where the claimant is relying on the evidence of a medical practitioner he must attach to, or serve with, the particulars of claim a report from the medical practitioner about the personal injuries which he alleges in his claim.

Court fees

When you issue a claim form you have to pay a fee, quantified according to the amount of your claim. Appendix 1 gives the table of fees as of April 1999. These change from time to time, but the court will tell you

Starting legal action

about this. You add the fee to your claim – it should be inserted into the appropriate box on the claim form. The fee is of course *recoverable* from the defendant if you win your case. You can pay by cash, postal order or cheque, accompanied by cheque card, payable to 'HM Paymaster General'. If you cannot afford to pay the fee, you can ask the court for a fee exemption application form. A request can only be considered if it is made in this form. You will have to produce evidence of income support by producing a valid benefit book or giro cheque.

Are you allowed interest on your claim?

You can claim contractual interest on your claim, if you think you are entitled, from the date the money claimed first became payable to the date of issue of the claim and continuing interest from issue until payment by specifying a daily rate.

Contractual interest can only be claimed where there is an agreement that the defendant will pay interest on any unpaid debts. The amount of interest depends on what has been agreed. Where this does not apply, the claimant can claim statutory interest of 8 per cent per annum from the date that the money became due to the date of judgment. The claim for statutory interest must be set out in the claim form, the amount due to the date of issue of the claim form calculated, and a daily rate given. Interest where claimed should therefore run from the date when the right to payment arose. In cases involving invoices, this is normally when 28 days have passed since delivery of the invoice.

One important difference between statutory and contractual interest is that the former is not taken into account in deciding whether the claim is for more than £5,000, whereas the latter is – i.e. if the basic claim is for £4,990 + £50 interest, it will be a small claim if the interest claimed is 'pursuant to statute' but not if it is payable under an agreement. Of course the excess can be waived.

What happens after you have paid your fee?

- You are given a form N205A (specified amount) (see page 81) or N205B (unspecified amount) (see page 82) which is a receipt for your fee, and also gives your case a reference number. This is called the 'Notice of Issue'. The case number is important and should be quoted in all correspondence. Keep this form safe. It is important and you will need it later. It will also give you the date of service and incorporates a Request for Judgment for use where the defendant does not file a defence or dispute the jurisdiction of the court.
- The court will send by first class post to each defendant a copy of the claim form and a Response Pack (form N9) including forms for defending claim, for admitting claim and for acknowledgement of service. This is known as service. The forms N9A and N9B allow the other party to admit or defend your claim. The court then

Starting legal action

sends you a notice (N215) informing you of the date when the claim form was served on the defendant.
- The person to whom you have sent the claim form has 14 days to respond.

The period allowed for response runs for 14 days after service is deemed to have been effected. This is normally two days after posting by the court, which will use first class post, of the originating process.

The defendant may respond by:
- filing an acknowledgement of service;
- filing or serving an admission;
- filing a defence.

(See Chapter 8.)

(c) Multiple claims

Large organisations such as utilities, finance companies or mail order firms obviously have to issue many thousands of claim forms every year for non-payment. In order to assist both them and the county courts themselves, where particular courts could have become completely overloaded with work, the Production Centre has existed since December 1989 to deal with the issuing of claim forms in large numbers for particular claimants.

Those interested in using the Centre should write to the Bulk Issue Liaison Officer, County Court Bulk Issue, St Katherine's House, St Katherine's Street, Northampton NN1 2LH (Tel: 01604 601636).

Any reader of this book who obtains permission to use the Production Centre is likely to be issuing a significant number of claims and will need to take careful note of Practice Direction – Production Centre which is issued pursuant to CPR r 7.10.

(d) Money claims online

A pilot scheme commenced on 17 December 2001 to last until 16 June 2003 whereby claims for money only, not exceeding £100,000 in sterling, can be started electronically in the Northampton County Court and the court fee paid by credit card. A defence may be filed by delivering it by post, or otherwise, to the Northampton County Court office or, provided it does not include a counterclaim, by e-mail.

Details are set out in the Court Service pamphlet which is reproduced on page 61.

Starting legal action

Money Claim Online

- Do you want to issue a county court claim – and have it issued and posted within 48 hours?
- Do you have access to the Internet – to send us your claim details at any time of the day or night?
- Do you have a credit or debit card – to pay your court fees more conveniently?

If you have answered yes to all three of these questions, why not issue your claim online?

If your claim is against:

- no more than two defendants
- who have a postal address within England and Wales; and
- you wish to recover a fixed amount of money (a 'specified amount'); and
- that amount is less than £100,000

you can use *Money Claim* Online.

This is a brand new service that the Court Service is offering its customers.

To find out more, visit our website at:

www.courtservice.gov.uk

© Crown copyright

Note for direct access to money claims online use www.courtservice.gov.uk/mcol

Starting legal action

3. Service

Service of the claim form may be the most trying and difficult part of the process for many people. Do not be surprised if it goes wrong. At one time all originating process had to be personally served. Service of the originating process may now be by the court or the claimant, and where by the court, will normally be by first class post.

The methods of service available are:

- personal service (except where a solicitor is authorised to accept service and has confirmed this in writing);
- by first class post;
- by leaving the document at the place of service;
- through a document exchange (provided there has been no indication that service will not be accepted by this method);
- by fax or other means of electronic communication (provided it has been indicated in writing that service will be so accepted);
- by any contractually agreed method.

(a) By post

Most claim forms are now served by post, and this method should be used by litigants in person. The other methods are less easy to use.

It is important that you provide a correct and up-to-date address for the defendant. If this is done, service by post will usually be successful. If the address at which the defendant lives or carries on business is not known, you will either have to serve personally or obtain an order for substituted service. Very occasionally you may have had correspondence with the defendant's solicitor; if the solicitor agrees to accept service on the defendant's behalf, the claim form must be sent to the solicitor. Service is deemed to be effective two clear days after the court posts the claim form by first class post. If the particulars of claim are not served with the claim form, they must be served within 14 days of the claim form.

Where the claim form is served by the claimant, he must file a certificate of service with the court within seven days of service.

The general rule is that service of the claim form must be effected within four months after the date of issue, but the time for service out of the jurisdiction is extended to six months.

A word of warning is appropriate at this point. Many judgments are obtained as a result of documents being sent to the wrong address or not received by the defendant. If this happens, the defendant may later apply for judgment to be set aside.

(b) By court bailiff

Where the court is to serve a document it is for the court to decide which of the methods permitted by the rules is to be used. In practice it will choose first class post, rather than bailiff service.

Starting legal action

(c) Personal service

You may serve the claim form yourself, if you know where the person you are claiming against lives or works. Where you or your solicitor effect personal service, this is proved by filing a certificate of service within seven days of service of the claim form.

A document is served personally on an individual by leaving it with that individual; on a company or other corporation by leaving it with a person holding a senior position within the company or corporation; and on a partnership, where partners are being sued in the name of the partnership, by leaving it with a partner or person having control or management of the principal place of business of the partnership at the time of service (CPR r 6.4).

(d) Service by alternative method

This is relatively rare, particularly in small claims. If it appears to the court that there is good reason to authorise service by a method not permitted by the Civil Procedure Rules 1998, the court may make an order permitting service by an alternative method.

An application for such an order should be made on form N244 which incorporates in Part C space for the reasons for the application, and in Part D a statement of truth. Form N244 should be used when making most applications to the court after the issue of proceedings and is reproduced at pages 64–65.

An order permitting service by an alternative method must specify:

- the method of service; and
- the date on which the claim form is deemed to be served.

The application for service by an alternative method may be made without notice to the defendant and the requirement that it be supported by evidence may be satisfied by completion of Part C and the statement of truth.

(e) Service on special parties

Suing a partnership

Service may be effected personally on any partner at any place or by any other permitted method (see page 62) on the partnership at its principal place of business. Additionally service can be effected by service at the principal place of business on a person who at the time of such service has control or management of such business.

Limited companies registered in England and Wales

A company may be served by any method permitted by the Civil Procedure Rules 1998 as an alternative to service in accordance with section 725(1) of the Companies Act 1985. The fact that the company has vacated its registered office without leaving a forwarding address does not

Starting legal action

Form N244 – application notice

Application Notice

- You must complete Parts A **and** B, **and** Part C if applicable
- Send any relevant fee and the completed application to the court with any draft order, witness statement or other evidence; and sufficient copies of these for service on each respondent

In the

Claim no.

Warrant no. (If applicable)

Claimant (including ref.)

Defendant(s) (including ref.)

Date

You should provide this information for listing the application

1. Do you wish to have your application dealt with at a hearing? Yes ☐ No ☐ If Yes, please complete 2

2. Time estimate _____ (hours) _____ (mins)

Is this agreed by all parties? ☐ Yes ☐ No

Level of judge _____

3. Parties to be served: _____

Part A

1. Enter your full name, or name of solicitor
   I (We)(1) _____ (on behalf of)(the claimant)(the defendant)

2. State clearly what order you are seeking and if possible attach a draft
   intend to apply for an order (a draft of which is attached) that(2) _____
   because(3) _____

3. Briefly set out why you are seeking the order. Include the material facts on which you rely, identifying any rule or statutory provision

Part B

I (We) wish to rely on: *tick one box*

the attached (witness statement)(affidavit) ☐   my statement of case ☐

evidence in Part C in support of my application ☐

4. If you are not already a party to the proceedings, you must provide an address for service of documents

Signed _____   **Position or office held** _____
(Applicant)('s solicitor)('s litigation friend)   (if signing on behalf of firm or company)

Address to which documents about this claim should be sent (including reference if appropriate)(4)

	if applicable
fax no.	
DX no.	
Tel. no. _____ Postcode _____	e-mail

The court office at _____ is open from 10am to 4pm Monday to Friday. When corresponding with the court please address forms or letters to the Court Manager and quote the claim number.

N244 Application Notice (4.99)   *Printed on behalf of The Court Service*

© Crown copyright

(Cont'd)

Starting legal action

Part C Claim No.

I (We) wish to rely on the following evidence in support of this application:

Statement of Truth

*(I believe)(The applicant believes) that the facts stated in this application are true

Signed _____   **Position or office held** _____
(Applicant)('s solicitor)('s litigation friend)   (if signing on behalf of firm or company)

Date _____

*delete as appropriate

© Crown copyright

Starting legal action

usually affect the validity of the service. The district judge will generally require proof that the address was up to date before deeming service to have been made. CPR r 6.6 permits service on a company registered in England and Wales 'at any place of business of the company which has some real connection with the claim in issue'. This means you can serve on the local branch of a national retailer.

In the case of service by post under the Companies Act, delivery is presumed by 'ordinary course of post'. The presumed date of service is the second working day for first class and fourth working day for second class. There is no presumption if the letter is returned by the Post Office undelivered.

(f) How do you know on what date the person receives the claim form?

The court will tell you when the other person has been sent the claim form. The date should be shown on your 'notice of issue' together with the date on which service will be deemed to have taken place and the date by which the defendant must respond.

The certificate of service (N215) must state:

- that the document has not been returned undelivered; and
- the date of posting, personal service, or as the case may be.

(g) What happens if the defendant does not receive the claim form?

- If the address is wrong or the defendant has moved the Post Office will return the claim form to the court.
- The court will then send you 'a notice of non-service'. Such reasons as 'Not known' or 'Gone away' are set out in the form. Where this happens you should try to serve by a different method.
- You must check on the defendant's new or correct address and begin the process of service again. The court will tell you when he or she receives the claim form.
- The defendant must receive the claim form within four months of the date of starting the claim. After a lapse of time or if you have difficulty, contact the court as soon as possible, and in the event of non-service, apply to the court to extend the time for service before the expiry of the four-month period (use form N244). Many people have a very frustrating experience, trying unsuccessfully to serve defendants who are determined or devious enough to avoid service. Unfortunately there is no real answer to this. It may be worthwhile trying to serve personally.
- If you receive no reply at all to a claim form which has been duly served you can then proceed to judgment. The next chapter deals with this, and also how to deal with a claim form from the defendant's point of view.

Chapter 8

Judgment in default; admitting or defending a claim; summary judgment

1. What to do when you receive a claim form

Up to this point we have concentrated on the action from the point of view of the claimant. It is now appropriate to consider the position of the defendant. The service of the claim form will usually have been preceded by a letter threatening legal action, though it may come as a bolt out of the blue. The claim form will usually arrive through the post but may be personally served by handing it to you, or to someone else for you or by putting it through your letter box. It must be treated seriously, and acted upon promptly, or you will find yourself with a judgment debt. A register of such debts is kept by the courts, and these records can be inspected (see Chapter 13). Unpaid judgment debts can seriously damage your credit rating. Summonses for non-payment of council tax are not part of the system being described and go to the magistrates' courts rather than the county courts. The rules of magistrates' courts are entirely different.

The defendant normally receives two documents:

- a claim form which will normally include the particulars of claim;
- a Reply Pack (N9) including a form of admission and a form of defence and counterclaim

On the claim form there is a section which should tell you what the claim is about. You should look first at the particulars of the claim to see why the claimant issued the claim form. The claim form tells you how much the claimant is claiming and also states that judgment may be obtained without further notice unless there is a defence or you pay the amount of claim and court costs to the claimant within 14 days from the date of receiving it. The person who receives a claim form should read the instructions on it carefully. If you are uncertain as to what to do, seek advice (see Chapter 4) – or if you think some mistake has been made, contact the claimant urgently.

Judgment in default; admitting or defending a claim; summary judgment

Notes

1. If the particulars of claim are not contained in or served with the claim form, they should be served within 14 days after its service. The defendant's time to respond is extended to 14 days after their receipt.
2. Certain types of claims will include a notice of the hearing date; they include claims for possession by mortgagees of land. This will be apparent from the claim form. They will not be allocated to the small claims track.

There are a number of ways of dealing with a claim form where the claim will fall to be allocated to the small claims track after the filing of a defence. These depend on whether the claim is for a specified or unspecified amount, and whether the claim is defended either entirely or in part.

  (a) Ignore the claim form and do not bother to reply. The claimant will then be entitled to judgment in default.
  (b) If the claim is for a specified amount and you admit liability for all the claims, pay the money claimed, together with any interest and costs claimed, direct to the claimant within 14 days.
  (c) If the claim is for a specified amount which you admit but you need time to pay, complete form N9A and send it to the claimant within 14 days. If the claimant accepts your offer he can request judgment on the agreed terms, and if he does not accept, the court will decide how payment is to be made and enter judgment accordingly.
  (d) If the claim is for a specified amount and you admit only part of it, complete forms N9A and N9B and send them to the court within 14 days. If the claimant accepts your offer he may request judgment for the admitted amount, but if he rejects the offer the case will proceed as a defended claim.
  (e) If the claim is for an unspecified amount which you admit but do not offer to satisfy, complete form N9C and send it to court within 14 days. The claimant may request judgment to be entered for an amount to be decided by the court and costs.
  (f) If the claim is for an unspecified amount and you admit liability and offer a sum of money to satisfy the claim, complete form N9C and send it to the court within 14 days. If the claimant accepts the sum offered he can request judgment for that sum, and if he does not accept, he can request judgment for an amount to be decided by the court.
  (g) If you are disputing the claim and need longer than 14 days to prepare your defence or dispute the court's jurisdiction, you can complete the Acknowledgement of Service form and send it to the court within 14 days. This will extend your time to respond to 28 days from the service of the particulars of claim.
  (h) If you are disputing the full amount of a claim for a specified

68

Judgment in default; admitting or defending a claim; summary judgment

       amount or want to make a claim against the claimant, complete form N9B and send it to the court within 14 days.

(i) If you are disputing part only of a claim for a specified amount, proceed as in (d) above.

(j) If you are disputing a claim for an unspecified amount or a claim for return of goods or a non-money claim or wish to make a claim against the claimant, complete form N9D and send it to the court within 14 days.

       If the claim is for personal injuries and the claimant has attached a medical report to the particulars of claim, in your defence you should state whether you:

- agree with the report; or
- dispute all or part of the report, and give your reasons for doing so; or
- neither agree with nor dispute the report, or have no knowledge of the report.

       Where you have obtained your own medical report, you should attach it to your defence.

       If the claim is for personal injuries and the claimant has attached a schedule of past and future expenses and losses, in your defence you must state which of the items you:

- agree with; or
- dispute, and supply alternative figures to where appropriate; or
- neither agree with nor dispute, or have no knowledge of.

Notes

1. In all cases the defendant must give an address to which notices are to be sent: his solicitor's address, his own residential or business address in England and Wales, or if the defendant lives outside England and Wales, some other address in England and Wales.

2. In all forms of admission or defence the statement of truth must be signed by the defendant, his solicitors or his litigation friend. Where the defendant is a registered company or corporation there are particular rules as to who can sign the certificate of truth (see the Practice Direction to CPR Part 22) but generally an officer of the company and the town clerk of the corporation may do so.

3. The court may strike out a statement of case (which includes the claim form and particulars of claim) on application or of its own motion if it:

    - discloses no reasonable ground for bringing or defending the claim;
    - is an abuse of process;
    - fails to comply with a rule, practice direction or order of the court.

    Any application to use these powers should be on form N244.

Judgment in default; admitting or defending a claim; summary judgment

4. There is power in Part 24 of the Civil Procedure Rules 1998 (CPR) for a claimant or defendant to apply for summary judgment; see paragraph 9 below.

2. Judgment in default

The essence of the default procedure is that if the person does not either pay the claim to the claimant or file with the court a defence or counterclaim, the claimant may have judgment entered against the defendant by default.

(a) Calculation of time

The defendant has 14 days from the *day after* he is deemed to have received the claim form, or if the particulars of claim were served later, from receipt of the particulars of claim, to reply. The 14-day period includes weekends and other days when the court is closed. It is important to note that the claimant should not begin the calculation of the number of days from the date of posting of the claim form but from two days later. This means 16 days from posting. The notice of issue or form N222 (notice of service) will tell you when the claim form was posted. Once the day has arrived and nothing has been heard from the defendant, the claimant then asks the court to 'enter judgment by default'. Form N205A is usually used for this. Thousands of judgments are obtained annually in this way.

Throughout the procedure for small claims there are references to time limits for doing certain things or periods of waiting time before a step can be taken. Periods of time fixed by the rules or by an order of the court are clear days before a return day, which means that in computing the number of days–

(a) the day on which the period begins, and
(b) if the end of the period is defined by reference to an event, the day on which that event occurs,

are not included.

There are also two provisions concerning computation of time when the court office is closed:

- Where a time period for doing an act *at the court office* expires on a day on which the office is closed, 'the act shall be in time if done on the next day on which that office is open'.
- In computing time periods of *five days or less*, Saturdays, Sundays, bank holidays, Christmas Day and Good Friday are not counted. However, for longer time limits they are.

Where the court imposes a time limit for doing an act, the last date for compliance must, wherever practicable:

Judgment in default; admitting or defending a claim; summary judgment

- be expressed as a calendar date; and
- include the time of day by which the act must be done.

If you do run out of time for some reason, for example you have been away on holiday, application can be made to a district judge to extend any time period fixed by the rules. There must be good reason for the failure to comply with the time limit, and where faced with such a difficulty the application should, if possible, be made before the expiry of the time limit. You can ask the district judge to deal with your application without a hearing, but he may decide that a hearing of the application should take place. If he does so decide, you and the other party will be sent notice of the hearing appointment.

(b) If the defendant ignores the claim form

If the defendant does nothing about the claim form, the claimant, having waited the requisite number of days, should request judgment in default by immediately completing the Request for Judgment form (form N205A, N205B or N225 – reproduced at the end of this chapter).

Make sure that you do not forget to do any of the following:

- Tick box A.
- Sign and date.
- Complete the box at top right – details can be copied from the corresponding box on the front of the form.
- In the section for judgment details:
  - complete to show how you would like the money paid. You may want the whole amount in a lump sum – but if you think that the defendant will be unable to manage this, then ask for instalments in reasonable amounts;
  - state the amount claimed, adding the fee for the claim form (and solicitors' costs on issue and entry of judgment, if appropriate);
  - deduct any payment that you may have received from the other party;
  - include interest at 8 per cent, but only if asked for on the claim form.
- Tear off the Request for Judgment section of the form and return it to the court.

(c) Entering judgment

Once the request for judgment has been received, the court staff will then issue a judgment. The form is given an official stamp by the court and copies are then sent to both claimant and defendant.

The form tells the defendant:

- how much he or she has to pay;

71

- when to pay it;
- the address the money has to be sent to.

If the defendant still does not pay, you have to take steps to enforce judgment and you should proceed to Chapter 13. In order to enforce judgment you will have to pay a further fee.

The defendant may apply to have the judgment set aside. Such applications are commonplace and often abused. However, many such cases are not an abuse. The claimant may have got the wrong address or even the wrong defendant (see Chapter 10).

3. Admitting the claim

(a) The defendant

If the defendant decides to admit that he owes the claimant money, he should fill in the admission form N9A (specified amount), or N9C (unspecified amount and non-money claims), which is enclosed with the summons. The defendant should send form N9A to the claimant and not to the court. Form N9C should, however, be sent to the court.

The defendant can ask to pay the money in instalments or on a future date.

(b) The claimant

It is up to the claimant to decide whether or not to accept the defendant's proposal. Look at the defendant's offer and decide whether it is reasonable, bearing in mind what the defendant has said about his or her circumstances. Though the offer may not seem much, it is worth remembering that this may be the best you can hope to get. If you decide to accept the offer, complete the Request for Judgment form (form N205A, N205B or N225).

When completing form N205A:

- Tick box B, and the box accepting the defendant's proposal for payment.
- Sign and date.
- Complete the box at top right – details can be copied from the corresponding box on the front of the form.
- In the section for judgment details:
    - if you have accepted the defendant's proposal show the payment instalments as accepted otherwise complete to show how you would like the money paid. You may want the whole amount in a lump sum – but if you think that the defendant will be unable to manage this, then ask for instalments in reasonable amounts;
    - state the amount claimed, adding the fee for the claim form, and where appropriate, solicitors' costs;

Judgment in default; admitting or defending a claim; summary judgment

- deduct any payment that you may have received from the other party;
- include interest at 8 per cent, but only if asked for on the claim form.
- Tear off the Request for Judgment section of the form and return it to the court.

The court will complete the judgment order form. This is called entering judgment on acceptance and tells the defendant how much to pay, when to pay and the claimant's address. This is stamped with the court seal, and copies are sent to both parties.

If you think the defendant can pay bigger instalments than he offers, put your reasons on the reverse side, part D of form N205A, saying why you object, how much you would be willing to accept and when it should be paid. You can accept an offer for a limited period but ask for a larger amount, for example, after six months. Tear off the Request for Judgment section of the form and return it to the court office along with a copy of the defendant's form N9A. You should keep a photocopy of form N9A for yourself.

Faced with a disagreement between the parties over how the money should be paid, the court staff will look at the information supplied by the defendant (N9A) and the claimant (form N205A), and will then decide what would be a fair way to pay. The court then enters a judgment pursuant to CPR r 14.10. This is called 'entering judgment by determination', and tells the defendant:

- how much to pay;
- when to pay it; and
- the address to which money must be sent (i.e. the claimant's address).

It is stamped with a seal, and is sent to both parties – the claimant and the defendant.

(c) Reviewing the decision of the court staff – CPR r 14.13

Either party, if not willing to accept the decision of the court staff, can ask a district judge to review the decision of the court staff, and to decide a fair way to have the money paid. In order to make such an application, you should:

- obtain application form N244 from the court;
- fill in the form saying why you object to the rate of payment determined by the court staff. You may also write a letter giving this information, if you wish;
- send form N244 back to the court within 14 days of service of the determination.

The court staff will then give you a date for an appointment to see the district judge. Copies of form N244 giving the time, date and place of the

Judgment in default; admitting or defending a claim; summary judgment

appointment will be sent to both the claimant and defendant. The case will be transferred to the court *nearest the defendant* for the appointment if the defendant is an individual. You may therefore have to travel quite far (see Transfer to another court, page 79).

If the decision, which is the subject of redetermination, was made by a court officer the redetermination may take place without a hearing unless a hearing is requested in the application notice.

(d) The appointment

The appointment is held in the judge's room, called chambers. The hearing will be in private, with only the district judge, claimant and defendant present (the general rule that hearings are in private is displaced where personal financial matters are involved).

It is obviously important to arrive in good time, particularly as you may be unfamiliar with the court building. The court usher will be able to tell you where the district judge's room is located. Scheduling hearings is notoriously difficult for court staff and judges, so you should not be too upset if you have to wait. It is also wise and courteous to be reasonably smartly dressed. You can ask someone else to attend for you if you do not want to lose time at work, although strictly the court can refuse to allow that person to attend the hearing.

The appointment is unlikely to last for very long. The district judge is likely to read the reasons why each side has argued for a different mode of payment. He may ask questions about the defendant's income and expenses. The judge will wish to know the defendant's income per week or per month, including overtime, and also the income of other members of the family. It is helpful if the defendant can produce pay slips or other documents to confirm his statement of earnings – if he is unemployed, it helps if he can bring evidence in order to prove this. Having heard both sides, the judge will decide how the debt is to be paid. The court will then send both the claimant and defendant an order which confirms what the district judge decided at the appointment. This tells the defendant:

- how much to pay;
- when it has to be paid; and
- the address to which the claimant wishes the money to be sent.

A financial statement by the defendant is essential for a properly prepared application. CAB will often help to prepare this.

(e) Admitting part of the claim

If this is really an admission, then it should be treated in the manner described above. In fact, it is more likely to be a defence to the claim – see below for defending a claim.

Judgment in default; admitting or defending a claim; summary judgment

4. Payment of money claimed

If you wish to pay the amount claimed, then you should quickly post payment to the claimant at the address for payment which appears on the claim form. It is not safe to send cash except by registered post. Courts used to accept money as part of their 'banking function'. This has been almost entirely discontinued. The courts will no longer accept payments from litigants – except for some payments in enforcing judgment (see Chapter 13).

Postage on any payment sent by mail must be prepaid – and a stamped, addressed envelope should be enclosed so that a receipt can be sent to you. The case number which appears in the top right corner of the claim form or judgment must always be stated when making payment. Allow at least four days for payments to reach the claimant or his representative.

Keep records and make sure that you can account for all payments made. Proof may be required if there is any disagreement.

A leaflet giving advice about payment is obtainable from the county courts. If you need more information, contact the claimant or his solicitor if he has one.

Payment made before receipt of the claim form

Sometimes the defendant pays the amount claimed after the claim form had been issued, but before it had been served. The question then arises as to whether the defendant must pay the costs shown on the claim form. The claimant is put to expense the moment he files the claim form and provided he was justified in starting the proceedings, it is fair that the defendant should bear this cost. In the normal course of events a court will order a defendant to pay the costs even though the money was sent before the defendant actually received the claim form. If the claimant received the money before the claim form was issued, the defendant is not liable for the costs. You should therefore note the date when the claim form was issued and, if payment was made by cheque, the date that the cheque cleared.

If you paid by post, it is possible that the claimant may not have received your letter until after the claim form was issued. If no specific time had been fixed for payment, and the claimant gave you no warning that they intended to start proceedings, you may be able to persuade the court not to make any order as to the cost of issuing the claim form. However, you will have to attend court.

5. Defending the claim

You must have a valid defence to the claim in order to defend. You should therefore seek advice if you are unsure. If you wish to defend, fill in the 'Defence' section in the form of Defence and Counterclaim enclosed with the claim form (N9B where the amount is specified, as is usually the case, or form N9C where the amount is unspecified or is not for money) and return it to the court office within the period of 14 days mentioned in the instructions on the back of the claim form. A simple denial of liability is not sufficient – the claimant is entitled to know your reasons for disputing the claim. Study the particulars of the claim, and then in your defence deal with each of the claimant's allegations. Some you may agree with, others you will wish to deny. If your version of events is different, you must give your own account. An example defence is set out below. The further progress of the case now depends upon the strength of the claimant's case. On receipt of your defence, the court will send allocation questionnaires to all parties (see Chapter 9).

Example Defence – form N9B

(Note parts 1 and 2 of form N9B must be completed to show:

- amount disputed;
- any amount admitted;
- any payment made in respect of the claim.)

Part 3 – Defence to claim that goods supplied are defective

DEFENCE

1 I admit that I sold the goods to the claimant at the price stated as set out in the particulars of claim following an oral contract made between us.

2 I did not sell the goods [if sale was not a business sale] in the course of a business and accordingly the sale is not subject to the provisions for reasonable fitness nor satisfactory condition contained in s 14 of the Sale of Goods Act 1979 nor to any other implied condition.

[Or, if the sale was a business sale:]

2 Before making the contract I pointed out to the defendant the following defects: [list the defects].

3 Having had this information and before entering into the contract the claimant tested the goods by [specify] or had an expert [Mr XY] examine the goods on his behalf.

4 Accordingly the contract was not subject to the terms of reasonable fitness nor satisfactory condition so far as the defects I pointed out are concerned.

(Note:

- paragraph 4 of form N9B must be completed if the defendant wishes to counterclaim;
- paragraph 5 of form N9B incorporating a certificate of truth must be completed and signed.)

Sometimes a defendant is sued for payment of money that should really have been paid by someone else. For example, this can happen if a party

Judgment in default; admitting or defending a claim; summary judgment

has signed a guarantee to enable another to obtain goods on hire purchase. If that other then fails to keep up the payments, the guarantor has no defence to the claim and judgment will be entered against them. But they are entitled to be repaid by the defaulter.

If two friends agree to share a flat, but the tenancy is taken in the name of only one of them, that tenant will have to pay any arrears of rent if sued by the landlord – but naturally will want their friend to contribute.

In cases such as these, the defendant may ask that the person who should repay him or her be made a party to the action pursuant to CPR r 20.7. Such a person is called a Part 20 defendant. It is usually wise to seek advice before taking this step – Part 20 proceedings are discussed in Chapter 9.

It sometimes happens that the claimant's claim is not fully particularised. If the defendant requires further information, he is entitled to send a request for information and if the claimant does not respond to that request, an application can be made to the district judge for an order either staying the proceedings until the information is given, or for an order requiring the information to be given within a specified time. Similarly one of the parties may wish to see documents in the possession of the other party, and a request can be made for these to be produced for inspection. If an application is made to the court for information or for the production of documents and the claimant does not comply with the order, an application can be made to strike out the claimant's claim.

However, once the claim has been allocated to the small claims track the right to further information (under CPR Part 18) and to disclosure and inspection (under CPR Part 31) ceases to apply. If the requested information or documents are not received when the time for filing a defence has almost elapsed, an application for an extension of time for filing a defence will have to be made to prevent judgment being entered in default of defence.

6. Counterclaims – CPR Part 20

A counterclaim is a separate claim by the defendant against the claimant. Instead of the defendant having to bring his own action, it is easier to deal with both claims in the same proceedings. Very often a counterclaim is connected with the claimant's action, as in the case of two cars damaged in the same collision. However, a counterclaim need not be related to the claim. There is no need for a separate document, as there is a special section for counterclaim on form N9B which is enclosed with the claim form. The defendant must answer the questions in this section and return the form to the court office within 14 days after service of the claim form. The defendant will have to pay an additional court fee in respect of the counterclaim.

It is necessary for the claimant to file a defence to counterclaim if he disputes it or judgment on the counterclaim may be entered against him in default.

7. Setting aside judgment

A claim form does not have to be handed to the defendant personally, so it is possible that he may know nothing about it until the court order arrives by post, or the bailiff knocks on the door with power to seize goods in satisfaction of the judgment. A defendant who suddenly learns of the situation should go without delay to the county court office where the officials will be able to provide information about the claim. Take the copy of the court order with you or, if you have only learned about the judgment from the bailiff, you should ask the bailiff for the case number so that the court officials can trace the court papers.

(a) Grounds for setting aside judgment

A judgment entered because no defence was filed or because the defendant did not attend the hearing can be set aside by the court. Whether the district judge will do so will depend on the circumstances. If the claim form was not properly served and consequently you had no knowledge of the proceedings, you are entitled to have the judgment set aside as a matter of right, although you will have to attend court to satisfy the district judge that this is the case. If you received the claim form but failed to send the Defence (form N9B) to the court in time, or failed to attend the preliminary hearing, or even the small claim hearing, you may still apply for the judgment to be set aside but the district judge will then have a discretion whether or not to grant your application.

The court may set aside or vary a judgment entered in default of defence if:

(i) the defendant has a real prospect of defending the claim; or
(ii) there is some good reason why the judgment should be set aside or varied or the defendant should be allowed to defend the claim.

In exercising its discretion the court must have regard to whether the application to set aside was made promptly.

If you failed to file a defence, you must convince the district judge that you have real prospects of successfully defending the action before he will set aside the judgment. This is in your own interest because you would have to pay extra costs if it turned out that you had no real defence to the claim. If the court is satisfied that the claim form was served upon you and you have had notice of the hearing, the judge may require you to pay any costs or expenses incurred by the claimant as a result of your default before the judgment is set aside. Setting aside judgment is also dealt with on page 120.

8. Defended actions: which court? – CPR r 26.2

As we have already noted, the case is normally sent to the defendant's court once a defence has been received provided the claim is for a specified sum of money and the defendant is an individual. This is often very inconvenient to the claimant. When this happens you can ask for a change of venue to your own local court when completing the allocation questionnaire (see Chapter 9).

(a) Transfer to another court

The claimant or defendant may apply to have the action transferred or re-transferred to another county court more accessible to themselves. If you wish to do so, you must set out your reasons in the allocation questionnaire (form N150) at paragraph G. The decision is usually based on balance of convenience to the parties. Where there is conflict over this, the court may require parties to attend a hearing to determine the matter. Normally you have to show that on balance it would be cheaper and more convenient for the action to be tried in the court nearer you. The judge will take into account any prejudice that may result to one or both parties by ordering or refusing to order a transfer. If the transfer results in greater travelling expenses for a claimant and his witnesses, these may be claimed against the defendant if the action is successful.

(b) Possible grounds for arguing for change of court

- you are old or handicapped and cannot travel without difficulty;
- you cannot afford to defend the action if you have to travel so far;
- witnesses will have to travel;
- contract or subject-matter of the dispute is situated in your own district. This might be property that you wish the judge to inspect before reaching his decision.

9. Summary judgment

If a claimant thinks he can establish that the defendant has no real prospect of successfully defending the claim or a defendant thinks he can establish that the claimant has no real prospect of succeeding on the claim; then the claimant or defendant, as the case may be, may apply for summary judgment.

If the application for summary judgment is made prior to allocation the court is likely to defer allocation to track until the application has been dealt with. This is of considerable importance on the small claims track because the 'no costs rule' only comes into effect after allocation to the small claims track. Solicitors' costs may be awarded at a summary judgment hearing prior to the allocation to the small claims track.

The application cannot generally be made against a defendant until he has filed an acknowledgement of service or defence.

The application must be made using form N244 that must identify or be accompanied by any evidence relied on. The applicant must state in the notice or evidence that his opponent has no real prospect of success and there is no reason why the disposal of the claim should await a trial. The

Judgment in default; admitting or defending a claim; summary judgment

person against whom the application is made must file and service the evidence he relies on at least seven days prior to the hearing and the applicant must file any evidence in reply at least three days before the hearing.

The application will be heard before a district judge who may grant the application and give summary judgment or he may dismiss the application and give directions for the claim to proceed to trial. He may impose conditions to be complied with before the action may proceed to trial, for example the payment of money into court to await the outcome of the case. Costs will also be dealt with.

Judgment in default; admitting or defending a claim; summary judgment

10. Forms

(a) Form N205A – notice of issue (specified amount)

(Sample only)

© Crown copyright

Judgment in default; admitting or defending a claim; summary judgment

(b) Form N205B – notice of issue (unspecified amount)

Notice of Issue
(unspecified amount)

To the Claimant['s Solicitor]

In the

The court office at

is open between 10 am & 4 pm Monday to Friday
Tel:

Claim No.	
Claimant (including ref.)	
Defendant(s)	
Issue fee	£

Your claim was issued on [ ].
The court sent it to the defendant by first class post on [ ]
and it will be deemed to be served on [ ].
The defendant has until [ ] to reply.

The defendant may either

- **Pay an amount into court to satisfy your claim.** This is called a 'payment in satisfaction'. The court will notify you of the payment and you will have to decide whether to accept the amount offered.
- **Offer to pay you an amount to satisfy your claim and/or ask for time to pay.** The court will send you a copy of the defendant's reply and you will have to decide what you want to do.
- **Admit liability for your claim but not offer an amount in satisfaction.** The court will send you a copy of the defendants's reply and you will be able to request judgment for amount to be decided by the court and costs.

- **File an acknowledgment of service.** This will allow the defendant 28 days from the date of service of your particulars of claim to file a defence or contest the court's jurisdiction. The court will send you a notice that an acknowledgment has been filed.
- **Dispute your claim.** The court will send you a copy of the defence and tell you what to do next.
- **Not reply at all.** You may ask the court to enter judgment for an amount to be decided by the court by completing the tear off portion on this form. A hearing will be arranged to determine the amount the defendant should pay you. **If you do not request judgment within 6 months of the date for filing a defence, your claim will be stayed. This means that the only action open to you would be to apply to a judge for an order lifting the stay.**

✂ --

Request for Judgment

Notes:

- The court will notify both you and the defendant of any steps you should take to prepare for the hearing at which the court will decide what amount you are entitled to.
- You should notify the court immediately if your claim is settled or you decide that you do not wish to proceed.

In the

Claim No.	
Claimant (including ref)	
Defendant(s)	

To the court

The defendant has not filed an admission or defence to my claim, or an application to contest the court's jurisdiction and the time for doing so has expired.

I request that judgment be entered for an amount including costs, to be decided by the court.

Signed		Date	

(Claimant)(Claimant's solicitor)(Litigation friend)

N205B Notice of Issue (unspecified amount) and request for judgment

(Sample only)

© Crown copyright

Judgment in default; admitting or defending a claim; summary judgment

(c) Form N225 – request for judgment and reply to admission (specified amount)

Request for Judgment and reply to Admission (specified amount)

- Tick box A or B. If you tick box B you must complete the details in that part and in part C. Make sure that all the case details are given. Remember to sign and date the form. Your signature certifies that the information you have given is correct.
- If the defendant has given an address on the form of admission to which correspondence should be sent, which is different from the address shown on the claim form, you must tell the court.
- Return the completed form to the court.

In the	
Claim No.	
Claimant (including ref)	
Defendant (including ref)	

A ☐ **The defendant has not filed an admission or defence to my claim**

Complete all the judgment details at C. Decide how and when you want the defendant to pay. You can ask for the judgment to be paid by instalments or in one payment.

B ☐ **The defendant admits that all the money is owed**

Tick only **one** box below and complete all the judgment details at C.

☐ I accept the defendant's proposal for payment

Say how the defendant intends to pay. The court will send the defendant an order to pay. You will also be sent a copy.

☐ The defendant has not made any proposal for payment

Say how you want the defendant to pay. You can ask for the judgment to be paid by instalments or in one payment. The court will send the defendant an order to pay. You will also be sent a copy.

☐ I do NOT accept the defendant's proposal for payment

Say how you want the defendant to pay. Give your reasons for objecting to the defendant's offer of payment in the space opposite. (Continue on the back of this form if necessary.) Send this form to the court with defendant's admission N9A. The court will fix a rate of payment and send the defendant an order to pay. You will also be sent a copy.

C Judgment details

I would like the judgment to be paid

☐ (immediately)

☐ (by instalments of £ _____ per month)

☐ (in full by _____)

Amount of claim as admitted
(including interest at date of issue) ....
Interest since date of claim (if any) ....
Period from .... to ....
Rate ...... %
Court fees shown on claim
Solicitor's costs (if any) on issuing claim

Sub Total

Solicitor's costs (if any) on entering judgment

Sub Total

Deduct amount (if any) paid since issue

Amount payable by defendant

I certify that the information given is correct

Signed		Position or office held	
(Claimant)(Claimant's Solicitor)(Litigation friend)		(if signing on behalf of firm or company)	
Date			

The court office at
is open between 10 am and 4 pm Monday to Friday. When corresponding with the court, please address forms and letters to the Court Manager and quote the Claim number.

N225 Request for Judgment and reply to Admission (specified amount) (4.99)   *Printed on behalf of The Court Service*

© Crown copyright

Chapter 9

Before the hearing

Between the date of receipt of a defence to a claim and the date fixed for the small claims hearing, several weeks – indeed months – may elapse. The period of delay varies from one court to another due to their unequal sizes and workloads. The average is a little under two months. This does not mean that nothing is happening, nor that you have to be inactive. Many important matters need to be considered by the litigants before the hearing. These are often time consuming, and unfortunately can drag out the procedure but getting this stage right is in many ways as important to the ultimate success of the case as the actual hearing itself. A word of warning: you may be required to attend for a preliminary hearing. This is not a hearing of your case, nor should you go along to court expecting one. Sadly, quite a number of people still do. Do not take witnesses with you.

The following matters may have to be considered before the hearing itself.

- Should the claim be discontinued?
- The allocation of the claim to a track.
- Is the case going to the small claims track?
- Attending a preliminary hearing, if there is one, and complying with the directions given by the court.
- Asking for a change of date or venue.
- Dropping the action or settling.
- Amending the claim or defence.
- Counterclaims and defence to counterclaim.
- Indemnity and contribution.
- Preparing your case – witnesses, documents, expert evidence etc.

1. Should the claim be discontinued?

The defence should be considered carefully and you must ask yourself the question 'Am I going to be able to persuade the judge that my version of events is more likely to be right than the defendant's version?' If the

Before the hearing

realistic answer is 'no' that fact should be faced and the claim withdrawn to avoid the waste of time involved in pursuing a claim likely to fail. See further paragraph 6 below and consideration of compromising the dispute by agreement.

2. Allocation to track

Once a defence is filed in a claim (unless the defence is that the money claimed has been paid, or there is a part admission, or the court dispenses with the need for a questionnaire) an allocation questionnaire will be served by the court on each party. This is form N150, which is reproduced at the end of this chapter. If the claim is to be automatically transferred to another court it will be served before transfer.

Each party must file the completed questionnaire no later than the date specified, which must be at least 14 days after its deemed service.

The claimant must also pay an allocation fee (see Appendix 1 for a list of current county court fees). This fee is payable even if the court has dispensed with the allocation questionnaire. The fee is not payable if the only claim is to recover a sum of money not exceeding £1000.

If there is a failure by either party to return the completed questionnaire, the court is likely to make an order that it should be filed within three days, with the additional provision that if there is a continued default the claim or defence will be struck out. A similar order is likely if the claimant defaults in paying the allocation fee.

If either party's statement of case is struck out, an application to restore can be made but such an application is only likely to be successful if there is a very good reason for the default. Form N150 contains instructions for the completion of the allocation questionnaire (reproduced with the form on pages 100–104).

The district judge will consider the allocation questionnaires and allocate the claim to the appropriate track: the small claims track, the fast track or the multi-track. If necessary he will require the parties to attend an allocation hearing when the appropriate track will be decided. (This will be very rare in a claim destined for the small claims track.)

The small claims track is the normal track for:

- Any claim which has a financial value of not more than £5,000, subject to the special provisions about claims for personal injuries and housing disrepair claims.
- Any claim for personal injuries where the financial value of the claim is not more that £5,000, and where the claim for damages for personal injuries is not more than £1,000.
- Any claim which includes a claim by a tenant of residential premises against his landlord for repairs or other work to the premises where the estimated costs of the repair or other work is not more than £1,000 and the financial value of any claim for damages in respect of those repairs or other work is not more than £1,000.

Before the hearing

- A claim for harassment or unlawful eviction relating, in either case, to residential premises shall not in any circumstances be allocated to the small claims track.

Notes

1. Claims for damages for personal injuries exceeding £1,000 are excluded from the small claims track.
2. 'Damages for personal injuries' means damages claimed as compensation for pain, suffering and loss of amenity, and does not include any other damages claimed (CPR r 26.6).
3. Small claims will generally be dealt with by a district judge but may be heard by a Circuit judge provided he consents to the small claim being listed before him.

Where a party is dissatisfied with an allocation order he may appeal or apply to the court to re-allocate the claim.

The parties may consent to allocation, if the court considers the claim suitable, to the small claims track where the value is above the financial limit and in that event the rules provide for costs to be in the discretion of the court as if the claim was on the fast track, except that the trial costs will be at the discretion of the court with the upper limit of what would be ordered on the fast track.

3. Small claims track or fast or multi-track

If the claim is allocated to the fast or multi-track:

- it will be heard in open court by a circuit judge or district judge (usually a district judge if on the fast track);
- the rules of ordinary civil procedure will apply;
- the rules of evidence will apply;
- the parties are likely to need legal representation;
- the losing party will probably have to pay the legal costs of his opponent – these could be quite substantial;
- there is usually a right of appeal to a higher court.

If the case is allocated to the small claims track:

- it will almost invariably be heard by a district judge;
- the procedure will be informal; evidence need not be on oath;
- the strict rules of evidence do not apply;
- parties normally appear in person, or with a lay representative;
- the loser pays only very limited costs, and expenses.

For the average person the advantages of the small claims track greatly outweigh any disadvantages, and you should seek to avoid allocation to the fast or multi-track unless you are prepared to use a solicitor and face

Before the hearing

the full costs and uncertainties of civil litigation. However, solicitors acting for personal injury claimants may wish to preserve their right to full costs (see Chapter 12).

It is for the court to assess the financial value of the claim (CPR r 26.8(2)), but it is directed to apply the following general principles:

- any amount for which the defendant does admit liability is in dispute;
- any part of the claim for which judgment has been entered (e.g. by summary judgment) is not in dispute;
- any specific sum claimed as a distinct item for which the defendant admits liability is not in dispute;
- any sum offered by the defendant which the claimant has accepted in satisfaction of any item which forms a distinct part of the claim is not in dispute.

A case involving a disputed allegation of dishonesty will not usually be suitable for the small claims track.

The court will not normally allow more than one day for the hearing of a claim on the small claims track.

The claims allocated to the small claims track should be 'straightforward' (para 8.1 of the Practice Direction to CPR Part 26). It is not possible to give an exhaustive list of what might be regarded as straightforward as this is at the discretion of the judge. This is an area where the parties' interests may conflict. The following are examples of factors which may cause a claim not to be regarded as straightforward:

- Complexity of fact. This could arise in any type of action but more often in claims for personal injuries.
- Where a difficult question of law is alleged, it would seem natural for a solicitor to be the person making the application. The fact that there is a straightforward legal question involved should not be a ground for avoiding the small claims track. However, a party trying to conduct his own case might find that he is at a disadvantage if the other party is represented at a hearing by a solicitor.
- Both parties seek the fast or multi-track. The court will take account of the parties' views as an important factor but the decision remains one for the court.
- Fraud. This is a tort action or an action for fraudulent misrepresentation (see *Derry v Peek* (1889) 14 App Cas 337). There has to be knowledge that a statement is false or made with the purpose of deceiving someone. In civil cases the remedy is damages and the rescission of any contract.
- The dispute concerns money payable at recurring intervals, such as a service charge. The amount in question can be within the small claims limit but will be considerably more when multiplied on an annual basis. The district judge might feel this is not appropriate for the small claims track.

Before the hearing

- The nature of the remedy sought. Although the court may grant any final remedy on the small claims track that it can on any other track.
- The size of any counterclaim. A counterclaim under Part 20 of the Civil Procedure Rules 1998 (CPR) will not generally be aggregated with the claim to establish the value. Generally the largest of the claim and the Part 20 counterclaim will determine the financial value of the claim.
- The claim could affect the liability of others not party to the action, for example where a claim may be a test case for many others.
- The circumstances of the parties.

The Practice Direction to CPR Part 26 at paragraph 8.1 gives a list of cases that will generally be suitable to the small claims track. These are:

- consumer disputes;
- accident claims;
- disputes about the ownership of goods;
- most disputes between landlord and tenant other than those for possession.

The claim may be limited to bring the financial value of the claim within the small claims limit, but this may be a factor that the court will consider when allocating to track.

When a claim has been allocated to the small claims track, the following parts of the Civil Procedure Rules 1998 do not apply:

- Part 18 (further information);
- Part 25 (interim remedies) except as it relates to interim injunctions;
- Part 31 (disclosure and inspection);
- Part 32 (evidence) except CPR r 32.1 (power of court to control evidence);
- Part 33 (miscellaneous rules about evidence);
- Part 35 (experts and assessors) except CPR r 35.1 (duty to restrict expert evidence), CPR r 35.3 (experts – overriding duty to the court) and CPR r 35.8 (instructions to a single joint expert);
- Part 36 (offers to settle and payments into court); and
- Part 39 (hearings) except CPR r 39.2 (general rule – hearing to be in public).

The other Parts of the Civil Procedure Rules 1998 apply to small claims except to the extent that a rule limits such application.

Where a party disagrees with an allocation made in his absence, he can apply to the court for re-allocation (such application will be heard by a district judge). If the allocation was made at a hearing at which he was present, the aggrieved party can appeal (the appeal will be held before a Circuit judge).

4. Completing the allocation questionnaire

The design of the allocation questionnaire form was amended with effect from February 2001 and although the form is relatively easy to complete guidance is useful for the completion of some of the paragraphs which provide opportunities for a party to take advantage of the fact that a district judge will be reading this form and using the information it contains to give directions for the preparation and listing of the case.

Paragraph A – Settlement

If time is genuinely needed to negotiate a settlement a stay of up to one month can be requested. If the stay is granted it will mean that no step needs to be taken in the case until the period of the stay elapses.

Paragraph B – Location of the trial

Where there has been a transfer of the case to the defendant's home court the claimant may wish to achieve a transfer of the case back to his local court; this will be particularly so if he has witnesses who would have to travel a considerable distance to attend a hearing at the defendant's home court.

A transfer back can be requested but the reason the request is made and considered justified must be set out:

- the incident happened in the area of the claimant's court;
- there are witnesses in the case who live (or most of whom live) in the area of the claimant's court;
- the claimant cannot travel because of infirmity, lack of funds or being reliant on public transport that would not get him to the defendant's court in reasonable time.

If the application to re-transfer in the allocation questionnaire is ignored, a formal application using form N244 can be made if the venue of the hearing is sufficiently important.

Paragraph D – Case management information

The paragraph '**applications**' asks whether any application has been made to the court, for example for summary judgment (see pages 79–80). If the answer is 'yes' the appropriate box can be ticked and the nature of the application and the hearing date given. The court will probably delay allocation until after the hearing of an application for summary judgment. There is little point in stating an application will be made; if it has not actually been made the court is likely to ignore it.

Before the hearing

The paragraph '**experts**' is important because permission will have to be requested to produce any expert evidence whether by report or oral evidence. There is provision in the form for a joint expert to be appointed and although it is relatively rare, because of the expense, in the small claims court it is worthy of careful consideration in a suitable case. For example, if windows have been manufactured as 'georgian windows' and there is a dispute as to whether they fit this description how can a district judge make a reasoned decision without expert evidence? See part 10 of this chapter as to the amount that can be awarded in costs towards expert's fees and expert witnesses generally.

Paragraph H – Other information

The final paragraph of this section asks for details of any information that a party considers will help the judge to manage the claim. Requests for disclosure of documents or further particulars cannot be made by a party on the small claims track. Use can be made of this paragraph to try to persuade the court that it will want further documents or information from the other party. If the court is persuaded it may well make an order of its own volition for the provision of the documents or information.

4A. The small claims pilot scheme – CPR 27 Practice Direction 27B

This scheme operated from 8 July 2002 until 7 October 2002 at the Lincoln, Wandsworth and Wigan county courts only. It had no application to cases transferred to one of those courts after issue in another court.

The scheme dispensed with the provisions requiring the completion and filing of allocation questionnaires in cases to be allocated to the small claims track. The district judge allocated and gave directions without them.

The success of the pilot scheme will be evaluated before a decision is made on its permanent introduction. If this should occur before the next edition of this book reference should be made to Appendix 4 on pages 193–194 where PD 27B is reproduced.

5. Directions and preliminary hearings

(a) Directions

After allocation the court will normally give standard or special directions and fix a date for the hearing. The directions are set out in Appendix A to the CPR Part 27 Practice Direction.

> Form A – the standard directions.
> Form B – the standard directions for use in road traffic claims.
> Form C – the standard directions for building disputes, vehicle repairs and similar contractual claims.

Before the hearing

Form D – directions for tenants' claims for return of deposits and landlords' claims for damage.
Form E – directions for holiday and wedding claims.
Form F – some special directions.

These are set out at the end of this chapter (pages 105–109) and must be carefully read and complied with. Some directions may impose a sanction in the event of non-compliance:

- that the claim or defence, as the case may be, will stand struck out;
- that the defaulting party may not use a particular type of evidence;
- that an adjournment may be necessary and the costs of the extra hearing will fall to be paid by the defaulting party.

Such directions must be exactly complied with by the date specified. If, for some reason this cannot be done an application should be made to the court, before the specified time has elapsed, for an extension of time for compliance or modification of the direction.

The parties must be given at least 21 days' notice of the hearing unless they agree to accept shorter notice. The district judge will fix the length of time to be allowed from his perusal of the papers or from the information given to him at the allocation hearing (such a hearing is rare on the small claims track).

(b) A preliminary hearing? – CPR r 27.6

These are held:

- where special directions are needed to ensure a fair hearing and the judge wishes to see the parties to ensure that they fully understand what is required of them; or
- to enable the district judge to dispose of the case where:
  - the claim is ill-founded; or
  - there is no reasonable defence.

When the district judge decides to hold a preliminary hearing, the court will fix a date and must allow the parties at least 14 days' notice.

When deciding whether or not to hold a preliminary hearing the desirability of limiting the expense of the parties in attending court must be taken into account. The preliminary hearing may be treated as a final hearing if the parties agree.

At or after the preliminary hearing the court shall:

- fix the date of the final hearing;
- inform the parties of the time allowed for the final hearing;
- give appropriate directions.

The preliminary hearing takes place in the district judge's room. The meeting is likely to last only a matter of minutes. A lot of people confuse

91

Before the hearing

the preliminary hearing with the hearing itself and attend ready to argue their case. They are often angry and annoyed about the extra visit to court. For this reason, the idea of dropping the preliminary hearing altogether was canvassed and seriously considered. The Civil Procedure Rules 1998 have limited the situations when a preliminary hearing can be directed. In the majority of cases none will be held.

If you are requested to attend a preliminary hearing, give serious thought to meeting your opponent and trying to settle the dispute there and then. A large number of litigants do this, and it avoids any further court appointments and correspondence. If you cannot settle, use the preliminary hearing as an opportunity to ensure that you know what the issues are, and what you have to do or bring with you when the case goes to a hearing. The main purpose of the appointment is to give you this opportunity, and you should not hesitate to ask for advice. Remember that neither judge nor court officials can advise you on the legal outcome of your case.

If the preliminary hearing is listed because the claim or defence is considered ill-founded the notice will generally say so. The party whose case is to be considered should seek advice prior to the hearing as it may be that he should consider dropping his claim or withdrawing his defence, as the case may be. An example of such a case would be where the defendant is one of two people jointly responsible for a debt and defends on the basis that the other person should pay half and he should only be ordered to pay half. The defence cannot be successful because each of the joint debtors is responsible for the whole debt.

If you find that you cannot attend the preliminary hearing, or you wish to change the date, write to the court immediately. You should also send a copy to the other party out of politeness. The following letter is all that is required.

Request to the court manager of the county court to postpone the prehearing appointment

Dear Sir/Madam,
[*Reference: case number*]

I have just received your note of [*date*], giving a date of [*specify*] for the preliminary hearing in this case.

Unfortunately I will not be able to attend on that date because [*give reason*].

I would therefore be grateful if you would fix a new date. I should be able to attend court from [*date*] onwards.

I look forward to hearing from you in due course.

Yours sincerely,

The court may charge you an application fee for this.

Before the hearing

(c) Non-appearance at preliminary hearing

There are no specific provisions in Part 27 of the Civil Procedure Rules 1998 dealing with failure to attend a preliminary hearing, but the district judge may well exercise his powers under CPR r 3.4 to strike out the statement of case of the defaulting party and make any consequential orders that he considers appropriate. The party present should consider asking the court to treat the failure to attend as unreasonable behaviour when making its order for costs.

(d) Disposal without a hearing

The court has power to deal with the claim without a hearing. This can, however, only be done if all parties agree and is in fact comparatively rare.

(e) Changing the hearing date

If the date fixed for the hearing is impossible or inconvenient to you or someone representing you, write to the other party asking him or her to agree. If they do, write to the court enclosing the letter from the other party agreeing to the change, and request a new date. If the other party does not agree, then you have to make an application to the court. Form N244 should be used to make the application. An application fee will be payable.

6. Dropping the action or settling

This is known as discontinuance. If a claimant wishes to discontinue all or part of any proceedings against another party, then notice must be given (N279) (CPR Part 38). Notice must be given to the court with a certificate that notice has been given to the other parties. If the hearing date is close, the court office should be notified by telephone.

The following letter is typical:

Notice to the defendant that the case is discontinued following receipt of full and final payment.

> Dear
> [*Reference: case number*]
> Thank you for your letter of [*date*] proposing settlement [*describe*].
> I am pleased to accept your cheque for [£ . . .] in full and final settlement of my claim against you.
> I am therefore discontinuing my claim against you in the [*location*] County Court and am copying this letter to the court.
> Your sincerely,
>
> cc: The Court Manager, [*location*] County Court

Before the hearing

Part 36 of the Civil Procedure Rules 1998, dealing with offers to settle, does not apply to small claims, but an offer to settle on a compromise basis should always be considered. A typical letter by a defendant seeking such a settlement would be:

Offer from the defendant to the claimant to settle on a compromise basis

[Date]

Dear [*Name of claimant*]

Without Prejudice Save as to Costs.

You will have received notice of the allocation of this claim to the small claims track.

Whilst the defence is fully maintained I am prepared to pay you the sum of [*specify amount*] and also the court fee to settle your claim. On hearing that you accept I will pay the money within seven days in a single sum by cheque or, if you prefer, in cash.

The offer is made 'without prejudice save as to costs', so it cannot and must not be shown to the court until the case has been heard. At that point the fact that an offer was made but not accepted may be relevant to the question whether either side ought to pay the other's costs.

Should the offer not be accepted and the court proceed to a hearing, if you do not recover more than the amount offered I will rely on this letter to establish that your conduct in refusing the offer amounts to unreasonable conduct such as to entitle me to an order for payment of my costs from your receipt of this letter.

I would ask you to give my offer serious consideration and hope you will find it an acceptable resolution to our dispute.

Yours etc.

It is uncertain whether it will persuade the district judge to award the defendant costs if the offer is not beaten, but it is worth trying.

It is open to the claimant to make such an offer perhaps to accept a reduced sum, to forgo interest or forgo the court fee.

7. Amending the claim or defence – CPR Part 17

You may find that you have omitted something from your statement of case, or that as a result of further enquiries you wish to alter it. Provided it has not already been served, you may do this by sending copies of the amended statement of case to the other party and to the court (keeping a copy for yourself). If it has already been served, it can only be amended:

- with the written consent of all other parties; or
- with the permission of the court.

If consent to the amendment cannot be obtained, the application to amend should be made as soon as possible using form N244 and attaching a copy of the proposed statement of case to each copy of the

N244. An application fee will be payable. If the amendment is granted and its effect is to increase the amount of the claim, an additional fee will also be payable.

8. Counterclaims and defences to counterclaims – CPR Part 20

If the defendant wishes to make a claim against the claimant it is called a counterclaim and is made pursuant to Part 20 of the Civil Procedure Rules 1998. Provided that the counterclaim is filed with the defence, it can be made without the court's permission. However, if it is made later, the court's permission will be required.

Counterclaims figure frequently in road traffic claims where each driver says the other is at least partly to blame and the defendant has suffered damage.

Forms N9B and N9D have provision within them for the defendant to make a counterclaim. A fee will be payable.

A Part 20 counterclaim is treated as if it were a claim so that the claimant must file a defence to the counterclaim.

9. Indemnity or contribution – CPR Part 20

If the defendant claims that someone else is responsible wholly or in part for the damage which the claimant claims (whether that person is already a defendant to the claim or is not yet a party to the claim), he may issue a Part 20 claim against that person seeking an indemnity or a contribution to any damages from him. Form N211 may be used and, provided it is issued at the same time as filing the defence, the permission of the court is not required. If it is to be issued later, the court's permission must be obtained by application using form N244. The notes for claimants in form N211A set out instructions for the completion of form N211.

10. Preparing your case for the hearing

(a) Exclusion of rules of civil procedure

Certain rules of the Civil Procedure Rules 1998 are excluded from claims on the small claims track (see page 88 above). Accordingly, if information is required from the other party and it is not supplied on request and the court ignores an invitation in the allocation questionnaire to order it, the only way of obtaining it will be to apply to the court for an order that there be a preliminary hearing, in the hope that the district judge will order the other party to supply the information at that hearing.

Effectively in small claims the obligation of the parties is to comply fully with the directions given.

Before the hearing

(b) Proper evidence

Many people attend court believing that since they are convinced that they are in the right the judge is bound to find in their favour. They may leave court feeling angry and disillusioned having lost. Obviously if the case has gone as far as a hearing there must be two sides to the story. The district judge has to choose between them. Often it is very difficult on the conflicting versions of events presented to the court for the judge to be convinced either way. Here, a legal principle of some importance holds sway. The burden of proof is on the claimant. In other words, it is up to the claimant to prove his or her case, on the *balance of probabilities*. This means merely that it is more likely than not that the claimant's case is the correct one.

It is advisable to agree as many matters arising in a dispute as possible so as to save the expense of bringing witnesses to prove them. A common example is the cost of repairing a car damaged in an accident. Many disputes are concerned with the cause of the damage rather than the cost of putting it right. In such cases the parties often agree the cost to save the expense of calling the engineer who carried out the repairs to give evidence of the work that he did. By agreeing what the repairs will cost, you are not admitting that you are liable to pay for them – parties should always try and agree minor points to ensure that the hearing is confined to the questions that really matter.

In order to improve your chances of success, the key to establishing a case is *proper evidence*. In most actions the parties themselves are the principal, or even the only, witnesses. Both parties will give their version of the dispute. Their stories are likely to conflict. This does not necessarily mean that one of them is telling lies.

Recollections are often different – certain matters can be forgotten or perceived differently. Therefore it is important to try to provide yourself with other evidence, in the form of:

- witnesses;
- expert witnesses;
- faulty goods or equipment;
- documents or photographs.

The question that governs preparation should be 'How can I persuade the judge that my version is more likely to be right than the other party's version?'

(i) Witnesses

Husbands and wives can give evidence on each other's behalf, as can friends, neighbours or strangers who can give a relevant version of events. Although hearsay evidence can be admissible at small claims hearings, it is preferable to ask witnesses to attend the hearing. The rules of evidence are relaxed in small claims hearings and written statements by witnesses may be allowed.

Before the hearing

The claimant and the defendant must remember that they are witnesses as well as parties, so that a direction that witness statements will be filed requires statements from the parties as well as from people that they wish to rely on as witnesses. Whether there is a direction for witness statements or not, always prepare them with copies for the court and the opponent. This will save time at the hearing and will be welcomed by the district judge.

Compelling witnesses to attend

Witnesses are sometimes reluctant to come to court. Perhaps they do not like the idea of giving evidence, or maybe their employers would not wish them to take time off work. When you ask someone to act as a witness, find out whether he is prepared to come without being served with a witness summons. Ask him also whether there are any dates when he would not be able to attend court, so that a clash with the hearing date can then be avoided. If a witness is not prepared to come to court voluntarily, he can be compelled to do so, although this is very rare in small claims. You should ask the court office for a request for a witness summons; the court staff may help you to fill in the request or may accept a letter instead of a formal request. The witness summons is in form N20. There is a danger in compelling a witness to attend unless it is known beforehand that the witness will give evidence which is helpful to your case. A witness who is compelled to attend may prove uncooperative and therefore unhelpful to the party who insisted on attendance.

Witness expenses

Unless a witness is a personal friend, he can hardly be expected to come to court without payment of his expenses and compensation for any loss of earnings. You must be prepared to pay your witnesses' expenses in the first place, but if you win the action, the defendant will usually have to pay all or part of these expenses. The court will decide what is a reasonable sum in respect of travelling and other expenses, such as staying away from home, and for time lost attending court. The rules limit the amount that may be claimed. The present limit is £50 for loss of earnings plus travelling expenses. If the attendance makes it necessary for the witness to stay away from home the cost of doing so can also be awarded.

The witness summons should be served at least seven days before the witness is required to attend court. The witness must be offered a sum to cover his travelling expenses to and from court and his loss of earnings.

(ii) Expert witnesses

In cases involving small claims, the question of expert evidence is most likely to arise in respect of claims for faulty goods or services. An expert is a person who through knowledge or experience is skilled in the matters about which he is asked to give an opinion. For example, in a small claim

Before the hearing

relating to plumbing, electrical work, or repairs to a motor vehicle, you could ask any experienced local plumber, electrician or mechanic to let you have a report and, if need be, to give evidence at the hearing. No particular qualifications are required, and it will be for the court to decide how much reliance can be placed on an expert's opinion. If you do not know of an expert in the matters affecting your case, your local Citizens Advice Bureau or Consumer Advice Centre should be able to help you find the names and addresses of likely persons.

You may have obtained an expert's report before you started the action. You should ask the defendant if he is prepared to accept it in order to save the expense of bringing the expert to court. If the defendant does agree, the report can be shown to the judge at the hearing. If the defendant wants to obtain a report, you should give the defendant or his expert an opportunity to inspect the faulty equipment or whatever is in dispute. You are not obliged to part with possession of it for this purpose. If reports cannot be agreed and your expert has to give evidence, he may charge you a substantial fee for his services. There are special rules covering these fees. An allowance of up to £200 may be ordered to be paid by the unsuccessful party to the winner for each expert.

If an expert is to be instructed you should first inform your opponent and see whether you can agree on an expert who can be jointly instructed by you both and at joint expense. This concept of having jointly instructed experts lies at the heart of the protocols to the Civil Procedure Rules 1998.

No expert evidence may be given orally or by report without leave of the court.

(iii) Faulty goods or equipment

If you have any broken or damaged parts of the equipment which is the subject of your claim, it is important to keep them because they may be useful as evidence. If they are small enough you should bring them with you to the hearing. In the case of things which cannot easily be brought to court, photographs might be useful, or you can ask the district judge to make an on-the-spot inspection. If the judge is satisfied that this would assist in deciding the case, he may make an inspection at some suitable stage of the proceedings in the presence of the parties.

(iv) Documents and photographs

Although spoken evidence from witnesses is most important, documents can sometimes make all the difference between success and failure. Letters written by the parties, contracts and agreements, bills, invoices and receipts, bank statements, paid cheques etc., can all be vital to your case. If you are claiming the cost of repairs to a car or other equipment, or for rectification of faulty work, you should obtain written estimates if the work has not been done. You should remember to bring them with you when your case is heard, and to supply copies to the other party as required. It will save time and help the court if the documents are made into bundles. Each page should be separately numbered. Photographs of the site or of the work done can also be extremely helpful.

(v) Cross-examination

Each of the parties will be able to ask questions of the other party and that party's witnesses. Most litigants find it difficult to remember what they want to ask. It is best to prepare a list of the questions to be put to the other side; tick the questions off the list as they are asked. The questions must be just that and not statements that require no answer from the witness. The witness must be given the opportunity to complete his answer before the next question is put to him.

(vi) Closing address to the court

After all the evidence has been taken each party will be given an opportunity to address the court. A list should be prepared of the points that the party maintains make his version more credible than his opponent's.

11. Small claims on site

Small claims hearings may be held at any place convenient to the parties. If the property or work done upon it is the issue, it may well be to your advantage to ask the district judge to conduct the small claims hearing on site. You should write to the Court Manager if you wish this to be arranged. Some small claims are commenced in court but are adjourned to the site on the same day or at a later date.

District judges vary in their fondness for the hearing to be on site and frequently requests for on-site hearings are refused.

Before the hearing

12. Forms and directions

(a) Form N150 – allocation questionnaire

Allocation questionnaire

To be completed by, or on behalf of,

[   ]

who is [1st][2nd][3rd][   ][Claimant][Defendant] [Part 20 claimant] in this claim

In the

Claim No.

Last date for filing with court office

Please read the notes on page five before completing the questionnaire.

You should note the date by which it must be returned and the name of the court it should be returned to since this may be different from the court where the proceedings were issued.

If you have settled this claim (or if you settle it on a future date) and do not need to have it heard or tried, you must let the court know immediately.

Have you sent a copy of this completed form to the other party(ies)? ☐ Yes ☐ No

A Settlement

Do you wish there to be a one month stay to attempt to settle the claim, either by informal discussion or by alternative dispute resolution? ☐ Yes ☐ No

B Location of trial

Is there any reason why your claim needs to be heard at a particular court? ☐ Yes ☐ No

If Yes, say which court and why?

C Pre-action protocols

If an approved pre-action protocol applies to this claim, complete **Part 1** only. If not, complete **Part 2** only. If you answer 'No' to the question in either Part 1 or 2, please explain the reasons why on a separate sheet and attach it to this questionnaire.

Part 1 The* [   ] protocol applies to this claim.
*please say which protocol

Have you complied with it? ☐ Yes ☐ No

Part 2 No pre-action protocol applies to this claim.

Have you exchanged information and/or documents (evidence) with the other party in order to assist in settling the claim? ☐ Yes ☐ No

N150 Allocation questionnaire (10.01)   1   *Printed on behalf of The Court Service*

© Crown copyright

(Cont'd)

Before the hearing

D Case management information

What amount of the claim is in dispute? £ _____

Applications

Have you made any application(s) in this claim? ☐ Yes ☐ No

If Yes, what for? _____   For hearing on _____
(e.g. summary judgment, add another party)

Witnesses

So far as you know at this stage, what witnesses of fact do you intend to call at the trial or final hearing including, if appropriate, yourself?

Witness name	Witness to which facts

Experts

Do you wish to use expert evidence at the trial or final hearing? ☐ Yes ☐ No

Have you already copied any experts' report(s) to the other party(ies)? ☐ None yet obtained ☐ Yes ☐ No

Do you consider the case suitable for a single joint expert in any field? ☐ Yes ☐ No

Please list any single joint experts you propose to use and any other experts you wish to rely on. Identify single joint experts with the initials 'SJ' after their name(s).

Expert's name	Field of expertise (eg. orthopaedic surgeon, surveyor, engineer)

Do you want your expert(s) to give evidence orally at the trial or final hearing? ☐ Yes ☐ No

If Yes, give the reasons why you think oral evidence is necessary:

continue over ⮕

© Crown copyright

(*Cont'd*)

Before the hearing

Track

Which track do you consider is most suitable for your claim? Tick one box   ☐ small claims track   ☐ fast track   ☐ multi-track

If you have indicated a track which would not be the normal track for the claim, please give brief reasons for your choice

[   ]

E Trial or final hearing

How long do you estimate the trial or final hearing will take?   [days] [hours] [minutes]

Are there any days when you, an expert or an essential witness will not be able to attend court for the trial or final hearing?   ☐ Yes ☐ No

If Yes, please give details

Name	Dates not available

F Proposed directions *(Parties should agree directions wherever possible)*

Have you attached a list of the directions you think appropriate for the management of the claim?   ☐ Yes ☐ No

If Yes, have they been agreed with the other party(ies)?   ☐ Yes ☐ No

G Costs

Do **not** complete this section if you have suggested your case is suitable for the small claims track **or** you have suggested one of the other tracks and you do not have a solicitor acting for you.

What is your estimate of your costs incurred to date?   £ [   ]

What do you estimate your overall costs are likely to be?   £ [   ]

In substantial cases these questions should be answered in compliance with CPR Part 43

© Crown copyright

(Cont'd)

Before the hearing

H Other information

Have you attached documents to this questionnaire? ☐ Yes ☐ No

Have you sent these documents to the other party(ies)? ☐ Yes ☐ No

If Yes, when did they receive them?

Do you intend to make any applications in the immediate future? ☐ Yes ☐ No

If Yes, what for?

In the space below, set out any other information you consider will help the judge to manage the claim.

Signed   Date

[Counsel][Solicitor][for the][1st][2nd][3rd][   ]
[Claimant][Defendant][Part 20 claimant]

Please enter your firm's name, reference number and full postal address including (if appropriate) details of DX, fax or e-mail

	if applicable
fax no.	
DX no.	
e-mail	

Tel. no.   Postcode

Your reference no.

© Crown copyright

(*Cont'd*)

Before the hearing

Notes for completing an allocation questionnaire

- If the claim is not settled, a judge must allocate it to an appropriate case management track. To help the judge choose the most just and cost-effective track, you must now complete the attached questionnaire.
- If you fail to return the allocation questionnaire by the date given, the judge may make an order which leads to your claim or defence being struck out, or hold an allocation hearing. If there is an allocation hearing the judge may order any party who has not filed their questionnaire to pay, immediately, the costs of that hearing.
- Use a separate sheet if you need more space for your answers marking clearly which section the information refers to. You should write the claim number on it, and on any other documents you send with your allocation questionnaire. Please ensure they are firmly attached to it.
- The letters below refer to the sections of the questionnaire and tell you what information is needed.

A Settlement
If you think that you and the other party may be able to negotiate a settlement you should tick the 'Yes' box. The court may order a stay, whether or not all the other parties to the claim agree. You should still complete the rest of the questionnaire, even if you are requesting a stay. Where a stay is granted it will be for an initial period of one month. You may settle the claim either by informal discussion with the other party or by alternative dispute resolution (ADR). ADR covers a range of different processes which can help settle disputes. More information is available in the Legal Services Commission leaflet 'Alternatives to Court' free from the LSC leaflet line Phone: 0845 3000 343

B Location of trial
High Court cases are usually heard at the Royal Courts of Justice or certain Civil Trial Centres. Fast or multi-track trials may be dealt with at a Civil Trial Centre or at the court where the claim is proceeding. Small claim cases are usually heard at the court in which they are proceeding.

C Pre-action protocols
Before any claim is started, the court expects you to have exchanged information and documents relevant to the claim, to assist in settling it. For some types of claim e.g. personal injury, there are approved protocols that should have been followed.

D Case management information
Applications
It is important for the court to know if you have already made any applications in the claim, what they are for and when they will be heard. The outcome of the applications may affect the case management directions the court gives.

Witnesses
Remember to include yourself as a witness of fact, if you will be giving evidence.

Experts
Oral or written expert evidence will only be allowed at the trial or final hearing with the court's permission. The judge will decide what permission it seems appropriate to give when the claim is allocated to track. Permission in small claims track cases will only be given exceptionally.

Track
The basic guide by which claims are normally allocated to a track is the amount in dispute, although other factors such as the complexity of the case will also be considered. A leaflet available from the court office explains the limits in greater detail.

Small Claims track	Disputes valued at not more than £5,000 except · those including a claim for personal injuries worth over £1,000 and · those for housing disrepair where either the cost of repairs or other work exceeds £1,000 or any other claim for damages exceeds £1,000
Fast track	Disputes valued at more than £5,000 but not more than £15,000
Multi-track	Disputes over £15,000

E Trial or Þnal hearing
You should enter only those dates when you, your expert(s) or essential witness(es) will not be able to attend court because of holiday or other committments.

F Proposed directions
Attach the list of directions, if any, you believe will be appropriate to be given for the management of the claim. Agreed directions on fast and multi-track cases should be based on the forms of standard directions set out in the practice direction to CPR Part 28 and form PF52.

G Costs
Only complete this section if you are a solicitor and have suggested the claim is suitable for allocation to the fast or multi-track.

H Other Information
Answer the questions in this section. Decide if there is any other information you consider will help the judge to manage the claim. Give details in the space provided referring to any documents you have attached to support what you are saying.

© Crown copyright

Before the hearing

(b) Appendix A to the CPR Part 27 Practice Direction

FORM A – THE STANDARD DIRECTIONS
(for use where the district judge specifies no other directions)
The court directs:

1. Each party shall deliver to every other party and to the court office copies of all documents (including any experts' report) on which he intends to rely at the hearing no later than [   ] [14 days before the hearing].
2. The original documents shall be brought to the hearing.
3. [Notice of hearing date and time allowed.]
4. The court must be informed immediately if the case is settled by agreement before the hearing date.

FORM B – STANDARD DIRECTIONS FOR USE IN CLAIMS ARISING OUT OF ROAD ACCIDENTS
The court directs:

1. Each party shall deliver to every other party and to the court office copies of all documents on which he intends to rely at the hearing. These may include:
   - experts' reports (including medical reports where damages for personal injury are claimed),
   - witness statements,
   - invoices and estimates for repairs,
   - documents which relate to other losses, such as loss of earnings,
   - sketch plans and photographs.
2. The copies shall be delivered no later than [   ] [14 days before the hearing].
3. The original documents shall be brought to the hearing.
4. Before the date of the hearing the parties shall try to agree the cost of the repairs and any other losses claimed subject to the court's decision about whose fault the accident was.
5. Signed statements setting out the evidence of all witnesses on whom each party intends to rely shall be prepared and copies included in the documents mentioned in paragraph 1. This includes the evidence of the parties themselves and of any other witness, whether or not he is going to come to court to give evidence.
6. The parties should note that:
   (a) In deciding the case the court will find it very helpful to have a sketch plan and photographs of the place where the accident happened,
   (b) The court may decide not to take into account a document or the evidence of a witness if no copy of that document or no

Before the hearing

        copy of a statement or report by that witness has been supplied to the other parties.
7   [Notice of hearing date and time allowed.]
8   The court must be informed immediately if the case is settled by agreement before the hearing date.

FORM C – STANDARD DIRECTIONS FOR USE IN CLAIMS ARISING OUT OF BUILDING DISPUTES, VEHICLE REPAIRS AND SIMILAR CONTRACTUAL CLAIMS

The court directs:

1   Each party shall deliver to every other party and to the court office copies of all documents on which he intends to rely at the hearing. These may include:
- the contract,
- witness statements,
- experts' reports,
- photographs,
- invoices for work done or goods supplied,
- estimates for work to be done.

2   The copies shall be delivered no later than [   ] [14 days before the hearing].

3   The original documents shall be brought to the hearing.

4   [The   shall deliver to the   and to the court office [no later than   ] [with his copy documents] a list showing all items of work which he complains about and why, and the amount claimed for putting each item right.]

5   [The   shall deliver to the   and to the court office [no later than   ] [with his copy documents] a breakdown of the amount he is claiming showing all work done and materials supplied.]

6   Before the date of the hearing the parties shall try to agree about the nature and cost of any remedial work required, subject to the court's decision about any other issue in the case.

7   [Signed statements setting out the evidence of all witnesses on whom each party intends to rely shall be prepared and included in the documents mentioned in paragraph 1. This includes the evidence of the parties themselves and of any other witness, whether or not he is going to come to court to give evidence.]

8   The parties should note that:
    (a) in deciding the case the judge may find it helpful to have photographs showing the work in question,
    (b) the judge may decide not to take into account a document or the evidence of a witness if no copy of that document or no copy of a statement or report by that witness has been supplied to the other parties.

Before the hearing

9 [Notice of hearing date and time allowed.]
10 The court must be informed immediately if the case is settled by agreement before the hearing date.

FORM D – TENANTS' CLAIMS FOR THE RETURN OF DEPOSITS/LANDLORD'S CLAIMS FOR DAMAGE CAUSED

The court directs:

1. Each party shall deliver to every other party and to the court office copies of all documents on which he intends to rely at the hearing. These may include:
   - the tenancy agreement and any inventory,
   - the rent book or other evidence of rent and other payments made by the   to the
   - photographs,
   - witness statements,
   - invoices or estimates for work and goods.
2. The copies shall be delivered no later than [   ] [14 days before the hearing].
3. The original documents shall be brought to the hearing.
4. The   shall deliver with his copy documents a list showing each item of loss or damage for which he claims the   ought to pay, and the amount he claims for the replacement or repair.
5. The parties shall before the hearing date try to agree about the nature and cost of any repairs and replacements needed, subject to the court's decision about any other issue in the case.
6. [Signed statements setting out the evidence of all witnesses on whom each party intends to rely shall be prepared and included in the documents mentioned in paragraph 1. This includes the evidence of the parties themselves and of any other witness whether or not he is going to come to court to give evidence.]
7. The parties should note that:
   (a) in deciding the case the judge may find it helpful to have photographs showing the condition of the property,
   (b) the judge may decide not to take into account a document or the evidence of a witness if no copy of that document or no copy of a statement or report by that witness has been supplied to the other parties.
8. [Notice of hearing date and time allowed.]
9. The court must be informed immediately if the case is settled by agreement before the hearing date.

FORM E – HOLIDAY AND WEDDING CLAIMS

The court directs:

1. Each party shall deliver to every other party and to the court office copies of all documents on which he intends to rely at the hearing.

Before the hearing

These may include:
- any written contract, brochure or booking form,
- photographs,
- documents showing payments made,
- witness statements,
- letters.

2   The copies shall be delivered no later than [   ] [14 days before the hearing].
3   The original documents shall be brought to the hearing.
4   Signed statements setting out the evidence of all witnesses on whom each party intends to rely shall be prepared and copies included in the documents mentioned in paragraph 1. This includes the evidence of the parties themselves and of any other witness, whether or not he is going to come to court to give evidence.
5   If either party intends to show a video as evidence he must:
   (a) contact the court at once to make arrangements for him to do so, because the court may not have the necessary equipment, and
   (b) provide the other party with a copy of the video or the opportunity to see it (if he asks) at least 2 weeks before the hearing.
6   The parties should note that the court may decide not to take into account a document or the evidence of a witness or a video if these directions have not been complied with.
7   [Notice of hearing date and time allowed.]
8   The court must be told immediately if the case is settled by agreement before the hearing date.

FORM F – SOME SPECIAL DIRECTIONS

The   must clarify his case. He must do this by delivering to the court office and to the   no later than [a list of   ] [details of   ] [   ]

The   shall allow the   to inspect   by appointment within   days of receiving a request to do so.

The hearing will not take place at the court but at

The   must bring to court at the hearing the

Signed statements setting out the evidence of all witnesses on whom each party intends to rely shall be prepared and copies included in the documents mentioned in paragraph 1. This includes the evidence of the parties themselves and of any other witness, whether or not he is going to come to court to give evidence.

The court may decide not to take into account a document [or video] or the evidence of a witness if these directions have not been complied with.

Before the hearing

If he does not [do so] [   ] his [Claim] [Defence] [and Counterclaim] and will be struck out and [(specify consequence)].

It appears to the court that expert evidence is necessary on the issue of [   ] and that that evidence should be given by a single expert [   ] to be instructed by the parties jointly. If the parties cannot agree about who to chose and what arrangements to make about paying his fee, either party may apply to the court for further directions.

If either party intends to show a video as evidence he must

(a) contact the court at once to make arrangements for him to do so, because the court may not have the necessary equipment, and

(b) provide the other party with a copy of the video or the opportunity to see it at least [   ] before the hearing.

Chapter 10

The hearing

1. To appear on your own or with a representative?

At some point before going to court you have to decide whether to argue the case on your own at the hearing or seek assistance in the form of a legal or lay representative. This is entirely up to the individual. It is largely a question of confidence and depends also on the type of case involved. Many parties do have solicitors in spite of the no costs rule, particularly large and even small businesses. However, litigants who are private citizens usually act in person. The private individual who appears in person may be surprised or even annoyed by the presence of legal practitioners in what he thought would be an informal atmosphere where the parties would present their case on their own. However, legal representation does not materially improve a party's chances of winning. Before acquiring the services of a lawyer for this type of hearing, bear in mind:

- the cost of legal services is likely to be large in relation to the amount at stake, and you will have to pay for this yourself;
- your chances of success at the hearing are usually just as good without a lawyer;
- the small claims rules are designed to help people appearing on their own;
- many solicitors will rarely if ever have appeared in a small claims court, and may be unfamiliar with what is required;
- the district judge, while remaining even handed, will try to assist you in the presentation of your case.

For the less confident there is a good deal to be said for having a friend or relative or an adviser of some sort with you at the hearing to provide moral support and to advise. Such people who were not legally qualified and who appeared in this way used to be known as 'McKenzie friends', after a case in 1970 in which they were first recognised. A litigant in person could have a lay adviser with him, subject to the court's discretion and the judge's power to maintain order and to regulate proceedings before him. The courts have stated that the expression 'McKenzie friend'

The hearing

is misleading and should be avoided (*R v Leicester City Justices, ex p Barrow* [1991] 3 All ER 935). Advice centres have limited resources to help in this way, and they sometimes tell those who seek advice that their best option is to appear in person. If you are particularly nervous or have language difficulties, then you should find someone to appear for you.

2. Lay representatives

Section 11 of the Courts and Legal Services Act 1990 gave the Lord Chancellor power to remove restrictions on those who may exercise rights of audience or conduct litigation in specified proceedings, and this has now been implemented by rule changes. The Civil Procedure Rules 1998 (CPR) specifically provide that a party may be represented by a lay representative or by a lawyer on the small claims track. See paragraph 3.2 of the Practice Direction 27 – Small Claims.

A lay representative may only present a party's case if the party is present at the hearing, unless:

- the lay representative is an employee of a corporate party; or
- the court gives permission; permission may be given to a lay representative who does not have a right of audience under the 1999 Order (see below, under (b)).

The lay representative is in the same position as a lawyer at the hearing in that he can address the court, call witnesses and examine them, cross-examine witnesses called by the other party and present documents to the court. Any person may be a lay representative.

Usually lay representatives are advisers from the Citizens Advice Bureau or an advice centre, a friend or a relative. In many cases a claimant will find it more effective to represent himself and have a friend or relative present for moral support if that friend or relative has no relevant experience.

If a lay representative is to represent the party, this decision should be made in good time before the hearing so that there is ample time for preparation.

(a) Companies in court

Any of its officers or employees may represent a corporate body. The form of written statement required to be produced by the officer or employee is set out in paragraph 5.2 of the Practice Direction to Part 39. The judge hearing a small claim is unlikely to require this.

(b) The Lay Representatives (Rights of Audience) Order 1999

This provides:

A lay representative may not exercise any right of audience:

- where his client does not attend the hearing;

The hearing

- at any stage after judgment; or
- on any appeal brought against any decision made by the district judge in the proceedings.

Conduct of proceedings in which lay representatives take part

- A key purpose in giving litigants a free choice of representative is to give them the confidence to pursue or defend their cases in court. This consideration should guide the court in the conduct of proceedings in which lay representatives take part, in its expectations of the standards of conduct and competence exhibited by lay representatives, and in its use of the sanctions of refusing to hear, or of disqualifying, a lay representative. The court is entitled to expect every representative to behave honestly, reasonably and responsibly. However, the standard of competence may vary greatly. A higher standard of competence may be expected of a person who provides such services commercially than of one who simply represents a friend or relative.
- Judges now have a responsibility actively to conduct small claims proceedings in such a way as to ensure that they and the parties are fully aware of all the relevant facts and issues. The court's responsibility does not cease where a lay representative is acting, except to the extent that the lay representative is clearly capable of conducting the litigant's case without the help of the court.
- Although the normal rule is that an advocate may not give evidence on behalf of the party he represents, the Lay Representatives (Rights of Audience) Order 1999 does not preclude a lay representative from giving evidence as a witness in the proceedings to which it applies. In small claims hearings there may be occasions when it would be difficult to avoid this, for example where one spouse is representing the other and both have witnessed the events in issue. However, parties should be warned that this may affect the weight which the court gives to the lay representative's evidence.

Refusal to hear a lay representative

- A Circuit judge or a district judge may refuse to hear a lay representative in particular proceedings if that representative behaves in an unruly manner. Examples might include ignoring directions of the court or otherwise impeding the proper progress of the proceedings.
- If a judge is minded to exercise this power, he should tell the lay representative and the affected party what his reasons are and state them in writing.
- If the judge considers that a refusal to hear a lay representative may prejudice the client's case for the remainder of the proceedings, the judge should consult the affected party on the possibility

The hearing

of adjourning the proceedings to provide an opportunity for the party, or another representative, to take over the presentation of the case.

- The court must specify which conduct warranted its refusal (s 11(5) of the Courts and Legal Services Act 1990). No central record is kept, but local administrative arrangements for records of refusal are made.

Disqualification of a lay representative

A judge may order a lay representative's disqualification if he has reason to believe that the representative intentionally misled the court or otherwise demonstrated unsuitability to exercise these rights. The judge must give reasons for the disqualification, though these do not have to be in writing. Disqualified persons have a right to appeal to the Court of Appeal.

The Lord Chancellor's Department maintains a central register of the names and addresses of disqualified persons; this is made available to all county courts so that litigants can obtain confirmation of a representative's status if they wish.

The rules for banning and disqualification of lay representatives are supplemented by rules requiring any person engaging in improper conduct to pay the wasted costs of the other party, where the court considers that costs have been unreasonably incurred as a result of 'any improper, unreasonable or negligent act or omission' on the part of the lay representative.

(c) The fees of a lay representative

As far as costs in small claims are concerned, those exercising rights of audience are allowed to charge for doing so. However, litigants claiming less than £5,000 will still have to meet any such costs themselves.

3. Lawyers – a barrister, solicitor or legal executive employed by a solicitor

Many small claimants use a lawyer for the hearing. Although most litigants should feel able to appear without a lawyer, they are perfectly entitled to use one if they wish, and may well find it useful. The idea of banning lawyers entirely from small claims courts, as happens in some American states, has not been adopted in the United Kingdom. However, you will have to pay your own costs (see Chapter 11). Lawyers more familiar with civil trials may find their role somewhat diminished in the more inquisitorial but informal atmosphere of a private hearing in the judge's private room.

Barristers appear mainly in road traffic claims where the parties are insured and where the insurers will be footing the bill.

The hearing

4. Attendance at court

The notice of the hearing gives a date and time of the small claims hearing. It also should give an estimate of the time that the hearing will take, and the name and address of the court which you must attend (names and addresses of all the county courts are reproduced in Appendix 4). You should receive a map from the court showing you where the hearing will take place. Hearings normally take place on weekdays between 10 am and 4 pm. There is no provision for evening or weekend sittings. It is very important to be sure about *which* county court your hearing has been scheduled for. This is likely to be the defendant's local court (if the defendant is an individual and the claim is for a specified amount) and not the court where you issued your claim form. Of course in many cases it will be the same court.

In many towns the court is not part of the same building as the court offices that you may have previously visited. Experience suggests that many people confuse the county court with the magistrates' court which is primarily a criminal court, and has no jurisdiction over small claims.

Many county courts are not in prominent places, so they may take a little while to find. It therefore pays to arrive early. This will also help in order to find out in which district judge's room your case is being heard. (If there is only one district judge, this problem is unlikely to arise.) Court ushers, recognisable by their black gowns, can help you, and court staff should assist. Unfortunately, like doctors' appointments, one can never estimate exactly how long each small claim will take, so there may be a delay before your case is heard. Parties should be warned that on arriving at court they may find that their case is listed with a large number of other small claims at the same time. This is known as 'block listing'. Experience shows that many people do not attend small claims hearings – indeed sometimes neither party does – so this cuts down on delay for others. Normally your case should begin quite promptly.

You should attend the hearing reasonably smartly dressed. This is courteous to the court and probably creates a good impression. As you wait outside the district judge's room to be called by the usher, try to stay calm. There is no reason to be nervous, as the judge should put you at your ease, and nerves are only likely to impede the presentation of your case. Nor is there any need for you to gird yourself up for a forensic battle – that is not appropriate for the process of an informal hearing. If you feel anger or frustration against your opponent, try to suppress it, as your case depends not on your indignation, righteous or otherwise, but on the facts you prove, the arguments you put forward and their basis in law. You will find the other party also waiting, if they have decided to attend. It may have been some time since you were face to face, or this may even be the first time. You might have an opportunity to speak about the possibility of a settlement. Lawyers do this all the time in the higher courts, where it is commonplace to settle on the morning of trial at the doors of the courtroom. Many district judges may indeed ask you if you have tried to settle the matter before you arrived. Beware of being

The hearing

too willing to conciliate or of making any dangerous admissions. These can only strengthen your opponent.

5. The judge

Small claims are almost always heard by a district judge or a deputy district judge. Deputy district judges are usually part-time but often go on to become district judges.

District judges are all lawyers of at least seven years' professional practice. Before the Courts and Legal Services Act 1990, they were known as county court registrars. They do not wear wigs and gowns when hearing small claims, and are attired in suits or, in the case of female district judges, the women's equivalent, without regalia of office. More like a local solicitor than the usual image of the British judiciary. The correct mode of address to a district judge is 'Sir' or 'Madam' and not 'Your Honour' which is appropriate for Circuit judges, who rarely hear small claims. Equally, addressing the district judge as 'Your Lordship' (the highest rank in the judiciary), though flattering, will not improve your chances of winning.

6. The hearing

Almost all small claims hearings take place in the district judge's room. This is intended to reduce the formality of proceedings. Although intended to be informal, you should not begin by shaking hands with the judge (as some litigants have been known to do). Civil trials are normally open to the public and anyone can sit and listen. In small claims this general rule applies unless the parties agree to a hearing in private or the hearing is on site (see page 99). CPR r 39.2 sets out situations where the hearing may be in private notwithstanding the general rule. The one most relevant to small claims is:

> 'it involves confidential information (including information relating to financial matters) and publicity would damage that confidentiality' (CPR r 39.2(3)(c)).

It is rare for the public to seek to attend a small claims hearing, although the press sometimes do if one of the parties is a celebrity or the facts are very unusual. Usually the parties sit around a table, while the judge sits at a desk beyond that table.

The key to small claims hearings is that the court may adopt any method of proceeding at a hearing that it considers to be fair. In order to minimise the differences between courts, the Lord Chancellor has issued guidance as to how small claims should be conducted. These are not mandatory, however, and practice varies from court to court and even between district judges within the same court. See Appendix 3 pages 189–192 for the rules on the conduct of a small claims hearing.

The hearing

- The hearing may be held at the court house, at the court offices, or at any other place 'convenient to the parties'. In fact it is almost invariably held in the district judge's room, although he may visit the site or property involved and hold the small claims hearing there. This can be time consuming, however, and will rarely happen.
- The hearing is informal and the strict rules of evidence do not apply.
- Unless the district judge orders otherwise, hearings are held in public, but normally evidence is not taken on oath.
- At the hearing the district judge may adopt any method of procedure which he considers to be fair and limit cross-examination to a particular subject or to a fixed time or both.
- Having considered the circumstances of the parties, and whether or not they are represented, the district judge questions witnesses or the other party, and should explain any legal terms or expressions which are used. Normally judges intervene quite regularly to ask questions, rather than merely listening to legal evidence as happens in court.
- The district judge may require the production of any documents or articles, and inspect any property or object concerning any which questions may arise.
- The district judge may refuse to allow cross-examination of any witness until all witnesses have given their evidence.
- The judgment (and any summing up given by the judge) will be recorded unless the judge otherwise orders. Normally the oral evidence will also be recorded.
- The district judge must inform the parties of his judgment and the central reasons for it. The reasons do not have to be, and are not normally, given in writing.

(a) Documents only?

This is possible but rare in small claims. Clearly it saves you attending a hearing, but you may feel that you would prefer to have your say in person, and to have 'your day in court'. Others may not feel competent at putting their case down accurately on paper.

(b) Hearings in Wales

By the Welsh Language Act 1967, in any legal proceedings in Wales or Monmouthshire (now Gwent) the Welsh language may be spoken by a party, witness or other person who desires to use it. There is a Practice Direction to Part 39 relating to the use of the Welsh Language in Cases in the Civil Courts in Wales and a supplementary Practice Direction applicable where such cases originate in North Wales.

The hearing

(c) Non-English speakers

Provision is made in the courts for allowing interpreters to attend on behalf of witnesses or parties. The cost of an interpreter in small claims will usually have to be met by the party themselves. Interpreters are normally treated as witnesses of fact rather than expert witnesses, for the purpose of recovering their costs. There are now restricted witness allowances (see Chapter 9).

(d) Putting parties or witnesses on oath

This is often not exercised in small claims. In some circumstances, however, such as where there is a real clash of evidence, the judge may choose to do so. There are alternative oaths for most religions (set out in *The Civil Court Practice*), and an affirmation for those who do not profess to hold any religious beliefs.

(e) Presenting your case

Having read the file relating to the case, the district judge will usually ask the claimant to tell him about his claim. He may even begin by asking if you have tried to settle your dispute or if there is still a possibility of settling without a consent. Judges also explain in outline the procedure of the hearing to the parties.

You should start at the beginning and tell your version of events. If you have a typed statement you should supply (if you have not already supplied) a copy to the court and to your opponent and then go through it. Remember to deal with the points in your opponent's statement of case with which you disagree. Imagine that perhaps you are telling the story to your family or a friend.

Stay calm and do not exaggerate. Address the district judge as 'Sir' or 'Madam'. A party who appears calm and reasonable creates a better impression than one who is filled with indignation. Remember to pause between sentences because the judge will be making a note of what you say in his notebook. It is a good idea to watch his pen: when he stops writing you may continue speaking. If you have difficulty in explaining what you want to say, the judge will usually help you by asking questions. When people are feeling nervous they often fail to hear questions, so make sure you listen carefully to any questions before answering. If you do not understand the question, you should not be afraid to say so. After you have given your evidence, the judge may hear what your witnesses (if any) have to say. He may then invite the defendant to ask questions and will probably ask a number of questions himself. You will find that the judge will usually ask quite a number of questions as the hearing progresses.

After the claimant has presented his case, the defendant will then give his evidence. If you are not invited to do so, and there are questions that you would like to ask, you should tell the judge that you wish to ask some questions.

The hearing

When hearing cases between parties appearing in person most judges prefer to hear what each of them has to say, and then, if any explanations are necessary, or there are points that require clarification, the judge will question each party in turn. At the same time he will give each of them an opportunity to qualify or explain anything that they have already said. This is known as interventionist procedure.

The practice of small claims has a basic structure which is capable of variation and can be tailored to suit the needs of the parties and the case itself. For example, one district judge produces small model cars in motor accident claims so that the parties can explain where they were when the accident occurred and how it came about. This informal aspect of the procedure often helps to get at the truth.

You are not expected to act as if you are a lawyer. Simply present your side of the dispute in the clearest possible terms. Remember that before you started proceedings or defended them, you should have established that you had some arguable legal case. If you did not, you will simply be wasting your own and the court's time. Some legal knowledge may help focus the disagreement between the parties, and there is no harm in coming with some points of law if you think them relevant. Faced with a solicitor, a non-lawyer may find this rather daunting, but it is better to make a point that seems worthwhile rather than be left with the thought that it might have made a difference if you haven't. The district judge should seek to establish a fair balance between the parties. He is also under a duty to explain legal terms and expressions used in the proceedings.

(f) The importance of evidence

It cannot be over-stressed that evidence to support your claim or defence is vital and likely to affect the outcome of the hearing. If you have relevant documents, invoices, receipts, and letters, then you must bring these with you. It is a good idea to have copies of all relevant papers and submissions so that you can hand a set to the judge and another to your opponent, if they have not already seen them. Make a bundle of the documents in date order and number each document. This will avoid delays in everyone locating the document. An index is not essential but is a sound investment of your time. Other evidence such as photographs can greatly assist the district judge as to the merits of a claim. Bringing a witness along to speak on your behalf or, if they cannot come, at least to provide a written statement can often make the difference between winning or losing. The strict rules of admissibility of evidence do not apply in the small claims court. Litigants must appreciate, however, that the burden of proof is on the claimant. If the case is simply one person's word against another's, the judge may have to find for the defendant because the case has not been proved on the balance of probabilities. This demonstrates the value of corroborative evidence.

(g) Experts

No expert may give evidence, whether written or oral, without the permission of the court (CPR r 27.5). The concept of evidence by a jointly instructed expert forms part of the basis of the Civil Procedure Rules 1998.

Where both parties have expert reports simultaneous exchange is normal.

Having an expert as a witness often proves invaluable. It should be emphasised that a written report is good evidence, even if not always as good as the expert attending. Experts tend to be expensive and the rate allowed is unlikely to cover the expert's charges for producing a report and attending the hearing. Parties are required to disclose expert reports prior to the hearing – you can therefore make a decision based on what your opponent discloses. If the other party does not disclose an expert report, it should normally be safe not to take your expert witness to the hearing.

If the opponent does disclose an expert report, the procedure will be to read through that report and compare it with your own. If there are significant differences it may be possible to balance the cost of losing on those points against the cost of calling an expert. In the last resort, if the expert does not attend and actually his presence would have been useful, the judge may grant an adjournment. It is sensible to ask your opponent if he agrees with your report – and, if not, what parts, if any, he does agree with. This should be done by letter so that there can be no argument later over what has been agreed.

(h) Non-attendance by the parties

If a party who does not attend the final hearing has given at least seven days' notice that he will not attend and has asked the court to decide the case in his absence, the court will take into account that party's statement of case and any other documents he has filed in deciding the claim.

If a claimant does not attend and has not given the seven days' notice, the court may strike out his claim.

If a defendant does not attend and has not given the seven days' notice and the claimant either attends or has given the seven days' notice, the court may decide the case on the basis of the evidence of the claimant alone.

If neither party attends or gives the seven days' notice, the court may strike out the claim and any defence and counterclaim.

These provisions do not affect the general power of the court to adjourn when it considers it just to do so.

There are often good reasons why one party cannot attend a hearing before the district judge. If one party is seeking an adjournment, e.g. due to illness or temporary incapacity, a letter should be sent as soon as possible to the court and to the other party giving the reason, and where appropriate a medical certificate should be enclosed with the letter.

The hearing

If no adjournment is being sought but the party cannot attend, e.g. due to the distance involved, he should give the seven days' notice and ask the judge to excuse his attendance and to reach a decision on the written representations of that party. Any relevant documents should be sent to the court and their significance explained. Copies of such documents should be served on the other party if they have not been previously disclosed.

(i) Setting aside judgment – CPR r 27.11

Where a party was neither present nor represented at the hearing and did not give the seven days' notice he can nevertheless apply for an order that the judgment be set aside and the claim reheard. He must apply within 14 days of receiving notice of the judgment.

The court may grant his application if:

- he had good reason for not attending or giving the seven days' notice; and
- he has reasonable prospects of success at the hearing.

If the judgment is set aside the court must fix a new hearing, which may be for it to take place immediately after the application (however, this is not common). The judge who set aside the judgment can conduct the rehearing.

There can be no application to set aside a judgment on a claim dealt with without a hearing.

All too often the application to set aside procedure is employed by those who know how to manipulate the rules, although there are many genuine cases. There is no real limit to the number of applications that can be made, and the process can be made to drag on unnecessarily. If you think this is happening, ask the district judge to make an order dismissing the application and directing that 'no other further applications (other than an appeal) be accepted by the court without leave'.

7. The judgment

Most hearings should be over within one or two hours or even less, but hearings of over three hours are not uncommon. The judge normally announces his decision *ex tempore* at the conclusion of the case, along with his reasons for doing so. The reasons are not normally given in writing. The judge may occasionally take time to consider the case, in which case he will deliver his decision later, after a short delay, or even occasionally in writing by post. This is called a reserved judgment.

The judgment is enforceable just like any other judgment of a civil court (see Chapter 13). If judgment is given for the claimant, recoverable costs and expenses will be awarded, and, in the case of a debt, interest at 8 per cent from the date the debt arose to the date of judgment if interest has been claimed in the claim form (see Chapter 11). If the claim form also

The hearing

includes a claim for interest from the date of issue up to judgment, a daily rate should be shown in the particulars of claim. The judgment must be based on law, not on the basis of what the judge considers a fair or just outcome. It may be, however, that in many cases that is exactly what the judge sets out to achieve. Unless the judgment is in writing, it is important to take a note of the judge's reasons in case either party seeks to appeal. If the hearing was recorded a party may apply for a transcript on payment of the proper transcribers' charges. Further, a party is entitled to a copy of any note made by the judge of the evidence or the reasons for his judgment. If you are successful but the judge does not award you the recoverable costs and interest and does not say why he is not doing so you should ask for them because he may simply have forgotten. This can be done politely by saying, 'Thank you but I have also asked for my costs and for interest'. He will tell you that only limited costs are recoverable, but by making your request you will have ensured that the matters of recoverable costs and interest have been addressed by the judge. In most cases the recoverable costs and interest will be awarded.

8. Appeals

(a) Permission required

Either the claimant or the defendant has the right to appeal against the decision of a district judge in a case allocated to the small claims track provided permission is obtained.

Permission should be requested orally at the conclusion of the hearing and if it is refused a note should be made of the reasons given for the refusal. If the district judge does not give reasons for the refusal he should be asked to do so.

If the permission of the district judge is not requested at the conclusion of the hearing, or the request is refused, permission can be sought in the appeal notice from the Circuit Judge.

- The person appealing is called 'the appellant'.

(b) The appellant's appeal notice

The appellant's notice of appeal (form N161) must be completed and filed within such period as the district judge has directed or, where there is no such direction, 14 days after the date of the decision being appealed.

If permission has not been obtained from the district judge it must be sought by completing paragraph 6 of form N161.

- The whole of form N161 must be completed so that if permission is granted the form will furnish the required information for the appeal hearing.

The hearing

If the Circuit Judge refuses permission without a hearing a request can be made for that refusal to be reconsidered at a hearing. If permission is refused at the hearing there is no right of appeal against that decision.

The appeal notice (form N161) must be served promptly on the other party and that must be within 7 days after it is filed.

(c) Grounds to be established to obtain permission

Permission will only be granted where:

- the court considers the appeal would have a real prospect of success; or
- there is some other compelling reason why the appeal should be heard.

(d) Documents to be filed with the appeal notice

Where an appeal relates to a claim allocated to the small claims track the appellant must file with his appeal notice:

- a sealed copy of the order being appealed; and
- any order giving or refusing permission to appeal together with the reasons given for that decision.

The court may order a suitable record of the reasons for the judgment deciding the small claims to be filed:

- to enable it to decide if permission should be granted; or
- if permission is granted to enable it to decide the appeal.

The appellant may file certain other documents in particular 'any other documents the appellant reasonably considers necessary to enable the appeal court to reach its decision. A brief summary of the appellant's argument (usually called a skeleton argument) will invariably be useful.

Notes

1. An approved transcript of the district judge's judgment can be obtained from the court if it was recorded. This will almost always be the case.
2. Where the appellant was not represented at the hearing of the small claim but the other party was, the legal representative is under a duty to make a note of the judgment, if it is not recorded, and to make that note available to the appellant promptly and free of charge.

(e) Respondent's notice

The appellant is the party who is making the appeal; the other party (or parties) to the appeal is called 'the Respondent'. If the respondent wishes the appeal court (the Circuit Judge) to uphold the order made on the hearing of the small claim, but for reasons additional to or different from those given by the district judge who heard the case, he must file and serve a respondent's notice.

The respondent's notice is form N162. The notice must be filed within 14 days of:

- the date the respondent was served with the appeal notice, if permission was given by the court hearing the small claims;
- the date the respondent is notified that the appeal court (the Circuit Judge) has given the appellant permission to appeal; or
- the date the respondent is notified that the application for permission to appeal and the appeal itself are to be heard together.

The respondent's notice must be served on the appellant and any other respondent as soon as possible and in any event no later than 7 days after it is filed.

- If the respondent also wishes to appeal he must in any event file a respondent's notice and seek permission to appeal (see sections 4 and 5 of form N162).

(f) Hearing of the appeal

Neither new evidence nor oral evidence will be permitted at the appeal unless the court otherwise orders. The appeal court will allow the appeal where the decision appealed against was:

- wrong; or
- unjust because of serious procedural or other irregularity.

If the appeal is allowed normally a new trial will be ordered.

(g) The order appealed against

The appeal does not prevent the other party from enforcing the order that is appealed against. Application must be made to the court for enforcement to be stayed; if this is granted no step to enforce the order appealed against can be taken until the appeal is decided. Use form N244 for the application (see pages 64–65).

(h) Costs

The 'no costs' phrase does not apply to costs summarily assessed in relation to an appeal.

- 'Summarily assessed' means costs quantified by the Circuit Judge immediately after giving his decision on the appeal.

The hearing

9. Small claims for more than £5,000

Parties seeking informality may apply, in any action, for allocation to the small claims track, but it is still for the court to decide if the claim is suitable for that track. If an order, with the consent of the parties, is made referring the claim to the small claims track notwithstanding that it exceeds the financial limits for that track, it will be governed by the rules for the small claims track in Part 27 of the Civil Procedure Rules 1998 (although the no costs rule does not apply – see Chapter 11). The amount of costs incurred, however, is likely to be less than if the claim was allocated to either of the other tracks.

10. Judgment of the court

The court's judgment after a hearing is embodied in an order which is stamped with the court seal and copies sent to the claimant and defendant. This tells the party required to pay:

- how much to pay;
- when to pay it.

Payment of the monies due under a judgment must be made to the person named at the address for payment shown at the end of the court order.

Chapter 11

No costs

The cost of civil litigation in England and Wales is still notoriously high. Legal help or legal representation paid for by the Legal Services Commission is almost invariably not available for small claims. People are expected to process their own claims. Therefore it is self-evident that small claims must be cheap and easy to pursue. Since the inception of the new small claims procedures, there has existed a 'no costs' rule. This is essentially the defining feature of English small claims, not the arbitration process which is also available elsewhere. The costs referred to are the legal costs of both parties – under the English system these usually have to be paid by the losing party. The definition of costs therefore comprises:

(a) solicitors' charges, including fees to barristers and other disbursements;
(b) sums allowed to a litigant in person (under CPR r 48.6);
(c) fees or reward charged by a lay representative.

In small claims, such costs may not be recovered in the ordinary way by the victorious party. The rule is designed to discourage lawyers in small claims and to provide litigants in person with the assurance that pursuing a claim for a smallish amount will not render them at risk of having to face a large legal bill if they lose. If small claimants wish to provide themselves with legal services, they have to do so at their own expense. It is obviously far easier for large firms to absorb such legal costs than it is for the average individual. Many companies therefore retain solicitors for debt and small claims actions on a recurring basis, though solicitors do not appear regularly at small claims hearings.

1. When costs can be claimed

'No costs' is not exactly an accurate description of the procedure, though it is universally used. The restrictions on allowance of costs in small claims are dealt with in CPR r 27.14.

Costs can be claimed for certain matters, even within small claims.

No costs

- The court fee paid on commencing the claim, but only the fee payable for the amount recovered (as opposed to the amount claimed), is likely to be awarded by the judge. The allocation fee and other court fees paid may also be awarded.
- If the claim was issued by a solicitor the fixed costs on issue set out in CPR Part 45, Table 1, may be awarded. These are:
  - where the value of the claim exceeds £25 but does not exceed £500 ....£50.00
  - where the value of the claim exceeds £500 but does not exceed £1,000 ....£70.00
  - where the value of the claim exceeds £1,000 but does not exceed £5,000 ....£80.00

  An additional £10 is allowed where the form is served personally by the claimant on the first or only defendant. Where there is more than one defendant, for each defendant personally served at separate addresses, an additional £15 is allowed.
- Where the proceedings include a claim for an injunction or for specific performance, a sum not exceeding a prescribed amount for obtaining advice and assistance relating to that claim may be claimed. The prescribed amount is presently £260.
- Costs incurred through having to enforce the award.
- Costs, which will be summarily assessed, in relation to an appeal.
- Expenses which a party or witnesses have reasonably incurred in travelling to and from a hearing or in staying away from home for the purposes of attending a hearing. Additionally, a sum not exceeding a specified amount (presently £50 per day) for loss of earnings, by a party or witness due to attending a hearing may be claimed.
- The fees of an expert which can be recovered are limited to £200 for each expert for preparing a report, and/or attending court as a witness, if necessary. There is no discretion to exceed either this or the previous limit.
- Where a claim is re-allocated from the small claims track to another track, the no costs rule will cease to apply after the claim has been re-allocated. Thereafter costs are based on the ordinary rules under the Civil Procedure Rules 1998 (CPR).
- Where costs are allowed, they will be awarded at the end of the hearing, normally along with judgment, and that will be the amount to which you are entitled.
- The only exception to the no costs rule is with regard to costs, which will be summarily assessed, ordered to be paid by a party who has acted unreasonably.
- There is no entitlement to costs which are always within the discretion of court.

2. Unreasonable behaviour

When the other party has acted unreasonably a litigant may apply for costs to be awarded in his favour, notwithstanding the 'no costs' rule, because of that unreasonable behaviour. The time available to persuade the court to make this order will be very short so preparation for the application is vital. A schedule of unreasonable behaviour should be prepared and handed to the court at the conclusion of the case.

It will be rare that there is a single point of itself sufficient to justify the order; it is more often an accumulation of a number of acts that show unreasonable behaviour.

Some examples of such behaviour are:

- ignoring the letter before action;
- ignoring a suggestion that a joint expert be appointed;
- failure to comply with a reasonable request, e.g. for a copy document;
- not complying or not properly complying with the directions issued by the court;
- rejecting an offer of settlement which would have provided him with a better outcome than that ordered by the court;
- pursuing an obviously hopeless case;
- failing to attend the fixed hearing or to give notice in accordance with CPR of his intention not to attend.

The schedule should have any necessary documents attached (e.g. a copy of the letter of offer) and a copy of the schedule should be available for the opponent.

There should also be a schedule showing the work done and the time taken so that if the judge accepts that he should make an order for costs he will have a clear idea of how much time has been taken up and what work has been done to prepare and present the case. A copy of this schedule should be served on the other party at least 24 hours before the hearing with documents to prove any financial loss suffered.

- For entitlement where an order for costs is obtained see further paragraph 6 below.
- Reducing the claim to stay within the small claims limit is not unreasonable although the object of so doing is to avoid the risk of an award of costs if the claim fails. If the other party opposes this he should seek to have the claim allocated to another track.
- There are pre CPR authorities (e.g. *Bloomfield v Roberts* [1989] CLY 2948) that state to defend proceedings following an objective consideration which concludes that there was no adequate defence is unreasonable behaviour.

3. Inflating a claim to recover costs

Inflating a claim to avoid allocation to the small claims track in order to avoid the 'no costs' rule is regarded as a misuse of process, and costs are not likely to be awarded in favour of the claimant when the judge is exercising his discretion as to costs, and costs may be awarded against him. The Civil Procedure Rules 1998 are likely to result in such attempts becoming apparent on the lodging of allocation questionnaires by the parties. The district judge is likely to block the attempt, but if he should fail to do so his allocation decision can be appealed.

It should also be borne in mind that the amount in issue does not include any sum for which liability is admitted. Such an admission, if appropriate, should be put clearly in the defence so that the district judge will be fully aware of the position when allocating the claim.

4. The question of costs considered

As Part 36 of the Civil Procedure Rules 1998 (offers to settle and payments into court) does not apply to small claims, a party to such a claim has limited scope to protect himself against an intransigent opponent. The best that can be done is to write a letter without prejudice as to costs setting out what he is prepared to accept or pay, as the case may be, to settle the claim reserving the right to produce the letter to the court at the conclusion of the hearing to support an application that the court find the other party to have behaved unreasonably and that a sum by way of additional costs should be awarded and assessed by summary procedure.

5. The fees or charges of a lay representative

Lay representatives may charge for their services. However, these are treated as legal costs for the purposes of small claims and are not recoverable if you win, subject to the rules above where there is unreasonable behaviour (CPR r 27.14(4)).

6. Litigants in Person (Costs and Expenses) Act 1975

This Act allows orders for costs to be made in favour of litigants in person as would have been allowed if the work and disbursements had been done by a solicitor on the litigant's behalf. Where such costs are allowed, the litigant can only recover two-thirds of the sum which would have been allowed a solicitor.

Costs allowed to the litigant in person shall be:

- such costs which would have been allowed if the work had been done or the disbursements incurred by a legal representative on the litigant in person's behalf;

- the payments reasonably made by him for legal services relating to the conduct of the proceedings; and
- the costs of obtaining expert assistance in connection with assessing the claim for costs.

The costs a litigant in person can recover for time reasonably spent if he fails to prove financial loss are at a specified rate, presently £9.25 per hour.

However, the Act only applies on the small claims track if you are awarded costs because of the unreasonable conduct of the other party.

7. Costs in small personal injury claims

Personal injury claims that do not exceed £1000 in value are treated like any other small claims. In due course it is possible that special costs rules for such claims will be introduced if the financial limit is increased.

8. Costs of an appeal – CPR r 27.14(2)(c)

These are not subject to the no costs rule and will be assessed under the summary procedure at the conclusion of the appeal hearing.

Chapter 12

Small personal injury claims

Personal injury claims account for a large part of the workload of the civil courts, particularly the county courts and the Queen's Bench Division of the High Court. Most of these are settled but some proceed to a full trial. Since the decision of the Court of Appeal in *Afzal v Ford Motor Co Ltd, The Independent*, 6 June 1994, most personal injury claims for not more than £1,000 have been regarded as suitable for the small claims procedure.

The Civil Procedure Rules 1998 (CPR) provide that:

> 'any claim for personal injuries where the financial value of the claim is not more than £5,000 and where the claim for damages for personal injuries is not more than £1,000'

will normally be allocated to the small claims track (CPR r 27.1(2)).

Rule 2.3 of the Civil Procedure Rules defines 'claim for personal injuries' as 'proceedings in which there is a claim for damages in respect of personal injuries to the claimant or any other person or in respect of a person's death'.

Rule 26.6(2) provides that '"damages for personal injuries" means damages claimed as compensation for pain, suffering and loss of amenity and does not include any other damages which are claimed'. That is vehicle damage, loss of use of vehicle, damage to clothing, loss of earnings, for example, will not form part of the 'damages for personal injuries' when considering the £1,000 limit, although they will be relevant when considering the £5,000 limit.

The term 'personal injury' includes any disease and any impairment of a person's physical or mental condition. It does not include damage to one's property. Damage to property – whether it be to clothing or spectacles or to more major items, such as a car – is also recoverable in tort.

To succeed with a personal injury claim, it is necessary to prove that the injury was caused by someone else or by something over which a human being has control. Most actions proceed against negligent drivers of cars, employers, owners of domestic or business premises or providers of services. The burden of proving negligence usually lies on the claimant although this can be made easier in certain circumstances – for example, in cases where a person has clearly been careless – where the legal maxim *res ipsa loquitur* ('the thing speaks for itself') applies. The case has to be proved on the balance of probabilities, not beyond reasonable doubt, as in criminal law. A frequent difficulty is to prove that the injury was actually *caused* for the reasons alleged by the claimant.

Most personal injury actions are in the tort of negligence. The principles of negligence are the same whatever the context, and involve broad general criteria; these are given much more precise meaning by lawyers applying case law. It is for this reason, in particular, that legal advice may be essential before embarking on any action in this area.

To succeed in negligence the claimant has to prove that:

(a) the defendant owed him a duty of care; and
(b) there was a breach of the duty of care by the defendant – the standard required is that of 'the reasonable man' (**Note** in actions against professionals, the standard is reasonable skill and judgment); and
(c) the defendant's conduct caused injury to the claimant; and
(d) the type of injury suffered was not 'too remote' from the original act of the defendant. The test here is whether the injury was reasonably foreseeable.

In employers' liability cases it may be possible to bring an action in the tort of breach of statutory duty. This can be combined with negligence, or as an alternative to it. The claimant has to argue that:

- the defendant was in breach of health and safety legislation or regulations which were designed to protect a class of persons which include the claimant; and
- the breach of statute caused injury to the claimant; and
- the defendant was in breach of the relevant standard of care laid down in the statute, e.g. 'reasonably practicable' or 'in so far as is reasonable'.

Breach of statutory duty is often more specific and therefore easier to prove than the wider principles of negligence. Where injury is caused by another employee, that person himself may be sued as tortfeasor ('wrongdoer'), but the action will also be against the employer, who will be the main defendant and who may ultimately be required to pay any compensation awarded. This is called vicarious liability. All employers have to be insured against liability for injuries at work, by the Employers' Liability (Compulsory Insurance) Act 1969.

If the person you are suing is insured, you may find that his insurance company will defend the action. They are likely to have considerable expertise in this area. Equally, if an insurance company has paid out on an insurance policy to a potential claimant they may take over the action to recover their payments by subrogation. Defendants may therefore find that the claimant is in reality the victim's insurers.

Small personal injury claims

Personal injuries which are deliberately inflicted are more usually dealt with by the criminal courts. Trespass to the person, which includes assault and battery, and false imprisonment can give rise to civil claims. Criminal action, for instance by the Health and Safety Executive or by local environmental health officers, generally leaves unaffected the right of injured persons to use the civil courts. The fact of conviction of a criminal offence is admissible in evidence in subsequent civil proceedings, if relevant.

- The Offences Against The Person Act 1861, sections 44–45, provides that summary criminal proceedings whether resulting in a conviction or an acquittal, after a hearing on the merits, bar any subsequent civil proceedings for the same injury.

A successful action for personal injuries will result in an award of damages. Unlike a debt, these have to be quantified by the judge and vary from case to case. You may claim for a specified amount but it is ultimately for the court to make the award. The purpose of most damages is to compensate the claimant for his loss. This usually entails putting the claimant in the position he would have been in, had the injury not occurred. In personal injury actions the main headings are:

(a) loss of earnings;
(b) other financial loss, or expenses (this includes being disadvantaged on the labour market);
(c) loss of amenity, or enjoyment of life;
(d) pain and suffering – this is an award which compensates for the injury itself;
(e) loss of expectation of life.

The award of a certain sum to a claimant does not mean that another court will award the same sum to another claimant with the same injury, as every case is regarded as different. Nevertheless, solicitors can usually advise you on how much you are likely to receive, as there is a kind of rough 'tariff' for particular types of injury.

1. The difficulties with personal injury claims

- the need for legal advice on personal injury liability;
- the need for legal advice on quantum (the amount of damages), and how much to claim;
- inexperience of claimants in negotiating settlements with insurers, employers and public authorities, all of whom have greater experience of the system;
- if the case goes to trial on the fast or multi-track, the risk of paying the costs of your opponent if you lose;
- the difficulty of obtaining proof, particularly medical evidence, and being able to prove negligence;

Small personal injury claims

- the cost of medical and other expert evidence;
- inequality between the claimant and defendant in terms of resources, legal knowledge and experience, and skill in co-ordinating the case;
- compared with, say, debt cases, the successful outcome of a personal injury claim is less assured;
- claimants may limit their claim to £1,000, when in fact their injury is worth much more;
- the need for legal advice and representation, and the cost such services necessarily entail.

The problems should not be overstated, however, as it is perfectly possible for an unrepresented litigant to win a small personal injury claim.

2. Seeking advice about personal injuries

Trade unions: If you are a member of a trade union, you should contact it immediately. Most unions offer free advice and representation to their members. This includes the services of solicitors and lawyers to appear in court on your behalf. This is a huge advantage for trade unionists and you will not have to pay costs if you lose. However, the union's legal advice may be that you will lose any civil action. If you then proceed, you will be on your own. Unions and insurers now operate compensation schemes for a number of common occupational injuries. These offer the possibility of quicker resolution of claims without the need to go to court. Your trade union may also advise you on how to proceed with your action on your own if your claim falls within the small claims limit.

Solicitors: Personal injuries are an area in which many firms specialise, and most solicitors will be able to advise you on the course of an action. The obstacles of being unable to recover full costs may, however, be an impediment to their acting for you. Certain firms work mostly for claimants, others specialise in working for the insurance industry.

Accident Line: Many firms of solicitors are now members of this service. They will offer help and advice with personal injury claims, including a free initial consultation. The Law Society now has a panel of personal injury practitioners – only those who are members of this panel may belong to Accident Line. The freephone number is 0800 19 29 39.

Advice centres: Since the difficulties involved in personal injuries are almost certain to be greater than for other types of claims, advisers are likely to suggest that you see a solicitor. They may be able to recommend a local solicitor who does personal injury work.

General practitioners: Medical evidence will be vital to your claim, so consult your GP.

Small personal injury claims

3. Pre-action protocol for personal injury claims

This protocol, attached to the Civil Procedure Rules 1998, and Annex A to it are reproduced at pages 136–149. The protocol provides that it is intended to apply to all claims which include a claim for personal injury, but is primarily designed for such claims as are likely to be allocated to the fast track. Nevertheless, it provides useful guidance where a claim is on the small claims track, in particular as to the contents of the letter making the claim and as to the instruction of a medical expert.

Paragraph 3.14 of the protocol provides:

> 'Before any party instructs an expert he should give the other party a list of the name(s) of one or more experts in the relevant speciality whom he considers are suitable to instruct.'

4. Issue of claim

In a claim for personal injuries the claimant must state in the claim form whether or not the amount he expects to recover for pain, suffering and loss of amenity exceeds £1,000. Further the particulars of claim must include:

- the claimant's date of birth; and
- brief details of the claimant's personal injuries.

The claimant must also attach to the particulars of claim a schedule of details of any past and future expenses and losses which he claims.

Where the claimant relies on the evidence of a medical practitioner, the claimant must attach to, or serve with, his particulars of claim a report from a medical practitioner about the personal injuries which he alleges in his claim.

5. Allocation of claim

Although the small claims track will generally be the normal track for a personal injury claim falling within the financial limits, the reference to 'straightforward' claims in paragraph 8.1 of the Practice Direction to CPR Part 26 should be noted. If the claim is for some reason complicated it may be allocated to another track. Proportionality, however, makes this unlikely.

6. Valuing a small personal injury claim

The basic rule must be to obtain advice about the value of a personal injury claim but it has to be faced that the value of some injuries is too small to justify paying out legal fees.

The tariff issued by the Criminal Justice Injuries Compensation Board provides some help for minor multiple injuries. Three separate injuries of

Small personal injury claims

the type listed below (of which at least one has significant residual effects six weeks after the accident and at least two visits to a doctor have been necessary in the six weeks period) give an entitlement to a claim of £1,000:

- grazing, cuts, lacerations (no permanent scarring);
- severe and widespread bruising;
- severe soft tissue injury (no permanent disability);
- black eye(s);
- a bloody nose;
- hair pulled from the scalp;
- loss of a fingernail.

These are not awards of damages but provide some guidance.

The Judicial Studies Board's Guidelines for the Assessment of General Damages is of little help with small injuries but the figure given for the loss of or damage to back teeth is £525 to £900 per tooth (£1,000 to £2,000 for loss of one front tooth).

There are few reported cases where the Court of Appeal has considered the damages of a claim that would fall within the Small Claims limit. However, in *Oxley v BCH Ltd*, 14 July 1997 (unreported) the Court of Appeal reduced an award of damages to £1,000 where the claimant received a blow to the head, causing a cut over one of his eyes and headaches. Five months after the accident he had completely recovered save for an insignificant scar over his eye.

A medical report will be necessary unless a virtually nominal figure is being sought. The doctor, in his report, should be asked to deal with the nature of the injury, its effect, the recovery period and whether there is any lasting effect or risk of recurrence.

7. Pre-action protocol for personal injury claims

1. INTRODUCTION

1.1 Lord Woolf in his final Access to Justice Report of July 1996 recommended the development of pre-action protocols:

'To build on and increase the benefits of early but well informed settlement which genuinely satisfy both parties to dispute.'

1.2 The aims of pre-action protocols are:
- more pre-action contact between the parties;
- better and earlier exchange of information;
- better pre-action investigation by both sides;
- to put the parties in a position where they may be able to settle cases fairly and early without litigation;
- to enable proceedings to run to the court's timetable and efficiently, if litigation does become necessary.

1.3 The concept of protocols is relevant to a range of initiatives for good litigation and pre-litigation practice, especially:
- predictability in the time needed for steps pre-proceedings;
- standardisation of relevant information, including documents to be disclosed.

1.4 The courts will be able to treat the standards set in protocols as the normal reasonable approach to pre-action conduct. If proceedings are issued, it will be for the court to decide whether non-compliance with a protocol should merit adverse consequences. Guidance on the court's likely approach will be given from time to time in practice directions.

1.5 If the court has to consider the question of compliance after proceedings have begun, it will not be concerned with minor infringements, e.g. failure by a short period to provide relevant information. One minor breach will not exempt the 'innocent' party from following the protocol. The court will look at the effect of non-compliance on the other party when deciding whether to impose sanctions.

2. NOTES OF GUIDANCE

2.1 The protocol has been kept deliberately simple to promote ease of use and general acceptability. The notes of guidance which follow relate particularly to issues which arose during the piloting of the protocol.

SCOPE OF THE PROTOCOL

2.2 This protocol is intended to apply to all claims which include a claim for personal injury (except industrial disease claims) and to the entirety of those claims: not only to the personal injury

Small personal injury claims

element of a claim which also includes, for instance, property damage.

2.3 This protocol is primarily designed for those road traffic, tripping and slipping and accident at work cases which include an element of personal injury with a value of less than £15,000 which are likely to be allocated to the fast track. This is because time will be of the essence, after proceedings are issued, especially for the defendant, if a case is to be ready for trial within 30 weeks of allocation. Also, proportionality of work and costs to the value of what is in dispute is particularly important in lower value claims. For some claims within the value 'scope' of the fast track some flexibility in the timescale of the protocol may be necessary, see also paragraph 3.8.

2.4 However, the 'cards on the table' approach advocated by the protocol is equally appropriate to some higher value claims. The spirit, if not the letter of the protocol, should still be followed for multi-track type claims. In accordance with the sense of the civil justice reforms, the court will expect to see the spirit of reasonable pre-action behaviour applied in all cases, regardless of the existence of a specific protocol. In particular with regard to personal injury cases worth more than £15,000, with a view to avoiding the necessity of proceedings parties are expected to comply with the protocol as far as possible e.g. in respect of letters before action, exchanging information and documents and agreeing experts.

2.5 The timetable and the arrangements for disclosing documents and obtaining expert evidence may need to be varied to suit the circumstances of the case. Where one or both parties consider the detail of the protocol is not appropriate to the case, and proceedings are subsequently issued, the court will expect an explanation as to why the protocol has not been followed, or has been varied.

EARLY NOTIFICATION

2.6 The claimant's legal representative may wish to notify the defendant and/or his insurer as soon as they know a claim is likely to be made, but before they are able to send a detailed letter of claim, particularly for instance, when the defendant has no or limited knowledge of the incident giving rise to the claim or where the claimant is incurring significant expenditure as a result of the accident which he hopes the defendant might pay for, in whole or in part. If the claimant's representative chooses to do this, it will not start the timetable for responding.

THE LETTER OF CLAIM

2.7 The specimen letter of claim at Annex A will usually be sent to the individual defendant. In practice, he/she may have no personal financial interest in the financial outcome of the claim/dispute because he/she is insured. Court imposed sanctions for non-compliance with the protocol may be ineffective against an insured. This is why the protocol emphasises the importance of passing the letter of claim to the insurer and the possibility that the insurance cover might be affected. If an insurer receives the letter of claim only after some delay by the insured, it would not be unreasonable for the insurer to ask the claimant for additional time to respond.

REASONS FOR EARLY ISSUE

2.8 The protocol recommends that a defendant be given three months to investigate and respond to a claim before proceedings are issued. This may not always be possible, particularly where a claimant only consults a solicitor close to the end of any relevant limitation period. In these circumstances, the claimant's solicitor should give as much notice of the intention to issue proceedings as is practicable and the parties should consider whether the court might be invited to extend time for service of the claimant's supporting documents and for service of any defence, or alternatively, to stay the proceedings while the recommended steps in the protocol are followed.

STATUS OF LETTERS OF CLAIM AND RESPONSE

2.9 Letters of claim and response are not intended to have the same status as a statement of case in proceedings. Matters may come to light as a result of investigation after the letter of claim has been sent, or after the defendant has responded, particularly if disclosure of documents takes place outside the recommended three-month period. These circumstances could mean that the 'pleaded' case of one or both parties is presented slightly differently than in the letter of claim and response. It would not be consistent with the spirit of the protocol for a party to 'take a point' on this in the proceedings, provided that there was no obvious intention by the party who changed their position to mislead the other party.

DISCLOSURE OF DOCUMENTS

2.10 The aim of the early disclosure of documents by the defendant is not to encourage 'fishing expeditions' by the claimant, but to promote an early exchange of relevant information to help in clarifying or resolving issues in dispute. The claimant's solicitor can assist by identifying in the letter of claim or in a subsequent letter the particular categories of documents which they consider are relevant.

Small personal injury claims

EXPERTS

2.11 The protocol encourages joint selection of, and access to, experts. Most frequently this will apply to the medical expert, but on occasions also to liability experts, e.g. engineers. The protocol promotes the practice of the claimant obtaining a medical report, disclosing it to the defendant who then asks questions and/or agrees it and does not obtain his own report. The Protocol provides for nomination of the expert by the claimant in personal injury claims because of the early stage of the proceedings and the particular nature of such claims. If proceedings have to be issued, a medical report must be attached to these proceedings. However, if necessary after proceedings have commenced and with the permission of the court, the parties may obtain further expert reports. It would be for the court to decide whether the costs of more than one expert's report should be recoverable.

2.12 Some solicitors choose to obtain medical reports through medical agencies, rather than directly from a specific doctor or hospital. The defendant's prior consent to the action should be sought and, if the defendant so requests, the agency should be asked to provide in advance the names of the doctor(s) whom they are considering instructing.

NEGOTIATIONS/SETTLEMENT

2.13 Parties and their legal representatives are encouraged to enter into discussions and/or negotiations prior to starting proceedings. The protocol does not specify when or how this might be done but parties should bear in mind that the courts increasingly take the view that litigation should be a last resort, and that claims should not be issued prematurely when a settlement is in reasonable prospect.

STOCKTAKE

2.14 Where a claim is not resolved when the protocol has been followed, the parties might wish to carry out a 'stocktake' of the issues in dispute, and the evidence that the court is likely to need to decide those issues, before proceedings are started. Where the defendant is insured and the pre-action steps have been conducted by the insurer, the insurer would normally be expected to nominate solicitors to act in the proceedings and the claimant's solicitor is recommended to invite the insurer to nominate solicitors to act in the proceedings and do so 7–14 days before the intended issue date.

3. THE PROTOCOL

LETTER OF CLAIM

3.1 The claimant shall send to the proposed defendant two copies of a letter of claim, immediately sufficient information is available to substantiate a realistic claim and before issues of quantum are addressed in detail. One copy of the letter is for the defendants, the second for passing on to his insurers.

3.2 The letter shall contain **a clear summary of the facts** on which the claim is based together with an indication of the **nature of any injuries** suffered and of **any financial loss incurred**. In cases of road traffic accidents, the letter should provide the name and address of the hospital where treatment has been obtained and the claimant's hospital reference number.

3.3 Solicitors are recommended to use a **standard format** for such a letter – an example is at Annex A: this can be amended to suit the particular case.

3.4 The letter should ask for **details of the insurer** and that a copy should be sent by the proposed defendant to the insurer where appropriate. If the insurer is known, a copy shall be sent directly to the insurer. Details of the claimant's National Insurance number and date of birth should be supplied to the defendant's insurer once the defendant has responded to the letter of claim and confirmed the identity of the insurer. This information should not be supplied in the letter of claim.

3.5 **Sufficient information** should be given in order to enable the defendant's insurer/solicitor to commence investigations and at least put a broad valuation on the 'risk'.

3.6 The **defendant should reply within 21 calendar days** of the date of posting of the letter identifying the insurer (if any). If there has been no reply by the defendant or insurer within 21 days, the claimant will be entitled to issue proceedings.

3.7 The defendant('s insurers) will have a **maximum of three months** from the date of acknowledgment of the claim **to investigate**. No later than the end of that period the defendant (insurer) shall reply, stating whether liability is denied and, if so, giving reasons for their denial of liability.

3.8 Where the accident occurred outside England and Wales and/or where the defendant is outside the jurisdiction, the time periods of 21 days and three months should normally be extended up to 42 days and six months.

3.9 Where **liability is admitted**, the presumption is that the defendant will be bound by this admission for all claims with a total value of up to £15,000.

Small personal injury claims

DOCUMENTS

3.10 If the **defendant denies liability**, he should enclose with the letter of reply, **documents** in his possession which are **material to the issues** between the parties, and which would be likely to be ordered to be disclosed by the court, either on an application for pre-action disclosure, or on disclosure during proceedings.

3.11 Attached at Annex B are **specimen**, but non-exhaustive, **lists** of documents likely to be material in different types of claim. Where the claimant's investigation of the case is well advanced, the letter of claim could indicate which classes of documents are considered relevant for early disclosure. Alternatively these could be identified at a later stage.

3.12 Where the defendant admits primary liability, but alleges contributory negligence by the claimant, the defendant should give reasons supporting those allegations and disclose those documents from Annex B which are relevant to the issues in dispute. The claimant should respond to the allegations of contributory negligence before proceedings are issued.

SPECIAL DAMAGES

3.13 The claimant will send to the defendant as soon as practicable a Schedule of Special Damages with supporting documents, particularly where the defendant has admitted liability.

EXPERTS

3.14 Before any party instructs an expert he should give the other party a list of the **name**(s) of **one or more experts** in the relevant speciality whom he considers are suitable to instruct.

3.15 Where a medical expert is to be instructed the claimant's solicitor will organise access to relevant medical records – see specimen letter of instruction at Annex C.

3.16 **Within 14 days** the other party may indicate **an objection** to one or more of the named experts. The first party should then instruct a mutually acceptable expert. It must be emphasised that if the claimant nominates an expert in the original letter of claim, the defendant has 14 days to object to one or more of the named experts after expiration of the period of 21 days within which he has to reply to the letter of claim, as set out in paragraph 3.6.

3.17 If the second party objects to all the listed experts, the parties may then instruct **experts of their own choice**. It would be for the court to decide subsequently, if proceedings are issued, whether either party had acted unreasonably.

3.18 If the **second party does not object to an expert nominated**, he shall not be entitled to rely on his own expert evidence within that particular speciality unless:

Small personal injury claims

(a) the first party agrees;
(b) the court so directs; or
(c) the first party's expert report has been amended and the first party is not prepared to disclose the original report.

3.19 **Either party may send to an agreed expert written questions** on the report, relevant to the issues, via the first party's solicitors. The expert should send answers to the questions separately and directly to each party.

3.20 The cost of a report from an agreed expert will usually be paid by the instructing first party: the costs of the expert replying to questions will usually be borne by the party which asks the questions.

3.21 Where the defendant admits liability in whole or in part, before proceedings are issued, any medical report obtained by agreement under this protocol should be disclosed to the other party. The claimant should delay issuing proceedings for 21 days from disclosure of the report, to enable the parties to consider whether the claim is capable of settlement. The Civil Procedure Rules Part 36 permit claimants and defendants to make offers to settle preproceedings. Parties should always consider before issuing if it is appropriate to make a Part 36 Offer. If such an offer is made, the party making the offer must always supply sufficient evidence and/or information to enable the offer to be properly considered.

ANNEX A
LETTER OF CLAIM

To
Defendant
Dear Sirs
Re: Claimant's full name
Claimant's full address
Claimant's Clock or Works Number
Claimant's Employer (name and address)

We are instructed by the above named to claim damages in connection with an *accident at work/road traffic accident/tripping accident* on   day of   (*year*) at (*place of accident which must be sufficiently detailed to establish location*)

Please confirm the identity of your insurers. Please note that the insurers will need to see this letter as soon as possible and it may affect your insurance cover and/or the conduct of any subsequent legal proceedings if you do not send this letter to them.

The circumstances of the accident are:
(*brief outline*)
The reason why we are alleging fault is:
(*simple explanation e.g. defective machine, broken ground*)

Small personal injury claims

A description of our clients' injuries is as follows:
(*brief outline*)
(*In cases of road traffic accidents*)

Our client (*state hospital reference number*) received treatment for the injuries at (*name and address of hospital*).

He is employed as (*occupation*) and has had the following time off work (*dates of absence*).

His approximate weekly income is (*insert if known*).

If you are our client's employers, please provide us with the usual earnings details which will enable us to calculate his financial loss.

We are obtaining a police report and will let you have a copy of the same upon your undertaking to meet half the fee.

We have also sent a letter of claim to (*name and address*) and a copy of that letter is attached. We understand their insurers are (*name, address and claims number if known*).

At this stage of our enquiries we would expect the documents contained in parts (*insert appropriate parts of standard disclosure list*) to be relevant to this action.

A copy of this letter is attached for you to send to your insurers. Finally we expect an acknowledgment of this letter within 21 days by yourselves or your insurers.

Yours faithfully

ANNEX B
STANDARD DISCLOSURE LISTS
FAST TRACK DISCLOSURE

RTA Cases

SECTION A

In all cases where liability is at issue–

  (i) Documents identifying nature, extent and location of damage to defendant's vehicle where there is any dispute about point of impact.
  (ii) MOT certificate where relevant.
  (iii) Maintenance records where vehicle defect is alleged or it is alleged by defendant that there was an unforeseen defect which caused or contributed to the accident.

SECTION B

Accident involving commercial vehicle as potential defendant–

  (i) Tachograph charts or entry from individual control book.
  (ii) Maintenance and repair records required for operators' licence where vehicle defect is alleged or it is alleged by defendants that there was an unforeseen defect which caused or contributed to the accident.

Small personal injury claims

SECTION C

Cases against local authorities where highway design defect is alleged. Documents produced to comply with Section 39 of the Road Traffic Act 1988 in respect of the duty designed to promote road safety to include studies into road accidents in the relevant area and documents relating to measures recommended to prevent accidents in the relevant area.

Highway Tripping Claims

Documents from Highway Authority for a period of 12 months prior to the accident–

- (i) Records of inspection for the relevant stretch of highway.
- (ii) Maintenance records including records of independent contractors working in relevant area.
- (iii) Records of the minutes of Highway Authority meetings where maintenance or repair policy has been discussed or decided.
- (iv) Records of complaints about the state of highways.
- (v) Records of other accidents which have occurred on the relevant stretch of highway.

Workplace Claims

- (i) Accident book entry.
- (ii) First aider report.
- (iii) Surgery record.
- (iv) Foreman/supervisor accident report.
- (v) Safety representatives accident report.
- (vi) RIDDOR report to HSE.
- (vii) Other communications between defendants and HSE.
- (viii) Minutes of Health and Safety Committee meeting(s) where accident/matter considered.
- (ix) Report to DSS.
- (x) Documents listed above relative to any previous accident/matter identified by the claimant and relied upon as proof of negligence.
- (xi) Earnings information where defendant is employer.

Documents produced to comply with requirements of the Management of Health and Safety at Work Regulations 1992–

- (i) Pre-accident Risk Assessment required by Regulation 3.
- (ii) Post-accident Re-Assessment required by Regulation 3.
- (iii) Accident Investigation Report prepared in implementing the requirements of Regulations 4, 6 and 9.
- (iv) Health Surveillance Records in appropriate cases required by Regulation 5.

Small personal injury claims

(v) Information provided to employees under Regulation 8.
(vi) Documents relating to the employees health and safety training required by Regulation 11.

Workplace Claims – Disclosure Where Specific Regulations Apply

SECTION A – WORKPLACE (HEALTH SAFETY AND WELFARE) REGULATIONS 1992

(i) Repair and maintenance records required by Regulation 5.
(ii) Housekeeping records to comply with the requirements of Regulation 9.
(iii) Hazard warning signs or notices to comply with Regulation 17 (Traffic Routes).

SECTION B – PROVISION AND USE OF WORK EQUIPMENT REGULATIONS 1992

(i) Manufacturers' specifications and instructions in respect of relevant work equipment establishing its suitability to comply with Regulation 5.
(ii) Maintenance log/maintenance records required to comply with Regulation 6.
(iii) Documents providing information and instructions to employees to comply with Regulation 8.
(iv) Documents provided to the employee in respect of training for use to comply with Regulation 9.
(v) Any notice, sign or document relied upon as a defence to alleged breaches of Regulations 14 to 18 dealing with controls and control systems.
(vi) Instruction/training documents issued to comply with the requirements of Regulation 22 insofar as it deals with maintenance operations where the machinery is not shut down.
(vii) Copies of markings required to comply with Regulation 23.
(viii) Copies of warnings required to comply with Regulation 24.

SECTION C – PERSONAL PROTECTIVE EQUIPMENT AT WORK REGULATIONS 1992

(i) Documents relating to the assessment of the Personal Protective Equipment to comply with Regulation 6.
(ii) Documents relating to the maintenance and replacement of Personal Protective Equipment to comply with Regulation 7.
(iii) Record of maintenance procedures for Personal Protective Equipment to comply with Regulation 7.

Small personal injury claims

(iv) Records of tests and examinations of Personal Protective Equipment to comply with Regulation 7.
(v) Documents providing information, instruction and training in relation to the Personal Protective Equipment to comply with Regulation 9.
(vi) Instructions for use of Personal Protective Equipment to include the manufacturers' instructions to comply with Regulation 10.

SECTION D – MANUAL HANDLING OPERATIONS REGULATIONS 1992

(i) Manual Handling Risk Assessment carried out to comply with the requirements of Regulation 4(1)(b)(i).
(ii) Re-assessment carried out post-accident to comply with requirements of Regulation 4(1)(b)(i).
(iii) Documents showing the information provided to the employee to give general indications related to the load and precise indications on the weight of the load and the heaviest side of the load if the centre of gravity was not positioned centrally to comply with Regulation 4(1)(b)(iii).
(iv) Documents relating to training in respect of manual handling operations and training records.

SECTION E – HEALTH AND SAFETY (DISPLAY SCREEN EQUIPMENT) REGULATIONS 1992

(i) Analysis of work stations to assess and reduce risks carried out to comply with the requirements of Regulation 2.
(ii) Re-assessment of analysis of work stations to assess and reduce risks following development of symptoms by the claimant.
(iii) Documents detailing the provision of training including training records to comply with the requirements of Regulation 6.
(iv) Documents providing information to employees to comply with the requirements of Regulation 7.

SECTION F – CONTROL OF SUBSTANCES HAZARDOUS TO HEALTH REGULATIONS 1988

(i) Risk assessment carried out to comply with the requirements of Regulation 6.
(ii) Reviewed risk assessment carried out to comply with the requirements of Regulation 6.
(iii) Copy labels from containers used for storage handling and disposal of carcinogenics to comply with the requirements of Regulation 7(2A)(h).
(iv) Warning signs identifying designation of areas and installations which may be contaminated by carcinogenics to comply with the requirements of Regulation 7(2A)(h).

Small personal injury claims

(v) Documents relating to the assessment of the Personal Protective Equipment to comply with Regulation 7(3A).
(vi) Documents relating to the maintenance and replacement of Personal Protective Equipment to comply with Regulation 7(3A).
(vii) Record of maintenance procedures for Personal Protective Equipment to comply with Regulation 7(3A).
(viii) Records of tests and examinations of Personal Protective Equipment to comply with Regulation 7(3A).
(ix) Documents providing information, instruction and training in relation to the Personal Protective Equipment to comply with Regulation 7(3A).
(x) Instructions for use of Personal Protective Equipment to include the manufacturers' instructions to comply with Regulation 7(3A).
(xi) Air monitoring records for substances assigned a maximum exposure limit or occupational exposure standard to comply with the requirements of Regulation 7.
(xii) Maintenance examination and test of control measures records to comply with Regulation 9.
(xiii) Monitoring records to comply with the requirements of Regulation 10.
(xiv) Health surveillance records to comply with the requirements of Regulation 11.
(xv) Documents detailing information, instruction and training including training records for employees to comply with the requirements of Regulation 12.
(xvi) Labels and Health and Safety data sheets supplied to the employers to comply with the CHIP Regulations.

SECTION G – CONSTRUCTION (DESIGN AND MANAGEMENT) REGULATIONS 1994

(i) Notification of a project form (HSE F10) to comply with the requirements of Regulation 7.
(ii) Health and Safety Plan to comply with requirements of Regulation 15.
(iii) Health and Safety file to comply with the requirements of Regulations 12 and 14.
(iv) Information and training records provided to comply with the requirements of Regulation 17.
(v) Records of advice from and views of persons at work to comply with the requirements of Regulation 18.

SECTION H – PRESSURE SYSTEMS AND TRANSPORTABLE GAS CONTAINERS REGULATIONS 1989

(i) Information and specimen markings provided to comply with the requirements of Regulation 5.
(ii) Written statements specifying the safe operating limits of a system to comply with the requirements of Regulation 7.
(iii) Copy of the written scheme of examination required to comply with the requirements of Regulation 8.
(iv) Examination records required to comply with the requirements of Regulation 9.
(v) Instructions provided for the use of operator to comply with Regulation 11.
(vi) Records kept to comply with the requirements of Regulation 13.
(vii) Records kept to comply with the requirements of Regulation 22.

SECTION I – LIFTING PLANT AND EQUIPMENT (RECORDS OF TEST AND EXAMINATION ETC) REGULATIONS 1992

(i) Record kept to comply with the requirements of Regulation 6.

SECTION J – THE NOISE AT WORK REGULATIONS 1989

(i) Any risk assessment records required to comply with the requirements of Regulations 4 and 5.
(ii) Manufacturers' literature in respect of all ear protection made available to claimant to comply with the requirements of Regulation 8.
(iii) All documents provided to the employee for the provision of information to comply with Regulation 11.

SECTION K – CONSTRUCTION (HEAD PROTECTION) REGULATIONS 1989

(i) Pre-accident assessment of head protection required to comply with Regulation 3(4).
(ii) Post-accident re-assessment required to comply with Regulation 3(5).

SECTION L – THE CONSTRUCTION (GENERAL PROVISIONS) REGULATIONS 1961

(i) Report prepared following inspections and examinations of excavations etc to comply with the requirements of Regulation 9.
(ii) Report prepared following inspections and examinations of work in cofferdams and caissons to comply with the requirements of Regulations 17 and 18.

N.B. Further standard discovery lists will be required prior to full implementation.

ANNEX C
LETTER OF INSTRUCTION
TO MEDICAL EXPERT

Dear Sir

Re: (*Name and Address*)

D.O.B.:

Telephone No:

Date of Accident:

We are acting for the above named in connection with injuries received in an accident which occurred on the above date. The main injuries appear to have been (**main injuries**).

We should be obliged if you would examine our client and let us have a full and detailed report dealing with any relevant pre-accident medical history, the injuries sustained, treatment received and present condition, dealing in particular with the capacity for work and giving a prognosis.

It is central to our assessment of the extent of our client's injuries to establish the extent and duration of any continuing disability. Accordingly, in the prognosis section we would ask you to specifically comment on any areas of continuing complaint or disability or impact on daily living. If there is such continuing disability you should comment upon the level of suffering or inconvenience caused and, if you are able, give your view as to when or if the complaint or disability is likely to resolve.

Please send our client an appointment direct for this purpose. Should you be able to offer a cancellation appointment please contact our client direct. We confirm we will be responsible for your reasonable fees.

We are obtaining the notes and records from our client's GP and hospitals attended and will forward them to you when they are to hand/or please request the GP and hospital records direct and advise that any invoice for the provision of these records should be forwarded to us.

In order to comply with court rules we would be grateful if you would insert above your signature a statement that the contents are true to the best of your knowledge and belief.

In order to avoid further correspondence we can confirm that on the evidence we have there is no reason to suspect we may be pursuing a claim against the hospital or its staff.

We look forward to receiving your report within .... weeks. If you will not be able to prepare your report within this period please telephone us upon receipt of these instructions.

When acknowledging these instructions it would assist if you could give an estimate as to the likely time scale for the provision of your report and also an indication as to your fee.

Yours faithfully

Chapter 13

Enforcing judgment

1. Introduction

The successful litigant, having won his case, may feel already in receipt of what the court has ordered the other party to pay. Unfortunately in far too many cases this turns out to be over-optimistic, or certainly premature. Often the defendant may prove unwilling or unable to comply. It has to be stressed that this can become a complex and time-consuming area of law. In straightforward cases, warrants of execution, third-party orders and attachment of earnings orders may be sought by a determined litigant without recourse to a solicitor. With other methods of enforcement, such as charging orders and bankruptcy, there are difficulties involved, although both of these methods may be attempted by litigants in person.

When judgment is obtained, it will include an order that the defendant must pay the amount found due. If this order is not obeyed, responsibility for enforcing it rests with you and not with the court. The court provides the facilities and legal framework for enforcement but it is up to the individual as to how he proceeds. Once judgment has been obtained, the successful party is known as the *judgment creditor* and the one who has to pay as the *judgment debtor*. The judgment creditor is usually the claimant but could be the defendant if the claimant has lost the claim and the defendant has succeeded on a counterclaim. Before suing, it is always advisable to consider whether the other party is worth bringing action against; equally, having obtained judgment there remains the problem of whether or not the debtor has the means to pay. The proverbial problem of getting blood out of a stone remains apt.

The county courts have a number of procedures for enforcing judgment. It is always important to think of the circumstances of the judgment debtor and to decide which method is the most appropriate to them – otherwise a good deal of time and effort may be wasted.

Enforcement of judgment can be one of the most frustrating areas of law, particularly for the newcomer. Some businesses have their own practices and procedures for enforcement in place. Others may hand the matter over to debt collection firms. This chapter is intended as a basic outline on enforcement. The county courts will provide you, free of charge, with

Enforcing judgment

a series of leaflets on enforcement. It is best to start with the leaflet entitled 'I have a judgment but the defendant hasn't paid. What can I do?' Court staff and advice centres can also help. The costs of enforcing the award are recoverable but the costs of a solicitor dealing with enforcement of a judgment are not likely to be covered by the fixed costs generally recoverable.

Some of the forms referred to in this chapter are forms under the County Court Rules which have not, as yet at any rate, been replaced by CPR forms. Where there is a CPR form it is so described; otherwise the forms are those in existence before the Civil Procedure Rules 1998 were implemented.

2. The court order

Most judgments are entered without a hearing because judgment is entered in default of a defence or because the defendant has admitted the claim. The judgment sets out the amount to be paid, and when it is to be paid. If the defendant was present at the hearing the judge will probably have had a discussion as to his means of satisfying the judgment. An order for payment does not guarantee that the money will be paid. A defendant's circumstances may change so that he cannot pay. Some defendants will not pay unless they are forced to. The judgment creditor therefore has to decide whether it is worth enforcing a judgment, and also how to do so.

3. Payment of a judgment debt

(a) Immediate payment or instalment orders?

The debtor should pay all money directly to the creditor, not to the court. Any money sent wrongly to the court will be returned to the debtor. If payment is made by post, it is at the debtor's risk. If it does not arrive, the debtor will have to pay again. Keep an accurate record of the date and amount of all payments. This will prevent any arguments about how much money is owed. It is best for the creditor to issue receipts.

A money judgment may order the money to be paid forthwith or by a certain date or by weekly, monthly or other instalments. If the order does not specify when a money judgment is to be paid the rules provide payment must be made within 14 days from the date the order was made. An instalment order may be made at the request of the creditor or the debtor. Unless you are sure that the debtor will be able to pay the money all at once, you should ask for instalments. Many debtors are dependent on their earnings or income and may have little in the way of savings or goods which can be easily sold. It may be difficult, or even impossible, for them to pay other than by instalments although this may cause hardship to the creditor.

Enforcing judgment

The creditor may find that the district judge orders the debt to be paid by smaller instalments than the creditor might consider reasonable. Experience shows that if the debtor is ordered to pay more than he thinks he can really afford, he will be unlikely to keep up his payments – and the creditor will then be put to the trouble and expense of enforcement proceedings. If the judgment allows the debtor time to pay, either in a lump sum or by instalments, an order will be posted to him. A judgment for payment 'forthwith' is not usually made against the debtor if he asks for time and his financial circumstances are such as to necessitate an instalment order. Such an order should be requested only when the debtor is likely to try and avoid payment and immediate steps to enforce the judgment are necessary. Otherwise it is better to give him some time and the opportunity of paying before incurring the additional expense of enforcement.

(b) Variation of orders

When judgment has been entered for payment in a lump sum, and you decide later that it would be better to have an instalment order, or you wish the payments to be increased or reduced, as the case may be, you can seek a variation. It is open to either party to seek a variation – this is commenced by completing the relevant form at the court office, as follows:

- the creditor wishes variation of an order (form N294 – CPR);
- the creditor wishes the instalments to be increased, if there is evidence that the debtor's financial position has changed for the better (application form N244 – CPR) – there will be a hearing in this case (CCR Ord 22 r 10(3) and (4) – retained by the Civil Procedure Rules);
- the debtor applies for variation or reduction of an instalment order (form N245). Form N246 is the claimant's reply to the defendant's application to vary. This must be completed and returned within 14 days of service on him. If the creditor replies accepting the offer, the varied order will be drawn by the court in those terms. If the creditor does not reply, the varied order is drawn in accordance with the debtor's offer. If the creditor rejects the debtor's offer, the proper officer will carry out a determination based on the debtor's statement of means and the creditor's objections.

Hearings are normally arranged only if either party wishes an order made by the proper officer to be reconsidered by the district judge.

4. Registration of county court judgments

All county court money judgments are entered on a register on the same day that the court enters judgment except where the case is defended and the losing party does not request an instalment order. This register is kept pursuant to section 73 of the County Courts Act 1984 and is available for

Enforcing judgment

inspection at Registry Trust Limited, 173–175 Cleveland Street, London W1P 5PE (tel: 020 7380 0133). You may apply in person or write, enclosing a fee, and the register will be searched and the amount of judgment, date of judgment and court and case number of any judgment revealed will be supplied. It is *not* possible to undertake telephone searches of the register of county court judgments. At the time of writing, the fees to be paid in respect of searches of the register are as follows:

- £4.00 per name and address for a request in person; and
- £4.50 per name and address for a request by post.

(These fees are subject to change.)

Alternatively, credit agencies can provide this service as part of their standard charges (possibly at a more expensive rate, although speed of response may be better).

The register can be used by anyone seeking information as to the credit worthiness of prospective customers. If several judgments are registered against a debtor, it may help you to assess his ability to pay your debt. Once a judgment has been registered, it remains there for six years unless it has been paid within one month. This can obviously damage a person's credit rating and may prevent the defendant from obtaining a credit card or a mortgage. If the judgment is paid in full within one month from the date of its entry, the debtor can apply to the court for a certificate of cancellation. A fee of £10 is payable. The court will tell the keeper of the register that the entry on the register should be removed. A form of words to this effect appears on the relevant court forms. The debtor needs to ask the court to remove the entry and to provide proof of payment of the debt. If the judgment is paid in full after one month from the date of judgment, the debtor can apply to the court for a certificate of satisfaction. Again, a fee of £10 is payable. The entry on the register will be marked 'satisfied'.

If there is a dispute between the parties as to whether the debt has been paid, an application to the court, using form N244, will be necessary to decide the issue.

A judgment after a contested hearing is an exempt judgment if for:

(a) the payment of money otherwise than by instalments; or
(b) the payment of money (whether or not by instalments) and the judgment includes an order for costs to be assessed by way of a detailed assessment.

Such an exempt judgment does not fall to be registered unless the creditor takes steps to enforce it, or a request is made for an order to obtain information from the judgment debtor or for the payment of money by instalments. A case within (b) is also exempt from registration until the costs are assessed by way of detailed assessment.

- There are special provisions whereby an order for the payment of money is made in an action for the recovery of land.

Enforcing judgment

(a) Credit repair companies

The Lord Chancellor issued a press notice about these in July 1992. He advised consumers to beware of advertisements or literature sent out by certain so-called credit repair companies, purporting to be able to have most entries cancelled from the register of county court judgments and therefore from the files of the major credit information agencies. This literature suggested that, where the debt had already been satisfied or where the defendant had sufficient funds to settle the debt in full, the credit repair company could help in having the judgment which gave rise to the entry set aside. A substantial fee is often charged for this service, of which a large element is usually non-refundable, no matter what the outcome.

In the words of the Lord Chancellor:

> 'I am deeply concerned that consumers should think carefully before paying any fees for such a service. The procedures for having entries removed from the Register are described in the leaflet sent to defendants on entry of judgment; they are quite simple and can be followed easily and cheaply by defendants themselves. However, the circumstances in which entries can be removed are limited. Most entries stay on the Register for six years, even where payment has been made; they can only be removed where the defendant provides proof that the debt was paid within one month of judgment being entered, where the court, through administrative error, has wrongly registered the judgment, or where the defendant makes a successful application to have judgment "set aside". But the court will not set the judgment aside simply because the debt has been paid subsequently; a judgment will usually only be set aside on the grounds that there is a defence to the claim which ought to be heard'.

Consumers should therefore think carefully before paying any fee to these companies. As explained in the Lord Chancellor's Department leaflet *Paying your judgment – what do I do?* (sent to defendants on entry of judgment), it is possible to have an entry cancelled or deleted from the register if the total debt is paid within one month of the date of judgment. All that the defendant needs to do is provide proof of payment (the court can explain what is wanted) and pay a fee of £10. The court will do the rest automatically. The leaflet also explains what to do if the debt is paid after one month. The procedures are similar but the entry on the register cannot be cancelled or deleted – it can only be marked 'satisfied' and will remain there for six years. However, a search of the register will show that the debt has been paid and will give the date of the last payment.

Following the simple procedures described in the leaflet, defendants can have entries on the register removed or marked satisfied, depending on the date when final payment was made. However, if a defendant has reason to believe that the judgment should not have been entered, he can apply to the county court where judgment was entered for the judgment to be set aside. The application must give reasons. Where a successful application is made, the court will automatically have the entry on the

Enforcing judgment

register cancelled. In these circumstances, no fee is charged. There is also no fee for making an application.

Advice on making applications to set aside judgment can be obtained from a solicitor or Citizens Advice Bureau. Advice about court procedures in general is available free of charge from any county court office. Consumers should, however, be warned that, whatever some credit repair companies may claim, most entries cannot be removed from the register.

5. The effect of judgment

A judgment payable in a lump sum can be enforced if the whole amount is not paid within the time mentioned in the order. When an instalment order has been made, the outstanding balance becomes immediately payable if the debtor fails to pay any instalment on the date that it is due. Having ascertained that the debtor is in default, you must decide how you want the judgment to be enforced and make the necessary application. The court will then carry out the selected mode of enforcement. Enforcement usually involves the transfer of the case to the debtor's home court. This can be inconvenient for many creditors.

6. Orders to obtain information from the judgment debtor – CPR 71

After allowing the debtor a reasonable time to pay the judgment debt you will have to consider enforcement proceedings. It may be that you know enough information about the debtor's finances to decide which method of enforcement is most likely to be successful or that a search of the title of the debtor's house will provide sufficient information.

- Office copies of the title of any property can be obtained from the Land Registry even if you do not know the title number.
- The consent of the owner of a house is not necessary for office copies to be issued.
- Land Registry form N109 is the appropriate form of application and Practice Leaflet No 13, which provides full information is available free from any Land Registry office.
- For the addresses of the HM Land Registry, District Land Registries and Land Charges Department see Appendix 8 at pages 231–234.

If you do not have sufficient information you should seriously consider obtaining an order for the debtor to be examined by a court officer or, although it rarely happens, by a judge as to his financial position to establish the best way to obtain payment. The process will take time but delay is better than spending money on court fees for a form of enforcement that has little or no chance of success.

- An application is made by using form N316.
- The order can be obtained against an officer or director of a limited company – in this situation use form N316A.

Enforcing judgment

- It will be up to you to supply the address of the person who is to be examined.
- If the case is not proceeding in the debtor's home court a request in writing must be made for the transfer of the case to that court.
- A fee of £40 will be payable.
- The application must contain a certificate of the amount remaining due under the judgment.

If you have completed the form properly and you pay the fee the court will order the judgment debtor to attend court at a specified appointment to be questioned as to his finances and will warn the debtor of the consequences of failure to attend.

If the creditor is an individual litigant in person the order will be served by the court bailiff but otherwise service must be effected by the judgment creditor or his representative.

If the person ordered to attend, within seven days of being served asks you for a reasonable sum to cover his travelling expenses to and from the court you must pay this to him. You must either file or produce at the hearing an affidavit or affidavits:

- giving details of how and when the order was served;
- stating that the debtor has not requested travelling expenses or that he has asked for such expenses and they have been paid to him;
- stating how much of the judgment debtor remains unpaid.

If the person ordered to attend fails to attend his non-attendance will be certified and, provided the formalities have been properly complied with, the judge may, and normally will, commit the debtor to prison but the committal will be suspended provided he attends a further appointment that will be specified.

(a) Attending the examination hearing

The examination hearing will be in private and is usually conducted by a senior court official; the judgment creditor or his representative can attend to put questions to the debtor but you will save yourself time if you attach to the application form (N316 or N316A) a list of additional questions you wish the court officer to put to the debtor in addition to the standard questions (see (b) below).

(b) The questions

In Appendix 5 on pages 195–206 the form incorporating the questions the court officer will ask is reproduced.

- There is a different set of questions for an officer or a director of a limited company – see Appendix B to the Practice Direction to Part 71 of CPR.

Enforcing judgment

(c) Conclusion of the examination

The court officer writes down the debtor's replies and the debtor is requested to sign the document at the end of the examination. If he refuses to sign the court officer will endorse a certificate to that effect. You can obtain a photocopy of the debtor's answers. A copying fee may be charged.

Methods of enforcement

The four most common methods of enforcement are used against different resources of the debtor.

- Goods, or 'moveable' property. Use a *warrant of execution*.
- Bank account or building society savings account. Use a *third party debt order*.
- Income or earnings from regular employment other than self-employment. Use *attachment of earnings*.
- House, land and other buildings. Use a *charging order*.

7. Warrant of execution – seizure and sale of goods

This is the most common way to enforce a judgment. The creditor asks the court to issue a warrant of execution. A warrant authorises a county court bailiff to go to the defendant's house or business premises or anywhere else that the defendant might have goods that belong to him. If the debtor does not pay the amount of the warrant, the bailiff can remove and sell the goods. If this happens, the costs of removing and selling the goods are paid first.

The goods are sold by auction and often bring low prices – sometimes not enough to pay the costs. The bailiff can only take what belongs to the defendant. Cars, TVs, video equipment etc. are often on hire-purchase or rented. They do not belong to the debtor. If you know that the defendant has a car or anything else which is valuable, tell the court when you request the issue of the warrant.

Bailiffs cannot force entry into a private house to enforce a warrant. If they cannot enter the house to remove goods, they will make a report. County court bailiffs are required to give a return (progress report) on the warrant one month after issue. A copy is sent directly to the claimant, thus ensuring that he is kept up to date. If a defendant cannot pay a warrant all at once, he can apply to the court to suspend the warrant and to permit payment by instalments. It is often assumed that warrants of execution are slow as bailiffs generally have a backlog of work, but this is not true in all areas of the country. The bailiffs may go into action quite promptly.

Certain goods are exempt from seizure in execution; see paragraph (i) below.

Enforcing judgment

(a) Procedure

You should use the appropriate form N323, and pay the appropriate fee, which is based on the amount for which the warrant is issued. Fees currently range from £25 to a maximum of £45. Leave to proceed with a warrant of execution is not required unless special circumstances exist. On form N323 the creditor must certify the amount remaining due under the judgment or, where it is to be paid in instalments, that the whole or any part of an instalment remains unpaid. In addition the creditor must certify the amount for which the warrant is to be issued. The creditor must inform the court of any sums he receives from the debtor after the request form for issue of a warrant of execution has been sent to the court.

On receipt of the correctly completed request the court will issue the warrant of execution and forward it to the bailiff in whose area the warrant is to be executed. There is space on the request form for the creditor to supply details which may assist the bailiff in respect of the execution. If this space is insufficient, a separate letter should be written. The bailiff will then proceed with the execution and make a return on the warrant to the court office. The court staff will send the return to the creditor. The creditor can speak to the bailiff if he wishes, usually by telephone to the court before 10.00 am.

On issue of the warrant, form N326 is sent to the debtor warning him that the warrant has been issued and that he should pay the warrant in seven days or the bailiff will call on him. This means that a debtor has a seven-day breathing space before the bailiff attends. However, the creditor can ask for this form not to be sent.

Where a court has made an order for payment of a sum of money by instalments and default has been made in any instalment, a warrant of execution may be issued for the whole of the sum of money and costs then remaining unpaid, or for part of the money due, provided that that sum is not less than £50 or the amount of one monthly instalment, or four weekly instalments, whichever is the greater.

(b) Disputes as to ownership – retained County Court Rules, Order 33

One of the most common problems when a bailiff attends is that the debtor claims that particular goods belong to a third party and are therefore not available for execution. Obviously if hire-purchase documentation is presented and checked by the bailiff the matter can be clarified there and then, but it is often the case that ownership is claimed by the debtor's wife or another relative. There is a set procedure if a claim by a third party is made to goods seized. Notice is sent to the creditor or his solicitor, and interpleader proceedings may then follow. Once a formal claim is made, the creditor has four days to admit or dispute the claim of the third party. If the claim is not admitted within the time period set out, then an interpleader summons will be issued to resolve the issue as to who owns the goods. The procedure is set out in CCR Ord 33.

This can be both time consuming and expensive. Although a warrant of execution is valid for twelve months beginning with the date of issue, the interpleader procedure can drag on for a considerable time and the creditor must take care to renew the execution process if it becomes necessary.

(c) Effect of insolvency

A common problem in execution is that the process is part under way when either the debtor company goes into liquidation or the individual is adjudged bankrupt – and the judgment creditor may well find himself thereafter dealing with the insolvency practitioner appointed. The position is that a judgment creditor may only retain the benefit of his warrant of execution if it has been completed before the start of insolvency proceedings. An execution is completed when the goods and chattels that have been seized have been sold or any sums paid to avoid execution. Be careful when considering warrant of execution as an enforcement method if an individual or company is thought to be in difficulties.

(d) Other creditors

It can happen that when execution process is begun it is discovered that the debtor has other creditors. What if other warrants of execution exist against the debtor? The basic rule in the country court is that priority is governed by the time the request for issue is delivered to the court. If problems arise because of a lot of other warrants, bankruptcy may have to be considered.

(e) What if the goods are elsewhere?

A warrant issued in one court will automatically be sent to another court if the debtor lives outside the jurisdiction of the issuing court. However, if it becomes apparent in the course of executing a warrant that the debtor's goods are outside the jurisdiction of the court, the creditor will need to reissue the warrant.

(f) Withdrawal or suspension of execution process

Once the execution process has begun, it is not unusual for the debtor to attempt to come to some arrangement with the creditor. This may take the form of an application to suspend the warrant. This is made on form N245. If the creditor agrees, a court officer will make an order suspending the warrant. Only if the debtor asks for the warrant to be suspended and the creditor objects to suspending it *per se*, will the proper officer arrange a hearing before a district judge.

Enforcing judgment

(g) Fees

The fees chargeable for the enforcement by bailiffs of county court judgments and orders are set by order of the Lord Chancellor. County court fees are on a sliding scale depending on the amount of money (or value of goods) to be recovered. The fee payable is a once and for all fee throughout the life of the warrant (one year unless extended on the application of the creditor). If full payment of the warrant is not received during its life, it may be re-issued without further charge any number of times at the creditor's request.

On a request for a further attempt at execution of a warrant at a new address following a notice of the reason for non-execution (except a further attempt following suspension) a fee of £20 is payable.

(h) County court bailiffs

The bailiffs are usually attached to a particular county court. County court bailiffs, should not be confused with other types of bailiffs – for example those who are certificated to 'levy distress' for unpaid rent, and private bailiffs whose work is done on a purely contracted basis.

Apart from their enforcement functions – i.e. executing warrants of execution (money judgments), possession (of land), delivery (of goods), and committal (to prison) – county court bailiffs are also used for personal service of documents but only in very limited circumstances.

When performing their enforcement functions, county court bailiffs are acting as officers of the court. Impersonating an officer of the court is an indictable offence punishable on conviction with up to seven years' imprisonment. Assaulting an officer of the court while in the execution of his duty is also a summary offence. The police are under a statutory duty to assist in the execution of warrants.

County court bailiffs are the only class of civil enforcement agent employed by the state in that they are staff of the Lord Chancellor's Department. As part of the Court Service, they are subject to Civil Service and Departmental rules on recruitment, appraisal and general monitoring of their day-to-day work, including the procedure for handling any complaints. This means that the Lord Chancellor's Department can control directly the way in which they do their work and can take disciplinary action should this be necessary. There is no equivalent degree of control by any person or body over sheriffs, certificated bailiffs or other private bailiffs. However, if a complaint about a certificated bailiff is made to the judge of the court which granted the certificate and the complaint is upheld, the judge may revoke the certificate.

Apart from control by the Lord Chancellor's Department, county court bailiffs are subject to control by the court because the district judge is responsible for their acts and wrongdoings (County Courts Act 1984, s 123). In addition, section 124 of the County Courts Act 1984 allows any person aggrieved by a bailiff's failure to levy execution against goods through neglect, connivance or omission, to complain to a judge of that

Enforcing judgment

court. If satisfied that the complaint is proved, the judge may order the bailiff to pay damages, not exceeding the sum for which the execution was issued, to the person complaining.

(i) The levy procedure

There is no statutory requirement for a county court bailiff to identify himself to the debtor or a responsible person on the premises where execution is to be levied, but in practice he will always do so. Order 26 r 7 of the County Court Rules 1981 requires a bailiff on levying execution to deliver to the debtor, or leave at the place where execution is levied, a levy notice. This notice intimates that the warrant has been issued for a stated amount and costs, sets out briefly the debtor's rights and the procedures which may follow the levy, and any further costs which may become payable if the amount to be levied is not paid promptly.

The following goods are exempt from seizure:

- such tools, books, vehicles and other items of equipment as are necessary to the judgment debtor for use personally by him in his employment, business or vocation (there are no monetary limits on this);
- such clothing, bedding, furniture, household equipment and provisions as are necessary for satisfying the basic domestic needs of the judgment debtor and his family (again without limit);
- any money, banknotes or securities for money.

Time when distress may be levied

Distress is the legal name for taking goods out of the possession of a debtor or wrongdoer. It may not be levied on a Sunday, Good Friday or Christmas Day, without the leave of the court.

Sale of the goods seized

When goods seized in execution are removed, the court must deliver or send to the debtor an inventory of the goods removed and, not more than four days before the sale, give notice of the time and place of the sale (CCR Ord 26 r 12). Section 93 of the County Courts Act 1984 provides that no goods seized under execution shall be sold until the expiration of at least five days following the day on which the goods have been seized, unless the goods are perishable or the person whose goods have been seized so requests in writing. Section 94 requires goods seized in execution to be sold only by a broker or appraiser appointed by a district judge under section 95 of the Act. Sale of the debtor's goods worth more than £20 must be advertised and must be sold by public auction (s 97). When goods taken in execution are sold, the court must provide the debtor with a detailed account in writing of the sale and the application of the proceeds.

Enforcing judgment

In fact sales are few in number. This is because many debtors have very little worth selling, and second-hand household goods do not fetch a great deal. If goods are unlikely to realise the costs of removal and sale, the creditor may be asked by the court to provide an undertaking to be responsible for costs in excess of the sale price. The costs of sale and removal will be deducted from the proceeds of the sale before anything is paid to the creditor.

(j) Enforcement in the High Court

Creditors who have obtained a money judgment in the county court for more than £600 and are not regulated by the Consumer Credit Act 1974 can transfer the judgment to the High Court for enforcement. Enforcement will then be carried out by the sheriff's officer rather than the court bailiff.

Transfer and the issue of the writ of execution (called a writ of *fieri facias*) can be effected by the Sheriff's Lodgment Centre ('SLC') for the judgment creditor for a modest fee. Details of the SLC are:

address: 20–21 Tooks Court, off Chancery Lane, London EC4A 1LB
tel: 020 7025 2555
fax: 020 7052 2556
email: slc@sheriffs.co.uk
website: www.sheriffslodgmentcentre.co.uk

8. Third party debt orders – Part 72 CPR

A third party debt order will be an appropriate method of enforcement when a third party within the jurisdiction owes money to the judgment debtor. The order was previously called a 'garnishee order'.

- This procedure is not available in respect of a debt that is due to the judgment debtor and another person, who is not subject to the judgment, jointly.

(a) Making and serving the application

The application must be made by the judgment creditor, using form N349–CPR to the court in which the judgment was obtained. If the application is properly completed and the fee, presently £50, is paid, the judge may make **an interim third party debt order**.

You would be sensible to allow the court to deal with **service** although the judgment creditor may serve. The third party will be served first, to prevent him making payment to the debtor or on the debtor's instructions that would reduce the debt below the amount required to pay the judgment and the costs of the third party debt order. Subsequently the debtor will be served.

(b) Further consideration of the interim order

A date will be fixed for the judge to further consider the matter at a hearing of which all parties have been given notice. If the judgment debtor or the third party objects to the court making a **final order** he must file and serve his evidence setting out the grounds of opposition at least three days before the hearing.

The judgment creditor may file evidence to dispute the objection.

(c) Hearing of the application for a final third party debt order

The court may discharge the interim order or make it final and order the third party to pay to the judgment creditor the amount of the judgment and the costs of the third party debt application or the whole amount that the third party owes to the judgment debtor (whichever is the smaller). The judge has a discretion whether to make the order final and has to take account of the interests of the other creditors.

(d) Hardship payment orders

There is provision for the judgment debtor to apply for a hardship payment order if he is suffering hardship in meeting ordinary living expenses by reason of the third party debt order. Application for such an order should be made on form N244, see pages 64–65 above. The order will be in form N37–CPR.

9. Attachment of earnings order

If the judgment is for more than £50, and the debtor has an employer, you can ask for an attachment of earnings order. This works by deducting a fixed amount from the wages or salary of the debtor on a regular basis until the debt is paid. It does not apply if the debtor is unemployed or even self-employed; nor does it apply if the debtor is a company or firm. An order runs the risk of lapsing if the debtor loses or changes his employment.

Attachment of earnings is commonly used in the county courts. The money is deducted by the employer from the debtor's wages and is paid into court. Attachment of earnings payments are made into court and will be forwarded to the creditor when the court makes its periodic payout. Payments under a consolidated order are also made into court, but payment out to the creditor does not take place until 10 per cent of the total debt is paid in, or quarterly (whichever is the sooner).

An attachment of earnings order can only be made by the court in the area where the debtor lives. You will have to ask for a transfer if the debtor does not live in the area of the court where you obtained the judgment. A request in writing is made to the district judge of the court in which the judgment or order was obtained, stating the reasons for the transfer. However, if you do not know where the debtor resides, you can

Enforcing judgment

apply for an attachment of earnings order to the court where you obtained the judgment.

It is a wise step to search in the appropriate county court for existing attachment of earnings orders. Any person with a judgment can undertake this search. There is no fee for this search. If an attachment of earnings order is found to exist, then the creditor may wish to consider consolidation with an existing order. The appropriate county court is the one in whose area the debtor resides. This may of course not be the court in which proceedings had been commenced and the judgment obtained, in which case a transfer should be requested.

The law is to be found in the Attachment of Earnings Act 1971 and Ord 27 of the County Court Rules 1981. You must complete and file form N337 which is the request for an attachment of earnings order, and duly certify the amount due and owing. You must pay a fee – currently (unless the application is for a consolidated order) £50.

The court will normally serve the notice of application (form N55) on the debtor, together with an appropriate form of reply (form N56). He has eight days to file a reply and a copy is sent to the creditor. The court, acting through the proper officer, may make an attachment of earnings order on the basis of the information received from the debtor without the attendance of either party. If an order is made in this way it will be served on both parties, and either may then apply for it to be reconsidered. An application for reconsideration has to be made within 14 days of the making of the order.

On completing form N56, the debtor can ask the court not to send the order to his employer, in other words to suspend the order on condition that he pays regular installments direct to the creditor. If the court agrees, a suspended order will be made and a copy sent to the creditor. If the debtor does not make payments, the creditor can then ask the court to send the order to the employer thereafter without further ado. This is for the creditor to monitor.

An attachment of earnings order can be made in respect of certain pensions (Attachment of Earnings Act 1971, s 24).

(a) Obtaining information from the employer

Form N338 may be sent by the court to any person who has the debtor in his employment. It requires the employer to supply a statement of the debtor's earnings. If necessary, the court can threaten positive sanctions against an employer (form N61A) in order to force the employer to supply particulars of the debtor's earnings. A common problem is where the debtor changes his employment. The attachment of earnings order puts his old employer under an obligation to notify the court that the debtor is no longer in his employment. Unfortunately there is no positive obligation on a new employer to determine whether or not an attachment of earnings order is in force. If, however, he learns of one he must notify the court, and then probably the order will be redirected and continue as before.

Enforcing judgment

Although the debtor is under an obligation to notify the court of a change in employment, it is difficult in practice to enforce an attachment of earnings order if he is regularly changing employment. It is an offence for a debtor and/or his employers to fail to comply with the provisions of the Attachment of Earnings Act 1971 – under Ord 27 r 16 of the County Court Rules 1981 they can be ordered to attend before a district judge to explain any breach to avoid being punished for the alleged offence.

(b) The amount of the order

Two phrases need to be understood:

- normal deduction rate (NDR);
- protected earnings rate (PER).

The NDR is the amount which should be deducted regularly (normally weekly or monthly, depending on how the debtor is usually paid) by the employer from a debtor's wages.

The PER is the minimum amount that the debtor must retain from earnings and is calculated by having regard to his resources and needs. Although district judges and courts are given guidance in fixing the protected earnings rate, it is not binding. Practice can vary from court to court, but it is clearly accepted that no debtor should go below subsistence level as defined by social security. Employers are allowed to charge £1 per deduction.

10. Charging order – CPR Part 73

If the debtor owns or has an interest in a house or other buildings or property, a charging order can be an effective method of enforcement. It can be obtained in respect of any beneficial interest which the debtor may have in property. If the debtor is a joint owner, the charging order is made in respect of that interest. It is particularly appropriate if you know that the house is for sale. However, if there are any mortgages or earlier charges on the house, they must be paid first, and there may not be enough money left to pay you. In some cases, the court can order the debtor to sell his house to pay the debt. However, this is very unlikely for a small claim. The procedure to obtain and enforce an order to sell a house is complex, and you would need a solicitor's advice.

The charging order creates an equitable charge or security over the property which may give the creditor a right to be paid out of the proceeds of the sale. It is worth noting that this process must be applied for in the court where judgment was obtained unless the proceedings have been transferred to another court in which case the application must be to that court.

A charging order is usually made over land but can be obtained over property such as shares or funds in court. It is important to note that obtaining the charge itself does not automatically lead immediately to the

Enforcing judgment

money. There has to be a further application to enforce the sale of the property, or a voluntary sale which will provide enough money to satisfy the debt. The effect of the charging order is to give the creditor security for the debt. There has to be some equity in the property to make this process worthwhile. The creditor may then receive all or some of the money that he is owed from the proceeds of the sale.

The law is governed by Part 73 of the CPR and the Charging Orders Act 1979. The procedure is undertaken without notice by application in the prescribed form N379 (land) or N380 (securities). The application must contain a certificate of truth. A fee is payable (currently £50). Upon receipt of the documentation the court will bring the matter before the district judge. If the order is made, it will be drafted by the court as an interim order. The creditor is required to effect service of the order nisi and affidavit on such other of the debtor's creditors as the court shall direct.

At a further hearing the district judge has a discretion either to make the order absolute or final with or without modifications, or to discharge it (CPR 73.8(2)) – he has a duty to consider not only the parties to the application but also other joint owners of the property and creditors as far as they are known. It is for this reason that the application must disclose the names of other creditors who may be affected by the application.

The judge will need to be satisfied that the debtor has an interest in the property in question. Office copy entries of the title to the property are the best evidence. In exercising his discretion to make an order, the judge will take into account the amount of the debt sought to be charged. Although there is no rule about this, the smaller the debt the less likely the order will be made.

A charging order against land or the proceeds of sale of land must be registered appropriately in accordance with the provisions of the Land Registration Acts (where the title to the land is registered) or the Land Charges Act 1925 (where the title to the land is unregistered).

- Office copies of the registered title of a property can be obtained without the permission of the registered proprietor and without knowing the title number. The Land Registry form is 109. The address of HM Land Registry is Lincoln's Inn Fields, London WC2A 3PH; tel 020 7917 8888. The country is divided into a number of District Land Registries and the application will have to be sent to the District Registry for the area in which the home or land is situated. (See Appendix 8 for addresses of District Land Registries.)

11. Insolvency or bankruptcy

Individuals can be made bankrupt, and companies can be made insolvent. The law is governed by the Insolvency Act 1986. It may be a useful threat against debtors who do not pay up. However, this is very much a last resort, and will in most cases result only in a proportion of the debt being recovered. In the context of small claims this may be a negligible amount. It is worth noting that the debt must be £750 or more before the court has jurisdiction to hear a bankruptcy petition issued by a creditor.

12. Costs of enforcing judgment

The fees currently recoverable in enforcing judgment are set out in Appendix 1 – each step in a standard recovery action has its own fees, and these should be added to the debt at the end of the proceedings. Care should be taken to find out the correct fees, as they are frequently amended.

Solicitors often act for clients in debt recovery matters. Only fixed costs and not full legal costs are recoverable in respect of enforcement of judgments. This amounts only to fees paid and prescribed solicitors' charges. Obviously fees are only recoverable if the debtor pays or the debt is recovered by enforcement through the court.

Chapter 14

Alternatives to the county court

For many people, going to court may simply be too daunting or unpredictable, or they may not wish to spend the time and effort necessarily involved in pursuing legal action. Increasingly there are other methods of dealing with complaints which do not involve court proceedings. These have many advantages but there may be drawbacks also, so it is up to the individual to decide which method is most suitable. Alternative Dispute Resolution (ADR) now exists in a number of forms:

- negotiation;
- conciliation;
- mediation;
- arbitration;
- other complaint mechanisms.

Although all these options are available in respect of small claims, the most obvious are arbitration and mediation. A whole host of mechanisms for negotiation and for settling claims has evolved – and a range of complaints procedures for consumers to use against the privatised utilities are being developed by way of consumers' watchdogs and various Ombudsmen. You should seek advice about these to see if they provide a more appropriate forum for dealing with your claim. Unfortunately a full account of all the alternatives falls outside the scope of this book.

Mediation and conciliation

The Civil Procedure Rules 1998 lay great emphasis on seeking to reach a settlement by means other than going to court. They encourage pre-action negotiation and also allow for the district judge to adjourn (or 'stay') proceedings for mediation to take place.

Mediation is a voluntary non-judicial procedure by which the parties in dispute attempt to reach an agreed settlement with the help of an independent and impartial person. Essentially the mediator tries to bring the parties together to reach a settlement. The settlement need not be in accordance with legal rules. The parties can agree to settle on any terms.

Alternatives to the county court

The outcome will be binding only if the parties agree and express their agreement in writing. In many cases this may be a preliminary step before court proceedings or arbitration or a technique for dispute resolution in its own right. Similarly, with conciliation the procedure may differ in detail, but broadly:

- first the consumer takes up the complaint with the trader;
- if satisfaction is not obtained, then contact with a local advice agency is recommended;
- if the consumer remains dissatisfied, he can write to the trade association, which will attempt conciliation.

Under a conciliation scheme, when a consumer complains to a trade association about one of its members, the trade association contacts the trader and tries to bring the two sides to a mutually acceptable compromise. Disputes are often settled at this stage and do not go on to the next, more formal, stage – arbitration. The consumer is not charged for using a trade association conciliation scheme. It is an informal procedure, not bound by any legal framework. Its way of operating, and its effectiveness, depend on the individual trade association. If conciliation fails, the consumer may choose to go to arbitration.

Arbitration

Arbitration is the process by which two parties in dispute agree, usually in advance, to appoint an independent third person to make a binding award on the dispute. It is the main alternative to going to court. It always has to be in accordance with law. The third party should preferably be expert in the field of the dispute, in contrast to a judge who is essentially an expert in matters of law, or a mediator who may be neither but is an expert in mediation.

1. Arbitration clauses in contracts

Many contracts provide, often in small print, that all disputes will be referred to arbitration. Frequently these provisions will appear to rule out going to court. Such terms are not subject to the Unfair Contract Terms Act 1977. Mere signature is usually sufficient to make such clauses binding even if you did not read the document or terms beforehand – sometimes, however, a court may set aside such a contract on grounds of mistake or misrepresentation.

Arbitration is a highly complicated area of law, which has recently been addressed by the Arbitration Act 1996. For several centuries there existed a principle that you could not oust the jurisdiction of the courts entirely by contract. The 1996 Act provides that where there is an arbitration clause the court should not allow court proceedings to continue. Furthermore, once arbitration has begun the parties may be able to exclude the courts if they agree. In reality this may block any right of access to the courts of law, and unless the arbitrator has misconducted himself his award will be final. There still remains in most cases a right of appeal to the courts on a point of law. The courts will normally not grant leave to appeal unless they consider that the determination of the question of law could substantially affect the rights of the parties. The High Court also has jurisdiction, except where excluded by agreement, to determine any question of law arising in the course of a reference with the arbitrator's consent or the consent of all the parties. So there is in effect only a limited power for the courts to intervene.

2. Arbitration Act 1996, ss 89–91

If the sum involved is within the small claims limit, you may ignore the arbitration clause in the contract and go directly to court. This covers all the claims discussed in this book. The provisions apply only where one party is contracting as a 'consumer', as defined by section 12 of the Unfair Contract Terms Act 1977 (see Chapter 1). Many business contracts also fall within this definition.

3. Trade association arbitration schemes

There are many arbitration, mediation and conciliation schemes available to consumers. Many of these schemes are part of trade association codes of practice, drawn up with the support of the Office of Fair Trading (OFT). Appendix 9 contains the latest information on the codes of practice supported by the OFT. They include new and used cars, furniture, double glazing and package holidays. They will offer you cheap conciliation and/or independent arbitration of your claim without going to court. Under the Fair Trading Act 1973 the Director General of Fair Trading was under a duty to encourage traders to draw up codes of practice to safeguard the interests of consumers. In July 1999 the Department of Trade and Industry issued a White Paper entitled 'Modern Markets: Confident Consumers' which contained proposals for significant changes in the codes of practice (the White Paper is available on the internet at http://www.dti.gov.uk/consumer/whitepaper). Most of these codes offer conciliation or arbitration, and often both of these, for consumer complaints. Arbitration, conciliation and mediation now commonly exist outside the OFT-approved schemes.

A large number of schemes are administered by the Chartered Institute of Arbitrators. This is a professional body, set up for the training of arbitrators and for the promotion of arbitration in a wide range of commercial and consumer disputes. It also provides the services of arbitrators in relation to arbitrating small consumer matters.

Alternatives to the county court

(a) A better alternative?

Possible advantages of the schemes:

- they can be tailor-made to the needs of a particular industry;
- you do not have to deal with the courts at all;
- you will probably not have to attend any hearing;
- they are flexible;
- they are made by discussions between the members of the trade themselves, and so do not require legislation;
- you can arbitrate claims which are for more than the county court limit;
- they are often quicker than the courts;
- they are mostly cheap and do not run the risk of large legal bills.

Possible disadvantages of the schemes:

- not all traders are members of their trade association – often the worst traders do not belong;
- the codes are voluntary – there is no way of enforcing them directly. Members who break the rules can be expelled or fined, but this is rare;
- codes of practice are merely guidelines for correct behaviour – they are not legally binding;
- some trade arbitration schemes take longer than the courts;
- the fees payable may be more than the courts.

(b) Court or arbitration? Factors to consider

- An arbitration scheme does not usually involve any appearance at court. The case is normally resolved by documents alone. This means that you do not have to go to a hearing. On the other hand, you will not be able to argue your case in person, or cross-examine any witnesses. If your case is very complicated, it may well be better to go to court to explain it all. Under some of the arbitration schemes on offer, however, the claimant can request a hearing though this is usually at the discretion of the arbitrator.
- Arbitration can be expensive, compared with small claims in the county courts, but it is cheaper than civil litigation, generally.
- Arbitration schemes are an alternative to the county courts. They are voluntary to begin with, but the result is legally binding. The successful party can have the award enforced as a debt by the courts.
- Some claimants may feel that trade schemes are not truly independent.
- Arbitration is not limited to claims for less than £5,000. If your claim is for more than this there may be an advantage in using arbitration rather than risking the costs of a trial in the county

Alternatives to the county court

court. For instance, ABTA now runs a very well known procedure for package holiday claimants; often the claim for a family holiday which went wrong will be above the county court limit.

- According to the Office of Fair Trading, arbitration may have the advantage of procedural flexibility which can allow an informal approach that other means of dispute resolution cannot always match. Although arbitration resolves disputes according to the law, the process by which the law is applied can be less formal than in the courts. Procedures and solutions can be adapted to meet the particular needs of the parties and the nature of the dispute to a degree which is not always possible in litigation.

- Arbitration can provide a low-cost mechanism for a greater number of disputes than can be dealt with by way of the small claims procedure in the county courts. While the trade arbitration schemes do have financial limits they are frequently much higher than those of the small claims schemes and, thus, in some cases, offer the only realistic method of dispute resolution.

- Flexibility can often lead to a speedy resolution of a dispute which can help to ensure that costs are kept to a minimum and that the parties are satisfied with the outcome. Many arbitration agreements lay down clear time limits for each stage of the procedure. Speedy resolution does, however, require the co-operation of the parties with the arbitrator. It has the further advantage for the consumer that there is no once-and-for-all opportunity to address the court and present a case. The claimant can prepare his written case at leisure and revise it until satisfied that it is in the most satisfactory form, while still adhering to the rules of natural justice. Speed and low cost are also encouraged by the fact that appeals from the decisions of arbitrators are possible only on points of law, not of fact.

- The Office of Fair Trading (OFT) offers its support to those codes of practice which meet a series of criteria, regarded as 'best practice'. The guidelines provide that the trade association should have a significant influence on the industry in question, that the code should be mandatory on all members and that the code be drawn up in consultation with consumer organisations. The code should also give genuine benefits to consumers beyond legal requirements. Most of the schemes based on OFT guidelines offer arbitration on a 'documents only' basis.

(c) The Chartered Institute of Arbitrators

Most trade arbitration schemes are organised through the Chartered Institute of Arbitrators, using trained arbitrators to decide the dispute. In order to use an arbitration scheme, the consumer must pay a nominal registration fee. This varies considerably from scheme to scheme. Some schemes are free while others have fees of nearly £90 (in 1999). The main costs of the scheme are borne either by the trader or the trade association.

Alternatives to the county court

Consumers who win are usually refunded their registration fee. If they lose, they are not liable to pay more than another sum equivalent to the original registration fee. Some schemes include low-cost independent testing facilities. The Chartered Institute is discussing a new model arbitration scheme to be introduced in the near future.

The Chartered Institute maintains a panel of arbitrators, made up of those of its members who have passed its examinations and are approved by it. They continue in their normal jobs, accepting appointments as arbitrator as and when invited by the parties in dispute or by an appointing body such as the Institute. The Chartered Institute sees these low-cost schemes for resolving disputes between consumers and traders as a form of public service. Fees payable to arbitrators are on a lower scale than those charged in commercial matters.

(d) How to use the schemes

Details vary considerably from scheme to scheme. You must check each relevant scheme.

1. Check first that the trader you are in dispute with is a member of a trade association. Trade associations will tell you if they offer arbitration and how much it will cost.
2. Apply to the trade association for an arbitration form and a copy of the association's code of conduct. These may also be available from the Chartered Institute of Arbitrators, whose address is The International Arbitration Centre, 24 Angel Gate, City Road, London EC1V 2RS (Tel: 020 7837 4483).
3. Complete the form and send it to the trade association with the arbitration fee, which will be on a sliding scale depending on how much you are claiming. Once you have signed this form, you have lost your right to go to court on the matter with the exception of any rights of appeal.
4. You will be sent a claim form which you must fill in and return within a certain period, usually 28 days. You must send two copies of any evidence supporting your claim, for example witnesses' statements, photographs or receipts. Keep a copy yourself, and be as factual as possible. You are called the claimant; the trader is the respondent.
5. The administrators of the arbitration scheme then ask the trader to respond to your claim within another period, again 28 days. You are then allowed another period, perhaps a fortnight, to respond to the trader's response. The arbitrator can call for independent evidence but usually decides on the basis of the documents alone. Having considered all the evidence before him, he then makes the award, giving his reasons. He can also require the trader to pay back your arbitration fee if you win. The trader is usually given 21 days within which to pay the award and fee. The award is legally binding. If the trader does not pay up, you

Alternatives to the county court

should go to the county court for enforcement, as the award operates as a contractual debt.

(e) Codes of practice – the main schemes approved by the OFT

Information regarding the codes of practice supported by the Office of Fair Trading can be found in Appendix 9. The best known of these are probably the ABTA scheme for package holidays, and that for glass and double glazing (GGF).

(f) The Chartered Institute of Arbitrators

The Institute can be contacted via its web site at www.arbitrators.org It administers a variety of consumer dispute resolution schemes. A scheme is a set procedure under the rules of which parties in dispute agree to have their dispute resolved. A scheme is often more cost effective and expeditious than litigation. The parties in dispute are aware of the maximum cost of the procedure at the beginning and the tailor-made rules allow the parties to know what to expect in the procedure and with regard to the powers of the arbitrator. In the majority of consumer schemes the claimant, who will be a consumer, does not pay any fees, or may have to pay a small registration fee which may be reimbursed if the claimant is successful.

These schemes are available to a large percentage of the UK population. For example, the Association of British Travel Agents has over 2,000 members with more than 7,000 outlets on the high streets, dealing with the holidays of millions of consumers each year. The Royal Institution of Chartered Surveyors has 70,000 members and there are 44,000 intermediaries registered to the Mortgage Code.

The method of dispute resolution most frequently provided by the Institute is arbitration. There is, however, a growing use of mediation and other forms of alternative dispute resolution (ADR).

Occasionally the Institute has been asked to develop schemes that can be used both by consumers and by businesses, these are listed on the web site under the Consumer Dispute Resolution Services section.

For further information on any of the Consumer Dispute Resolution procedures contact Dispute Resolution Services on 020 7421 7444.

For disputes with an ABTA member email: arodriguez@arbitrators.org

For disputes with your mortgage lender or intermediary, BT, the Post Office, or a surveyor email: sprobets@arbitrators.org

Arbitration, administered by the Institute, would normally follow the timetable set out below:

- 1 week: Institute send claim form to the applicant and appoint arbitrator;
- 4 weeks: claim submitted to Institute who will copy it to the respondent;

Alternatives to the county court

3 weeks: defence submitted to Institute with a copy to the claimant;
2 weeks: reply to defence submitted to Institute with a copy to the respondent;
1 week: documents sent to arbitrator;
3 weeks: arbitrator publishes award (final decision).

The rules include provisions for counterclaims, site inspections and hearings as necessary but in most cases the arbitration would be based on documents only and should be complete within 14 weeks. The aim has been to give the arbitrator powers which ensure maximum flexibility of procedure and hence economic resolution of the dispute. Legal representation would not be necessary and the claimant would pay only a modest registration fee, with each party bearing their own costs. The trade body would meet the Institute's and the arbitrator's fees.

(g) Dispute Resolution Services of the Chartered Institute of Arbitrators
Association of Newspapers and Magazine Wholesalers
British Franchise Association
Chartered Institute of Housing
Elf Oil (GB) Ltd
Esso Petroleum Ltd
Hatton Garden Association
Honda Dealers (UK)
Institute of Field Archaeologists
Institute of Management Consultancy
National Association of Commercial Finance Brokers
Screen Printing Association
Total Oil Great Britain Ltd

Construction/Building
Arbitration Scheme for the Flat Roofing Industry
British Wood Preserving and Damp-proofing Association
Building Guarantee Scheme
Door and Shutter Manufacturers Association
Heating and Ventilation Contractors Association
National House Building Council
National Approved Letting Scheme

Financial Services
British Cheque Cashers Association
Consumer Credit Trade Association
Finance and Leasing Association
Mortgage Code Arbitration Scheme

Glass/Plastics
Glass and Glazing Federation
Network VEKA

Incorporation of Plastic Window Fabricators and Installers Ltd
Craftsman Guarantee Corporation

Household
British Association of Removers

E-Commerce
Ford Journey Dispute Resolution Procedure
Web Trader

Insurance
Denplan
AON Home Assistance (formerly AA Home Assistance)

Joint Consumer and Commercial Dispute Resolution Schemes
British Institute of Architectural Technologists
Careers and Education Business Partnership
Coal Mining Subsidence
NHBC
Recruitment and Employment Confederation
Surveyors' and Valuers' Arbitration Scheme
British Marine Federation and Royal Yachting Association Marine Dispute Resolution Scheme

Leaseholder
Brent Council Leaseholder Dispute Resolution Scheme
Tower Hamlet Leaseholder Dispute Resolution Scheme
Waltham Forest Leaseholder Dispute Resolution Scheme

Leisure/Travel
Arbitration Scheme for the Travel Industry
Direct Holidays
Peepul Ltd
Holiday Caravan Pitch Fee
Holiday Caravan Arbitration Scheme
Park Home Pitch Fee
Passenger Shipping Association
Land Rover Adventure Holidays
Saga Holidays
Seychelles Travel
The Mediterranean Experience
Virgin Trains

Miscellaneous Consumer Services
Chartered Institute of Arbitration Consumer Dispute Resolution Scheme
British Blind and Shutter Association
Mail Order Traders Association
National Association of Funeral Directors

Post Office (at the time of writing known as Consignia)

Surveying/Architecture
Royal Institute of Chartered Surveyors

Telecommunications
British Telecom
BT Cellnet
Kingston Communications (Hull)
Manx Telecom
NTL
T-Mobile (formerly OneZone)
Telewest
Orange
Vodafone

Water
Dwr Cymru (Welsh Water)
Northumbrian Water

Appendices

Contents

		page
1.	Some current county court fees	180
2.	Principles of allocation – CPR Part 26.5–26.10 and Practice Direction to Part 26 paragraphs 7 and 8	183
3.	Conduct of hearings on the small claims track – CPR Part 27 and associated Practice Direction	189
4.	Practice Direction – pilot scheme for small claims	193
5.	Appendix A to Practice Direction to Part 71 Orders to obtain information – Record of examination	195
6.	List of relevant civil court forms – CPR Part 4	207
7.	Addresses of county courts of England and Wales	210
8.	HM Land Registry, District Land Registries and Land Charges Department	231
9.	Trade association voluntary codes of practice supported by the OFT	235

Appendix 1

Some current county court fees

These fees are effective from 26 April 1999. They are regularly amended, so before sending payment to the court a check should be made that there has been no change.

Starting your claim

- To issue proceedings where your claim is for money only and the amount is not more than:

£200	£27.00
£300	£38.00
£400	£50.00
£500	£60.00
£1,000	£80.00
£5,000	£115.00
£15,000	£230.00
£50,000	£350.00

- To issue proceedings where your claim exceeds £50,000 .. £500.00
- To issue proceedings for an unlimited amount of money.....£500.00
- To issue proceedings where your claim is for something other than money £120.00

Counterclaim

- To make a counterclaim the above fees apply as if the remedy sought were the subject of separate proceedings.

Appeals

- To file notice of appeal, on small claims track where permission to appeal has been granted by the lower court £50.00
- To file notice of appeal on small claims track where permission to appeal is also sought £100.00

Preparing for trial

- To file an allocation questionnaire £80.00

    Notes
    1. This fee is payable by the claimant except where the case is proceeding on a counterclaim alone, when it is payable by the defendant. The fee must be paid when the allocation questionnaire is filed.
    2. If either:
        - the court decides that an allocation questionnaire is not required; or
        - the Civil Procedure Rules 1998 do not require an allocation questionnaire to be completed,

      the same fee must be paid.

    Warning If you do not pay the allocation fee when required, the court can make an order which may lead to your statement of case (claim or counterclaim) being struck out. This would mean that you could not proceed with your claim (or counterclaim).

    3. If the only claim is to recover money which does not exceed £1,000 this fee does not have to be paid.

Applications

- To apply for judgment to be set aside £50.00
- To apply to vary a judgment or suspend enforcement £25.00
- To make an application on notice £50.00
- To apply for a summons or order for a witness to attend ...£30.00
- To apply by consent or without notice for a judgment or order £25.00

    Note A request for a judgment or order on admission or in default does not constitute an application and no fee is payable.

Enforcing judgments

- To issue a warrant of execution to recover a sum of money:
    - where the sum to be recovered is not more than £125 ....£25.00
    - where the sum to be recovered is more than £125 ....£45.00
- To issue a warrant for recovery of land or property (possession) £80.00

    Note Where a warrant for recovery of land or goods also includes a claim for money, no additional fee is payable.

Some current county court fees

- To issue a warrant of delivery £80.00
- To reissue a warrant of execution at a new address, except a further attempt at enforcement following suspension £20.00

Attachment of earnings

- To issue an application for an attachment of earnings order £50.00

    Note On a consolidated attachment of earnings order, for every £1, or part of a £1, of the money paid into court, a fee of 10p is deducted from the money before it is paid out to you.

Charging orders

- To issue an application for a charging order £50.00

Third party debt orders

- To issue an application for a third party debt order £50.00

Application for judgment debtor to attend court to provide information

- To issue an application £40.00

Copies of documents

- A fee is charged for making photocopies in the court office:
    - for first five photocopies .... £1.00 per sheet
    - for subsequent photocopies .... 25p per sheet
- For copies of documents provided on computer disk or other electronic form .... £3.00 per copy

Registration of county court judgments

- To ask for a certificate of satisfaction when a debt is paid £10.00

Appendix 2

Principles of allocation

CPR 26.5 – Allocation

'(1) The court will allocate a claim to a track–
- (a) when every defendant has filed an allocation questionnaire, or
- (b) when the period for filing the allocation questionnaires has expired, whichever is the sooner, unless it has–
  - (i) stayed the proceedings under rule 26.4; or
  - (ii) dispensed with the need for allocation questionnaires.

(Rules 12.7 and 14.8 provide for the court to allocate a claim to a track where the claimant obtains default judgment on request or judgment on admission for an amount to be decided by the court)

(2) If the court has stayed the proceedings under rule 26.4, it will allocate the claim to a track at the end of the period of the stay.

(3) Before deciding the track to which to allocate the proceedings or deciding whether to give directions for an allocation hearing to be fixed, the court may order a party to provide further information about his case.

(4) The court may hold an allocation hearing if it thinks it is necessary.

(5) If a party fails to file an allocation questionnaire, the court may give any direction it considers appropriate.'

CPR 26.6 – Scope of each track

'(1) The small claims track is the normal track for–
- (a) any claim for personal injuries where–
  - (i) the financial value of the claim is not more than £5,000; and
  - (ii) the financial value of any claim for damages for personal injuries is not more than £1,000;

Principles of allocation

    (b) any claim which includes a claim by a tenant of residential premises against his landlord where–

        (i) the tenant is seeking an order requiring the landlord to carry out repairs or other work to the premises (whether or not the tenant is also seeking some other remedy);

        (ii) the cost of the repairs or other work to the premises is estimated to be not more than £1,000; and

        (iii) the financial value of any other claim for damages is not more than £1,000.

(Rule 2.3 defines "claim for personal injuries" as proceedings in which there is a claim for damages in respect of personal injuries to the claimant or any other person or in respect of a person's death)

    (2) For the purposes of paragraph (1) "damages for personal injuries" means damages claimed as compensation for pain, suffering and loss of amenity and does not include any other damages which are claimed.

    (3) Subject to paragraph (1), the small claims track is the normal track for any claim which has financial value of not more than £5,000.

(Rule 26.7 (4) provides that the court will not allocate to the small claims track certain claims in respect of harassment or unlawful eviction.)

    (4) Subject to paragraph (5), the fast track is the normal track for any claim–

        (a) for which the small claims track is not the normal track; and

        (b) which has a financial value of not more than £15,000.

    (5) The fast track is the normal track for the claims referred to in paragraph (4) only if the court considers that–

        (a) the trial is likely to last for no longer than one day; and

        (b) oral expert evidence at trial will be limited to–

            (i) one expert per party in relation to any expert field; and

            (ii) expert evidence in two expert fields.

    (6) The multi-track is the normal track for any claim for which the small claims track or the fast track is not the normal track.'

CPR 26.7 – General rule for allocation

'(1) In considering whether to allocate a claim to the normal track for that claim under rule 26.6, the court will have regard to the matters mentioned in rule 26.8 (1).

    (2) The court will allocate a claim which has no financial value to the track which it considers most suitable having regard to the matters mentioned in rule 26.8 (1).

Principles of allocation

(3) Any court will not allocate proceedings to a track if the financial value of the claim, assessed by the court under rule 26.8, exceeds the limit for that track unless all the parties consent to the allocation of the claim to that track.

(4) The court will not allocate a claim to the small claims track, if it includes a claim by a tenant of residential premises against his landlord for a remedy in respect of harassment or unlawful eviction.'

CPR 26.8 – Matters relevant to allocation to a track

'(1) When deciding the track for a claim, the matters to which the court shall have regard include–

  (a) the financial value, if any, of the claim;
  (b) the nature of the remedy sought;
  (c) the likely complexity of the facts, law or evidence;
  (d) the number of parties or likely parties;
  (e) the value of any counterclaim or other Part 20 claim and the complexity of any matters relating to it;
  (f) the amount of oral evidence which may be required;
  (g) the importance of the claim to persons who are not parties to the proceedings;
  (h) the views expressed by the parties; and
  (i) the circumstances of the parties.

(2) It is for the court to assess the financial value of a claim, and in doing so it will disregard–

  (a) any amount not in dispute;
  (b) any claim for interest;
  (c) costs; and
  (d) any contributory negligence.

(3) Where–

  (a) two or more claimants have started a claim against the same defendant using the same claim form; and
  (b) each claimant has a claim against the defendant separate from the other claimants,

the court will consider the claim of each claimant separately when it assesses financial value under paragraph (1).'

CPR 26.9 – Notice of allocation

'(1) When it has allocated a claim to a track, the court will serve notice of allocation on every party.

Principles of allocation

(2) When the court serves notice of allocation on a party, it will also serve–

(a) a copy of the allocation questionnaires filed by the other parties; and

(b) a copy of any further information provided by another party about his case (whether by order or not).

(Rule 26.5 provides that the court may, before allocating proceedings, order a party to provide further information about his case)'

CPR 26.10 – Re-allocation

'The court may subsequently re-allocate a claim to a different track.'

Practice Direction to CPR Part 26 – paragraphs 7 and 8

Allocation Principles

'7.1 Rules 26.6, 26.7 and 26.8

(1) Rule 26.6 sets out the scope of each track,
(2) Rule 26.7 states the general rule for allocation, and
(3) Rule 26.8 sets out the matters relevant to allocation to a track.

7.2 Objective of this paragraph
The object of this paragraph is to explain what will be the court's general approach to some of the matters set out in rule 26.8.

7.3 "the financial value of the claim"

(1) Rule 26.8(2) provides that it is for the court to assess the financial value of a claim.

(2) Where the court believes that the amount the claimant is seeking exceeds what he may reasonably be expected to recover it may make an order under rule 26.5(3) directing the claimant to justify the amount.

7.4 "any amount not in dispute"
In deciding, for the purposes of rule 26.8(2), whether an amount is in dispute the court will apply the following general principles:

(1) Any amount for which the defendant does not admit liability is in dispute,

(2) Any sum in respect of an item forming part of the claim for which judgment has been entered (for example a summary judgment) is not in dispute,

(3) Any specific sum claimed as a distinct item and which the defendant admits he is liable to pay is not in dispute,

(4) Any sum offered by the defendant which has been accepted

Principles of allocation

by the claimant in satisfaction of any item which forms a distinct part of the claim is not in dispute.

It follows from these provisions that if, in relation to a claim the value of which is above the small claims track limit of £5,000, the defendant makes, before allocation, an admission that reduces the amount in dispute to a figure below £5,000 (see CPR Part 14), the normal track for the claim will be the small claims track. As to recovery of pre-allocation costs, the claimant can, before allocation, apply for judgment with costs on the amount of the claim that has been admitted (see CPR rule 14.3 but see also paragraph 5.1 (3) of the Costs Directions relating to CPR Part 44 under which the court has a discretion to allow pre-allocation costs

7.5 "the views expressed by the parties"
The court will treat these views as an important factor, but the allocation decision is one for the court, to be taken in the light of all the circumstances, and the court will not be bound by any agreement or common view of the parties.

7.6 "the circumstances of the parties"
See paragraph 8.

7.7 "the value of any counterclaim or other Part 20 claim"
Where the case involves more than one money claim (for example where there is a Part 20 claim or there is more than one claimant each making separate claims) the court will not generally aggregate the claims. Instead it will generally regard the largest of them as determining the financial value of the claims.'

The small claims track – allocation and case management

'8.1 Allocation

  (1) (a) The small claims track is intended to provide a proportionate procedure by which most straightforward claims with a financial value of not more than £5,000 can be decided, without the need for substantial pre-hearing preparation and the formalities of a traditional trial, and without incurring large legal costs. (Rule 26.6 provides for a lower financial value in certain types of case.)

      (b) The procedure laid down in Part 27 for the preparation of the case and the conduct of the hearing are designed to make it possible for a litigant to conduct his own case without legal representation if he wishes.

      (c) Cases generally suitable for the small claims track will include consumer disputes, accident claims, disputes about the ownership of goods and most disputes between a landlord and tenant other than those for possession.

      (d) A case involving a disputed allegation of dishonesty will not usually be suitable for the small claims track.

Principles of allocation

    (2) Rule 26.7(3) and rule 27.14(5)

        (a) These rules allow the parties to consent to the allocation to the small claims track of a claim the value of which is above the limits mentioned in rule 26.6(2) and, in that event, the rules make provision about costs.

        (b) The court will not allocate such a claim to the small claims track, notwithstanding that the parties have consented to the allocation, unless it is satisfied that it is suitable for that track.

        (c) The court will not normally allow more than one day for the hearing of such a claim.

        (d) The court will give case management directions to ensure that the case is dealt with in as short a time as possible. These may include directions of a kind that are not usually given in small claim cases, for example, for Scott Schedules.

8.2 Case management

    (1) Directions for case management of claims allocated to the small claims track will generally be given by the court on allocation.

    (2) Rule 27.4 contains further provisions about directions and the practice direction supplementing Part 27 sets out the standard directions which the court will usually give.'

Appendix 3

Conduct of hearings on the small claims track – CPR Part 27 and associated Practice Direction

Conduct of the hearing – CPR r 27.8

'(1) The court may adopt any method of proceeding at a hearing that it considers to be fair.
(2) Hearings will be informal.
(3) The strict rules of evidence do not apply.
(4) The court need not take evidence on oath.
(5) The court may limit cross-examination.
(6) The court must give reasons for its decision.'

Non-attendance of parties at a final hearing – CPR r 27.9

'(1) If a party who does not attend a final hearing–
  (a) has given the court written notice at least 7 days before the date of the hearing that he will not attend; and
  (b) has, in that notice, requested the court to decide the claim in his absence,
  the court will take into account that party's statement of case and any other documents he has filed when it decides the claim.
(2) If a claimant does not–
  (a) attend the hearing; and
  (b) give the notice referred to in paragraph (1),
  the court may strike out the claim.
(3) If–
  (a) a defendant does not–
    (i) attend the hearing; or
    (ii) give the notice referred to in paragraph (1); and
  (b) the claimant either–
    (i) does attend the hearing; or
    (ii) gives the notice referred to in paragraph (1),

the court may decide the claim on the basis of the evidence of the claimant alone.

(4) If neither party attends or gives the notice referred to in paragraph (1), the court may strike out the claim and any defence and counterclaim.'

Representation at a hearing – paragraph 3 of the Practice Direction

'3.1 In this paragraph:

(1) a lawyer means a barrister, a solicitor or a legal executive employed by a solicitor, and

(2) a lay representative means any other person.

3.2 (1) A party may present his own case at a hearing or a lawyer or lay representative may present it for him.

(2) The Lay Representatives (Right of Audience) Order 1999 provides that a lay representative may not exercise any right of audience:

(a) where his client does not attend the hearing;

(b) at any stage after judgment; or

(c) on any appeal brought against any decision made by the district judge in the proceedings.

(3) However the court, exercising its general discretion to hear anybody, may hear a lay representative even in circumstances excluded by the order.

(4) Any of its officers or employees may represent a corporate party.'

Small claim hearing – paragraph 4 of the Practice Direction

'4.1 (1) The general rule is that a small claim hearing will be in public.

(2) The judge may decide to hold it in private if:

(a) the parties agree, or

(b) a ground mentioned in rule 39.2(3) applies.

(3) A hearing or part of a hearing which takes place other than at the court, for example at the home or business premises of a party, will not be in public.

4.2 A hearing that takes place at the court will generally be in the judge's room but it may take place in a courtroom.

4.3 Rule 27.8 allows the court to adopt any method of proceeding that it considers to be fair and to limit cross-examination. The judge may in particular:

(1) ask questions of any witness himself before allowing any other person to do so,

(2) ask questions of all or any of the witnesses himself before allowing any other person to ask questions of any witnesses,

(3) refuse to allow cross-examination of any witness until all the witnesses have given evidence in chief,

(4) limit cross-examination of a witness to a fixed time or to a particular subject or issue, or both.'

Recording evidence and the giving of reasons – paragraph 5 of the Practice Direction

'5.1 The judge may direct that all or any part of the proceedings will be tape recorded by the court. A party may obtain a transcript of such a recording on payment of the proper transcriber's charges.

5.2 Attention is drawn to section 9 of the Contempt of Court Act 1981 (which deals with the unauthorised use of tape recorders in court) and to the Practice Direction [1981] 1 WLR 1526) which relates to it.

5.3 The judge will make a note of the central points of the oral evidence unless it is tape recorded by the court.

5.4 The judge will make a note of the central reasons for his judgment unless it is given orally and tape recorded by the court.

5.5 (1) The judge may give his reasons as briefly and simply as the nature of the case allows.

(2) He will normally do so orally at the hearing, but he may give them later either in writing or at a hearing fixed for him to do so.

5.6 Where the judge decides the case without a hearing under rule 27.10 or a party who has given notice under rule 27.9(1) does not attend the hearing, the judge will prepare a note of his reasons and the court will send a copy to each party.

5.7 A party is entitled to a copy of any note made by the judge under sub-paragraphs 5.3 or 5.4.

5.9 Nothing in this practice direction affects the duty of a judge at the request of a party to make a note of the matters referred to in section 80 of the County Courts Act 1984.'

Non-attendance of a party at a hearing – paragraph 6 of the Practice Direction

'6.1 Attention is drawn to rule 27.9 (which enables a party to give notice that he will not attend a final hearing and sets out the effect of his giving such notice and of not doing so), and to paragraph 3 above.

6.2 Nothing in these provisions affects the general power of the court to adjourn a hearing, for example where a party who wishes to attend a hearing on the date fixed cannot do so for a good reason.'

Appendix 4

Practice Direction – pilot scheme for small claims

This practice direction supplements CPR Part 27

General

'1.1 This practice direction is made under rule 51.2. It provides for a pilot scheme ('the Small Claims Pilot Scheme') to operate from 8 July 2002 to 7 October 2002. The purpose of the Small Claims Pilot Scheme is to provide for allocation to the small claims track without the need for the court to serve allocation questionnaires or to make an order dispensing with them.

1.2 The Small Claims Pilot Scheme will operate in the county courts at–

(1) Lincoln;
(2) Wandsworth; and
(3) Wigan.

1.3 The Small Claims Pilot Scheme will apply to any claim–

(1) for which the normal track is the small claims track in accordance with rule 26.6; and
(2) where a defence is filed during the period of its operation.

1.4 Any claim subject to automatic transfer under rule 26.2 is not included in the Small Claims Pilot Scheme.'

Application of Part 27

'2.1 Part 27 and the practice direction which supplements it apply to claims operated under the Small Claims Pilot Scheme except where this practice direction provides otherwise.'

Practice Direction – pilot scheme for small claims

Dispensing with the allocation questionnaire

'3.1 When a defendant files a defence to a claim, rules 26.3, 26.4 and 26.5 shall not apply to the proceedings.'

Allocation

'4.1 When a defence has been filed the court will–

  (1) allocate the claim to the small claims track; and
  (2) serve notice of allocation on every party.

4.2 Where there are two or more defendants and at least one of them files a defence, the court will not allocate the claim under paragraph 4.1 until–

  (1) all the defendants have filed a defence; or
  (2) when the period for the filing of the last defence has expired,

  whichever is the sooner.

4.3 When allocating a claim the court will–

  (1) give any necessary further directions including, if it is appropriate, a stay for settlement;
  (2) consider whether expert evidence is necessary and, if so, give permission for it to be given; and
  (3) consider whether any party should be required to give additional information or clarify any matter which is in dispute in the proceedings and, if so, make such order as it thinks just specifying the time within which such information or clarification is to be provided.'

Request for re-allocation

'5.1 Any party may, within 7 days of receiving notice under paragraph 4.1(2), apply to the court to re-allocate the claim to a different track.

5.2 An application under paragraph 5.1 must include the reasons which justify re-allocation.

5.3 Where an application is made under paragraph 5.1 the court will consider whether the allocation should be set aside–

  (1) without a hearing; or
  (2) at a hearing, if the court considers a hearing is appropriate.'

Application for summary judgment

'6.1 If a party has applied to the court for summary judgment the claim will not be allocated until after that application has been determined.'

Appendix 5

Record of examination of judgment debtor pursuant to Part 71 order

Record of examination (Individual)

In the

Claim No.

Appn. No.

Judgment Creditor:

Judgment Debtor:

1 Personal Information

Full Name

Present address

Phone numbers:
- home
- mobile

Your age?

National insurance no.

Are you ☐ married? ☐ single? ☐ separated? ☐ divorced? ☐ living with partner?

- work
- other

Do you intend moving to another address? ☐ Yes ☐ No
If Yes, what will your new address be and when are you moving?

Date

Do you have any dependant children? ☐ Yes ☐ No
If Yes, what are their names and ages?

Name | Age

Do you have other dependants living with you, eg. elderly relatives? ☐ Yes ☐ No
If Yes, what are their names and ages and to what extent are they dependant?

EX140 Record of examination (individual) (03.02)   Printed on behalf of The Court Service

© Crown copyright

Record of examination of judgment debtor

② Employment Status

Are you ☐ employed? ☐ self employed? ☐ unemployed? ☐ retired?
Go to section 3 below / Go to section 4 page 3 / Go to section 5 page 5 / Go to section 6 page 5

③ Employment Details

What is your occupation? _____

What is the name and address of your employer and your employee number? _____
employee number

Where is your place of work if different? _____

What is your gross pay ie. before tax, national insurance deductions? £ _____ per _____

What is your average take home pay including overtime and commission? £ _____ per _____

How often are you paid? ☐ weekly ☐ monthly ☐ other _____

On which day are you paid? _____

Is your pay paid ☐ in cash ☐ by cheque ☐ direct to bank or building society account?

If direct to bank or building society account what is the name and address of the branch and account number? _____
account number _____

Do you have any jobs other than your main job? ☐ Yes ☐ No
If Yes, ask for all the above details in relation to all other jobs and set out information below.

—[Go to Section 7 page 5]—

© Crown copyright

Record of examination of judgment debtor

4. Self Employed

How long have you been self employed?

What work do you do?

What is the name of your business?

Do you have business premises? eg. shop, yard, lockup
☐ Yes
☐ No

If Yes, what is their address?

What is your annual turnover? £

What amount of profit did the business make over the last year? £

How much do you draw from the business? £ per

What were your total drawings in last 12 months? £

Are you a ☐ sole trader? ☐ partner? If a partner,
(a) How many partners are there?

How many employees do you have?

(b) What is your share of the partnership? %

Do you complete Inland Revenue self assessment?
☐ Yes ☐ No

Do you have accounts? ☐ Yes ☐ No

Do you employ an accountant?
☐ Yes
☐ No

If Yes, what is the accountant's name and address?

If you don't have an accountant are accounts audited by a third party?
☐ Yes
☐ No

If Yes, give name and address and say when audit takes place?

Will you allow the creditor to approach your accountant or auditor or Inland Revenue to verify the information you have given in this section?
☐ Yes
☐ No

Date of audit

Are you working on any contracts at the moment?
☐ Yes
☐ No

If Yes, give details below

Name and address of customer	Nature of work	Contract price £	Amount outstanding £	Date payment expected

© Crown copyright

Record of examination of judgment debtor

Is any money still due to you for work already done? ☐ Yes ☐ No   If Yes, give details below

Name and address of customer	Nature of work	Contract price £	Amount outstanding £	Date payment expected

If money (see above) is overdue what steps are you taking to recover it?

Do you have contracts for work in the future? ☐ Yes ☐ No   If Yes, give details below

Name and address of customer	Nature of work	Expected price £

—[Go to Section 7 page 5]—

© Crown copyright

Record of examination of judgment debtor

5 Unemployed

How long have you been unemployed?

What is your trade / training / profession?

What steps are you taking to obtain employment?

Do you have any outstanding job interviews?
☐ Yes
☐ No

If Yes, when?

What state benefits do you receive?
(Housing benefit, if any should be included section 8b on page 7)

Type of benefit	Amount	Frequency of payment	DSS/BA ref.

—[Go to Section 7 below]—

6 Retired

When did you retire?

By whom are your pension(s) paid, how much is paid and when? *(include both state and private pensions)*

Pension from	Amount	Frequency of payment

—[Go to Section 7 below]—

7 Other Income

Is there anyone else in your household who is employed? *(Do not include tenants/lodgers. See section 8 on page 6)*
☐ Yes
☐ No

If Yes, how much do they contribute to the running of the home?
£ _____ per _____

—[Go to Section 8 page 6]—

© Crown copyright

199

Record of examination of judgment debtor

8 Residence

Is your home
- [ ] your own property? Go to 8a below
- [ ] lodgings? Go to 8b page 7
- [ ] rented from a council or housing association? Go to 8b page 7
- [ ] rented unfurnished from a private landlord? Go to 8b page 7
- [ ] rented furnished from a private landlord? Go to 8b page 7
- [ ] other _____ (e.g. mobile home) Go to 8b page 7

8a Your own property

Are you the sole owner?
- [ ] Yes
- [ ] No   If No, name joint owner(s) [_____]

Do you own the
- [ ] freehold?
- [ ] leasehold?

When did you buy the property? [_____]

Is your home a
- [ ] house?
- [ ] bungalow?
- [ ] flat?

Is it
- [ ] detached?
- [ ] semi-detached?
- [ ] terraced?

How many of the following rooms does it have?
- [ ] living rooms?
- [ ] kitchens?
- [ ] bedrooms?
- [ ] bath/shower rooms?

How much Council Tax do you pay per year? £ [____]

What was the purchase price of property? £ [____]   What is its value now? £ [____]

Is your home mortgaged?
- [ ] Yes
- [ ] No

If Yes, what is the name and address of your mortgage lender? [_____]

How much are your mortgage payments per month? £ [____]

What type of mortgage do you have? *eg. repayment, endowment etc.* [_____]

How long is the mortgage for? [____] years

When did you take out the mortgage? [_____]

How much is currently owed under the mortgage? £ [____]

Is some or all of the interest paid by the Benefits Agency?
- [ ] Yes
- [ ] No

If Yes, how much is paid each month? £ [____]

6

© Crown copyright

200

Record of examination of judgment debtor

Do you let any part of your home?	☐ Yes ☐ No	If Yes, give names of the tenants/lodgers and details of rent received	
Do you have any loans secured on your home? (e.g. further mortgage)	☐ Yes ☐ No	If Yes, give the same details as for the first mortgage	

—[Go to Section 9 page 8]—

8b Rented property

Do you rent	☐ on your own? ☐ jointly?	What is the name and address of your landlord?	
How long have you lived at the property?	_____ months _____ years		
Do you share parts of your home with someone unconnected with you?	☐ Yes ☐ No		
Do you pay any additional service charges in connection with the premises?	☐ Yes ☐ No	If Yes, give details	£ _____ per _____
How much rent do you pay?	£ _____ per _____ none ☐	How much Council Tax do you pay a year?	£ _____ none ☐
Do you sub-let any part of your home?	☐ Yes ☐ No	If Yes, give names of tenants/lodgers and details of rent received.	
Do you receive housing benefit?	☐ Yes ☐ No	If Yes, give details	£ _____ per _____ paid to _____

—[Go to Section 9 page 8]—

© Crown copyright

Record of examination of judgment debtor

9 Savings, Investments and other Assets

Do you own any property other than your home? ☐ Yes ☐ No

If Yes, give the address and value and details of any mortgages and lettings

Do you have any bank, building society or other accounts? ☐ Yes ☐ No

If Yes, give details below

Name & Address of Bank Building Society	Account No.	Type of Account	Balance	Sole or joint A/c	Name(s) of joint account holder(s)

Do you have any shares, investments (eg. ISAs, Tessas etc.), insurance/assurance policies or premium bonds? ☐ Yes ☐ No

If Yes, give details below

Are you making contributions to a pension scheme? ☐ Yes ☐ No

If Yes, give details

Do you have any of the following items and how long have you had them?

Item	Age	Is it owned by you, on hire purchase credit sale or rented?	If not owned by you, give: Name of Creditor	Amount still owed	Payments
☐ Microwave					
☐ Hi-fi / surround sound					
☐ Television (No.____)					
☐ Video					
☐ Camcorder					
☐ Computer					
☐ Dishwasher					
☐ Camera					
☐ Dining Room suite					
☐ Caravan					
☐ Mobile telephone					
☐ Musical instruments..					
☐ Other items....					

8

© Crown copyright

Record of examination of judgment debtor

Do you own a motor vehicle?	☐ Yes ☐ No	If Yes, give age, make, model value and registration number. State whether it is owned by you, or subject to a hire purchase/ rental agreement.

Do you have any assets not previously mentioned?	☐ Yes ☐ No	If Yes, give details

Assets	Value

Does anyone owe you money, which is not a business debt or for work you have done?	☐ Yes ☐ No	If Yes, who owes you money and how much do they owe?	Value

10 Other Debts or regular payments and court orders

Expenses
Do not include payments made by other members of your household out of their own income or priority debts listed opposite

Priority Debts
This section is for arrears only. DO NOT include regular expenses listed left

Total arrears outstanding

Expenses	£	per	Priority Debts	£	per	£
Mortgage	£	per	Rent arrears	£	per	£
Rent	£	per	Mortgage arrears	£	per	£
Council tax	£	per	Council tax/Community charge arrears	£	per	£
Gas	£	per	Water charge arrears	£	per	£
Electricity	£	per				
Water charges	£	per	Fuel arrears: Gas	£	per	£
Housekeeping, food, school meals	£	per	Electricity	£	per	£
Travelling expenses	£	per	Other	£	per	£
Children's clothing	£	per				
Maintenance/child support payments	£	per	Maintenance arrears	£	per	£
Student loan repayments	£	per	Income tax	£	per	£
Mail order payments	£	per	VAT	£	per	£
HP repayments	£	per	National Insurance	£	per	£
Digital/satellite TV subscriptions	£	per	Others *(give details below)*	£	per	£
Telephone	£	per		£	per	£
Mobile phone	£	per		£	per	£
Other expenses *(not court orders, priority debts or credit debts listed left)*	£	per		£	per	£
	£	per				
Total Expenses	£	per	Total Priority Debts	£	per	£

© Crown copyright

Record of examination of judgment debtor

Have any court orders been made against you? ☐ Yes ☐ No   If Yes, give details below

Name of court and case number	Date of Judgment or order	Amount of Judgment or order	Instalments payable per month	Name of creditor	Total still owed	Are payments up to date? (yes/no)	If no, how much in arrears?
	TOTALS						

Do you owe money on credit cards or any other loans (not mortage or business)? ☐ Yes ☐ No   If Yes, give details below

Name of Creditor	Total amount owing	Instalments payable per month	Are payments up to date? (yes/no)	If no, how much in arrears?
TOTALS				

Have any bankruptcy proceedings been issued against you? ☐ Yes ☐ No   If Yes, what is the court name and case no.

Is the petition ☐ still pending? ☐ order made but discharged? ☐ order has been made but not discharged? ☐ other outcome? *(give details below)*

Has an Individual Voluntary Arrangement been made? ☐ Yes ☐ No   If Yes, give the date

If No, is there a current proposal for one? ☐ Yes ☐ No

Give details of Trustee/ Insolvency Practitioner/ Administrator, supervisor

10

© Crown copyright

Record of examination of judgment debtor

⑪ Offer of Payment

Can you make an offer of payment?   ☐ Yes   ☐ No

What is your offer of payment?

Pay in full by _____ day of _____

Instalments of £ _____ per _____ to start on _____

Method of payment
☐ postal order   ☐ cheque   ☐ direct debit
☐ standing order   ☐ payment book   ☐ cash

I certify that this is a correct record of the answers I gave to the questions in this document.

Signed _____ Judgment Debtor
Print name _____
Date _____

The judgment debtor refused to sign this record of evidence.

Signed _____ Court Officer
Print name _____
Date _____

The following costs of the examination have been allowed and added to the judgment debt £ _____

© Crown copyright

Record of examination of judgment debtor

12 Documents produced

The judgment debtor produced the following documents:

© Crown copyright

Appendix 6

List of relevant civil court forms – CPR Part 4

There are three tables of forms contained in the Practice Direction to Part 4 of the Civil Procedure Rules 1998 (CPR):

    Table 1 – forms required to be used by CPR which are applicable in both the High Court and county courts.
    Table 2 – High Court forms in use prior to the Civil Procedure Rules coming into effect and which remain in use.
    Table 3 – county court forms in use prior to the Civil Procedure Rules coming into effect and which remain in use.

A number of forms have been introduced and others replaced since the last amendment to Part 4 CPR. These are included in the list below and are treated as CPR forms, although they are not yet included in Table 1 of Part 4.

There are no forms from Table 2 in the following list. All forms listed and followed by '(CCR)' are retained forms in use prior to CPR.

ADMISSION	– forms of	N9A, N9C
	– notice of	N225A–N226
AFFIDAVIT	– general form of	N285 (CCR)
ALLOCATION	– notice of	N154, N155, N157–N160
APPLICATION	– general notice of	N244
	– suspension of warrant, reduction of instalments	N245 (CCR)
ATTACHMENT OF EARNINGS	– application, statement of means	N55 (CCR),
	– reply	N56 (CCR)
	– warrant of committal	N59 (CCR)
	– orders	N58 (CCR), N64–N66 (CCR), N118 (CCR)
	– request for order	N337 (CCR)

List of relevant civil court forms – CPR Part 4

	– request for statement of earnings .... N338 (CCR)
	– application for consolidated order, notice of .... N66A (CCR)
CHARGING ORDER	– interim N86
	– final N87
CLAIM FORM	– general N1
	– claim production centre ... N1 CPC
DEFENCE AND COUNTERCLAIM	– specified amount N9B
	– unspecified amount N9D
DISCONTINUANCE	– notice of.............. N279
EVIDENCE	– summons to give oral..... N20
EXECUTION	– suspension .... N41 (CCR)
	– against goods .... N42 (CCR)
	– interpleader summons .... N88 (CCR)
	– bailiff's report .... N317 (CCR)
	– request for warrant ...... N323 (CCR)
	– notice of issue of warrant.. N326 (CCR)
	– notice of sale or payment.. N330 (CCR), N333 (CCR)
FEE	– notice to pay fee N173
HEARING	– notice of trial date........ N172
INSTALMENT ORDER	– application for reduction of................... N245 (CCR)
INTERPLEADER PROCEEDINGS	– summons .... N88–N89 (CCR)
	– application for relief ..... N361 (CCR)
JUDGMENT	– request for entry N225, N227
LISTING	– questionnaire........... N170
	– notice of date for return... N171
JUDGMENT SUMMONS AND CERTIFICATE	– request for issue .... N342(CCR)
	– of service of judgment summons .... N67 (CCR)
LITIGATION FRIEND	– certificate of suitability.... N235
NOTICE	– allocation to small claims track................. N158–N160
NON-SERVICE	– notice of.............. N216
ORAL EVIDENCE	– summons to give N20
ORDERS TO OBTAIN INFORMATION	– judgment debtor N316
	– officer of debtor company.. N316A
ORDER	– general form N24
	– suspending warrant ...... N41A (CCR)
	– charging N86, N87
PAYMENT	– judgment for........... N30–N32(3), N34

208

List of relevant civil court forms – CPR Part 4

	– variation order (return of goods)	N32(4)
SALE	– notice of under execution	N330 (CCR)
	– notice of time and place	N333 (CCR)
SERVICE	– certificate of	N10
SUSPENSION	– attachment of earnings order	N64 (CCR)
	– of warrant	N245 (CCR), N246 (CCR), N35A (CCR)
THIRD PARTY DEBT ORDER	– interim	N84
	– final	N85
	– application for	N349
	– hardship order (application for)	N37
VARIATION ORDER		N35 (CCR)
WITNESS	– oral evidence, summons to give	N20

Appendix 7

Addresses of county courts of England and Wales

The details listed in this Appendix are likely to change from time to time as courts merge or close down. Telephone and fax numbers are also liable to change. It may therefore be necessary to check the details below in a local directory.

ABERDARE
Crown Buildings
Green Street
Aberdare
Mid Glamorgan
CF44 7DW
Tel: 01685 874779
Fax: 01685 883413

ABERYSTWYTH
Eddlestone House
Queen's Road
Aberystwyth
Dyfed
SY23 2HP
Tel: 01970 636370
Fax: 01970 625985

ACCRINGTON
Bradshawgate House
1 Oak Street
Accrington
Lancashire
BB5 1EQ
Tel: 01254 398173/237490
Fax: 01254 393869

ALDERSHOT & FARNHAM
Copthall House
78/82 Victoria Road
Aldershot
Hampshire
GU11 1SS
Tel: 01252 321639
Fax: 01252 345705

ALTRINCHAM
16 Grafton Street
Altrincham
Cheshire
WA14 1DX
Tel: 0161 928 1444/941 1674
Fax: 0161 926 8374

ASHFORD
Ground Floor
The Court House
Tufton Street
Ashford
Kent
TN23 1QQ
Tel: 01233 632464
Fax: 01233 612786

Addresses of county courts of England and Wales

AYLESBURY
2nd Floor
Heron House
49 Buckingham Street
Aylesbury
Buckinghamshire
HP20 2NQ
Tel: 01296 393498
Fax: 01296 397363

BANBURY
35 Parsons Street
Banbury
Oxfordshire
OX16 8BW
Tel: 01295 265799
Fax: 01295 277025

BARNET
St Mary's Court
Regent's Park Road
London
N3 1BQ
Tel: 020 8343 4272
Fax: 020 8343 1324

BARNSLEY
12 Regent Street
Barnsley
South Yorkshire
S70 2EW
Tel: 01226 203471
Fax: 01226 779126

BARNSTAPLE
The Law Courts
7th Floor
Civic Centre
North Walk
Barnstaple
Devon
EX31 1DY
Tel: 01271 372252
Fax: 01271 322968

BARROW-IN-FURNESS
Government Buildings
Michaelson Road
Barrow-in-Furness
Cumbria
LA14 2EZ
Tel: 01229 820046/827150
Fax: 01229 430039

BASILDON
The Gore
Basildon
Essex
SS14 2BU
Tel: 01268 458000
Fax: 01268 458100

BASINGSTOKE
3rd Floor
Grosvenor House
Basing View
Basingstoke
Hampshire
RG21 4HG
Tel: 01256 318200
Fax: 01256 318225

BATH
Cambridge House
Henry Street
Bath
BA1 1DJ
Tel: 01225 310282
Fax: 01225 480915

BEDFORD
29 Goldington Road
Bedford
MK40 3NN
Tel: 01234 760400
Fax: 01234 327431

BIRKENHEAD
76 Hamilton Street
Birkenhead
Merseyside
CH41 5EN
Tel: 0151 647 8826/8827
Fax: 0151 647 3501

Addresses of county courts of England and Wales

BIRMINGHAM
Civil Justice Centre
33 Bull Street
Birmingham
B4 6DS
Tel: 0121 681 3000
Fax: 0121 681 3001/3002

BISHOP AUCKLAND
Saddler House
Saddler Street
Bishop Auckland
Co Durham
DL14 7HF
Tel: 01388 602423
Fax: 01388 606651

BLACKBURN
64 Victoria Street
Blackburn
Lancashire
BB1 6DJ
Tel: 01254 680640/680654
Fax: 01254 692712

BLACKPOOL
The Law Courts
Chapel Street
Blackpool
Lancashire
FY1 5RJ
Tel: 01253 293178
Fax: 01253 295255

BLACKWOOD
County Court Office
Blackwood Road
Blackwood
Gwent
NP12 2XB
Tel: 01495 223197
Fax: 01495 220289

BODMIN
Cockswell House
Market Street
Bodmin
Cornwall
PL31 2HJ
Tel: 01208 74224
Fax: 01208 77255

BOLTON COMBINED COURT CENTRE
The Law Courts
Blackhorse Street
Bolton
Lancashire
BL1 1SU
Tel: 01204 392881
Fax: 01204 373706

BOSTON
55 Norfolk Street
Boston
Lincolnshire
PE21 6PE
Tel: 01205 366080
Fax: 01205 311692

BOURNEMOUTH COMBINED COURT CENTRE
Deansleigh Road
Bournemouth
Dorset
BH7 7DS
Tel: 01202 502800
Fax: 01202 502801

BOW
96 Romford Road
Stratford
London
E15 4EG
Tel: 020 8536 5200
Fax: 020 8503 1152

BRADFORD COMBINED COURT CENTRE
Exchange Square
Drake Street
Bradford
West Yorkshire
BD1 1JA
Tel: 01274 840274
Fax: 01274 840275

BRECKNOCK
Cambrian Way
Brecon
LD3 7HR
Tel: 01874 622671
Fax: 01874 611607

Addresses of county courts of England and Wales

BRENTFORD
Alexandra Road
High Street
Brentford
Middlesex
TW8 0JJ
Tel: 020 8560 3424
Fax: 020 8568 2401

BRIDGEND
Crown Buildings
Angel Street
Bridgend
Mid Glamorgan
CF31 4AS
Tel: 01656 768881
Fax: 01656 647124

BRIGHTON
William Street
Brighton
East Sussex
BN2 2RF
Tel: 01273 674421
Fax: 01273 602138

BRISTOL
Greyfriars
Lewins Mead
Bristol
BS1 2NR
Tel: 0117 929 4414
Fax: 0117 925 0912

BROMLEY
Court House
College Road
Bromley
Kent
BR1 3PX
Tel: 020 8464 9727
Fax: 020 8313 9624

BURNLEY COMBINED COURT CENTRE
The Law Courts
Hammerton Street
Burnley
Lancashire
BB11 1XD
Tel: 01282 416899
Fax: 01282 414911

BURTON-ON-TRENT
165 Station Street
Burton-on-Trent
Staffordshire
DE14 1BP
Tel: 01283 568241
Fax: 01283 517245

BURY
Tenterden Street
Bury
Lancashire
BL9 0HJ
Tel: 0161 764 1344/9201
Fax: 0161 763 4995

BURY ST EDMUNDS
Triton House
St Andrews Street North
Bury St Edmunds
Suffolk
IP33 1TR
Tel: 01284 753254
Fax: 01284 702687

BUXTON
1–3 Hardwick Street
Buxton
Derbyshire
SK17 6DH
Tel: 01298 23734
Fax: 01298 73281

CAERNARFON
Llanberis Road
Caernarfon
Gwynedd
LL55 2DF
Tel: 01286 678911
Fax: 01286 678695

CAMBRIDGE
Bridge House
Bridge Street
Cambridge
CB2 1UA
Tel: 01223 354416
Fax: 01223 324775

Addresses of county courts of England and Wales

CANTERBURY COMBINED COURT CENTRE
Chaucer Road
Canterbury
Kent
CT1 1ZA
Tel: 01227 819200
Fax: 01227 819329

CARDIFF
2 Park Street
Cardiff
CF10 1ET
Tel: 029 2037 6400
Fax: 029 2037 6469

CARLISLE COMBINED COURT CENTRE
Courts of Justice
Earl Street
Carlisle
Cumbria
CA1 1DJ
Tel: 01228 528182/520619
Fax: 01228 590588

CARMARTHEN
The Old Vicarage
Picton Terrace
Carmarthen
Carmarthenshire
SA31 1BJ
Tel: 01267 236598
Fax: 01267 221844

CENTRAL LONDON CIVIL JUSTICE CENTRE
13–14 Park Crescent
London
W1N 3PD
Tel: 020 7917 5000
Fax: 020 7917 5014/5026

CHELMSFORD
London House
New London Road
Chelmsford
Essex
CM2 0QR
Tel: 01245 264670
Fax: 01245 496216

CHELTENHAM
The Court House
County Court Road
Cheltenham
Gloucestershire
GL50 1HB
Tel: 01242 519983
Fax: 01242 252741

CHESTER
Trident House
Little St John Street
Chester
Cheshire
CH1 1SN
Tel: 01244 404200
Fax: 01244 404300

CHESTERFIELD
St Mary's Gate
Chesterfield
Derbyshire
S41 7TD
Tel: 01246 501200
Fax: 01246 501205

CHICHESTER COMBINED COURT CENTRE
41–42 Southgate
Chichester
West Sussex
PO19 1SX
Tel: 01243 520700
Fax: 01243 533756

CHORLEY
59 St Thomas's Road
Chorley
Lancashire
PR7 1JE
Tel: 01257 262778
Fax: 01257 232843

CLERKENWELL
33 Duncan Terrace
Islington
London
N1 8AN
Tel: 020 7359 7347
Fax: 020 7354 1166

Addresses of county courts of England and Wales

COLCHESTER
Falkland House
25 Southway
Colchester
Essex
CO3 3EG
Tel: 01206 572743
Fax: 01206 369610

CONSETT
Victoria Road
Consett
County Durham
DH8 5AU
Tel: 01207 502854
Fax: 01207 582626

CONWY & COLWYN
36 Princes Drive
Colwyn Bay
Clwyd
LL29 8LA
Tel: 01492 530807
Fax: 01492 533591

COVENTRY COMBINED COURT CENTRE
140 Much Park Street
Coventry
West Midlands
CV1 2SN
Tel: 02476 536166
Fax: 02476 520443

CREWE
The Law Courts
Civic Centre
Crewe
Cheshire
CW1 2DP
Tel: 01270 212255
Fax: 01270 216344

CROYDON COUNTY COURT
The Law Courts
Altyre Road
Croydon
Surrey
CR9 5AB
Tel: 020 8410 4797
Fax: 020 8760 0432

DARLINGTON
4 Coniscliffe Road
Darlington
County Durham
DL3 7RG
Tel: 01325 463224
Fax: 01325 362829

DARTFORD
Home Gardens
Dartford
Kent
DA1 1DX
Tel: 01322 223396
Fax: 01322 270902

DERBY COMBINED COURT CENTRE
Morledge
Derby
Derbyshire
DE1 2XE
Tel: 01332 622600
Fax: 01332 622543

DEWSBURY
County Court House
Eightlands House
Dewsbury
West Yorkshire
WF13 2PE
Tel: 01924 465860/466135
Fax: 01924 456419

DONCASTER
74 Waterdale
Doncaster
South Yorkshire
DN1 3BT
Tel: 01302 323733
Fax: 01302 768090

DUDLEY
Harbour Buildings
Waterfront West
Dudley Road
Brierley Hill
West Midlands
DY5 1LN
Tel: 01384 480799
Fax: 01384 482799

Addresses of county courts of England and Wales

DURHAM
Hallgarth Street
Durham
County Durham
DH1 3RG
Tel: 0191 386 5941
Fax: 0191 386 1328

EASTBOURNE
4 The Avenue
Eastbourne
East Sussex
BN21 3SZ
Tel: 01323 735195
Fax: 01323 638829

EDMONTON
Court House
59 Fore Street
Upper Edmonton
London
N18 2TN
Tel: 020 8807 1666
Fax: 020 8803 0564

EPSOM
The Parade
Epsom
Surrey
KT18 5DN
Tel: 01372 721801
Fax: 01372 726588

EVESHAM
87 High Street
Evesham
Worcestershire
WR11 4EE
Tel: 01386 442287
Fax: 01386 49203

EXETER COMBINED COURT CENTRE
The Castle
Exeter
Devon
EX4 3PS
Tel: 01392 210655
Fax: 01392 433546

GATESHEAD
5th & 6th Floors
Chad House
Tynegate Precinct
Gateshead
NE8 1BR
Tel: 0191 477 2445
Fax: 0191 477 8562

GLOUCESTER COMBINED COURT CENTRE
Kimbrose Way
Gloucester
GL1 2DE
Tel: 01452 529351/2/3
Fax: 01452 386309

GRANTHAM
10 Guildhall Street
Kingswalk
Grantham
Lincolnshire
NG31 6NJ
Tel: 01476 63638
Fax: 01476 570181

GRAVESEND
26 King Street
Gravesend
Kent
DA12 2DU
Tel: 01474 321771
Fax: 01474 534811

GREAT GRIMBSY COMBINED COURT CENTRE
Town Hall Square
Great Grimsby
South Humberside
DN31 1HX
Tel: 01472 311811
Fax: 01472 312039

GUILDFORD
Mary Road
Guildford
Surrey
GU1 4PS
Tel: 01483 595200
Fax: 01483 300031

Addresses of county courts of England and Wales

HALIFAX
Prescott Street
Halifax
West Yorkshire
HX1 2JJ
Tel: 01422 344700
Fax: 01422 360132

HARLOW
Gate House
The High
Harlow
Essex
CM20 1UW
Tel: 01279 443291/2
Fax: 01279 451110

HARROGATE
2 Victoria Avenue
Harrogate
North Yorkshire
HG1 1EL
Tel: 01423 503921/564837
Fax: 01423 528679

HARTLEPOOL
Law Courts
Victoria Road
Hartlepool
TS24 8BS
Tel: 01429 268198
Fax: 01429 862550

HASTINGS
The Law Courts
Bohemia Road
Hastings
East Sussex
TN34 1QX
Tel: 01424 435128
Fax: 01424 421585

HAVERFORDWEST
Penffynnon
Hawthorn Rise
Haverfordwest
Pembrokeshire
SA61 2AZ
Tel: 01437 772060
Fax: 01437 769222

HAYWARDS HEATH
Milton House
Milton Road
Haywards Heath
West Sussex
RH16 1YZ
Tel: 01444 456326/7
Fax: 01444 415282

HEREFORD
1st Floor
Barclays Bank Chambers
1–3 Broad Street
Hereford
HR4 9BA
Tel: 01432 357233
Fax: 01432 352593

HERTFORD
Sovereign House
Hale Road
Hertford
Hertfordshire
SG13 8DY
Tel: 01992 503954
Fax: 01992 501274

HIGH WYCOMBE
The Law Courts
Easton Street
High Wycombe
Buckinghamshire
HP11 1LR
Tel: 01494 436374
Fax: 01494 459430

HITCHIN
Park House
1–2 Old Park Road
Hitchin
Hertfordshire
SG5 1LX
Tel: 01462 434218
Fax: 01462 432161

Addresses of county courts of England and Wales

HORSHAM
The Law Courts
Hurst Road
Horsham
West Sussex
RH12 2EU
Tel: 01403 252474
Fax: 01403 258844

HUDDERSFIELD
County Court House
Queensgate House
Queensgate
Huddersfield
West Yorkshire
HD1 2RR
Tel: 01484 421043/535085
Fax: 01484 426366

HUNTINGDON
Ground Floor
Godwin House
George Street
Huntingdon
Cambridgeshire
PE29 3BD
Tel: 01480 450932
Fax: 01480 435397

ILFORD
Buckingham Road
Ilford
Essex
IG1 1BR
Tel: 020 8478 1132
Fax: 020 8553 2824

IPSWICH
8 Arcade Street
Ipswich
Suffolk
IP1 1EJ
Tel: 01473 214256
Fax: 01473 251797

KEIGHLEY
Yorkshire Bank Chambers
North Street
Keighley
West Yorkshire
BD21 3SH
Tel: 01535 602803
Fax: 01535 610549

KENDAL
Kendal Courthouse
Burneside Road
Kendal
Cumbria
LA9 4NF
Tel: 01539 721218
Fax: 01539 733840

KETTERING
Dryland Street
Kettering
Northamptonshire
NN16 0BE
Tel: 01536 512471
Fax: 01536 416857

KIDDERMINSTER
Comberton Place
Kidderminster
Worcestershire
DY10 1QR
Tel: 01562 822480
Fax: 01562 827809

KING'S LYNN
Chequer House
12 King Street
King's Lynn
Norfolk
PE30 1ES
Tel: 01553 772067
Fax: 01553 769824

KINGSTON-UPON-HULL COMBINED COURT CENTRE
Lowgate
Kingston-upon-Hull
Humberside
HU1 2EZ
Tel: 01482 586161
Fax: 01482 588527

Addresses of county courts of England and Wales

KINGSTON-UPON-THAMES
St James Road
Kingston-upon-Thames
Surrey
KT1 2AD
Tel: 020 8546 8843
Fax: 020 8547 1426

LAMBETH
Court House
Cleaver Street
Kennington Road
London
SE11 4DZ
Tel: 020 7735 4425
Fax: 020 7735 8147

LANCASTER
Mitre House
Church Street
Lancaster
LA1 1UZ
Tel: 01524 68112/3
Fax: 01524 846478

LEEDS COMBINED COURT CENTRE
The Courthouse
1 Oxford Row
Leeds
LS1 3BG
Tel: 0113 283 0040
Fax: 0113 244 8507

LEICESTER
PO Box 3
90 Wellington Street
Leicester
LE1 6ZZ
Tel: 0116 265 3400
Fax: 0116 265 3475

LEIGH
22 Walmesley Road
Leigh
Lancashire
WN7 1YF
Tel: 01942 673639
Fax: 01942 681216

LEWES COUNTY COURT
182 High Street
Lewes
East Sussex
BN7 1YB
Tel: 01273 480400
Fax: 01273 485269

LINCOLN COMBINED COURT CENTRE
360 High Street
Lincoln
LN5 7PS
Tel: 01522 883000
Fax: 01522 883003

LIVERPOOL COMBINED COURT CENTRE
Derby Square
Liverpool
L2 1XA
Tel: 0151 473 7373
Fax: 0151 227 2806

LLANELLI
Magistrates' Court Buildings
Town Hall Square
Llanelli
Carmarthenshire
SA15 3AL
Tel: 01554 757171
Fax: 01554 758079

LLANGEFNI
County Court Buildings
Glanhwfa Road
Llangefni
Gwynedd
LL77 7EN
Tel: 01248 750225
Fax: 01248 750778

LOWESTOFT
'Lyndhurst'
28 Gordon Road
Lowestoft
Suffolk
NR32 1NL
Tel: 01502 586047
Fax: 01502 569319

Addresses of county courts of England and Wales

LUDLOW
9–10 King Street
Ludlow
Shropshire
SY8 1QW
Tel: 01584 872091
Fax: 01584 877606

LUTON
5th Floor
Cresta House
Alma Street
Luton
Bedfordshire
LU1 2PU
Tel: 01582 735671
Fax: 01582 724752

MACCLESFIELD
2nd Floor
Silk House
Park Green
Macclesfield
SK11 7NA
Tel: 01625 422872/432492
Fax: 01625 501262

MAIDSTONE COMBINED COURT CENTRE
The Law Courts
Barker Road
Maidstone
Kent
ME16 8EQ
Tel: 01622 202000
Fax: 01622 202001

MANCHESTER
The Courts of Justice
Crown Square
Manchester
M60 9DJ
Tel: 0161 954 1800
Fax: 0161 954 1661

MANSFIELD
Beech House
58 Commercial Gate
Mansfield
Nottinghamshire
NG18 1EU
Tel: 01623 656406
Fax: 01623 26561

MAYOR'S & CITY OF LONDON
Guildhall Buildings
Basinghall Street
London
EC2V 5AR
Tel: 020 7796 5400
Fax: 020 7796 5424

MEDWAY
Anchorage House
High Street
Chatham
Kent
ME4 4DW
Tel: 01634 810720
Fax: 01634 811332

MELTON MOWBRAY
50–52 Scalford Road
Melton Mowbray
Leicestershire
LE13 1JY
Tel: 01664 568336

MERTHYR TYDFIL COMBINED COURT CENTRE
The Law Courts
Glebeland Place
Merthyr Tydfil
Mid Glamorgan
CF47 8BU
Tel: 01685 358200
Fax: 01685 359727

MIDDLESBROUGH–
See Teesside

Addresses of county courts of England and Wales

MILTON KEYNES
351 Silbury Boulevard
Witon Gate East
Milton Keynes
MK9 2DT
Tel: 01908 668855
Fax: 01908 230063

MOLD
Law Courts
County Civic Centre
Mold
Flintshire
CH7 1AE
Tel: 01352 700313
Fax: 01352 700297

MORPETH & BERWICK
Fountain House
Newmarket
Morpeth
Northumberland
NE61 1LA
Tel: 01670 512221
Fax: 01670 504188

NEATH & PORT TALBOT
Forster Road
Neath
SA11 3BN
Tel: 01639 642267/8
Fax: 01639 633505

NELSON
Phoenix Chambers
9–13 Holme Street
Nelson
Lancashire
BB9 0SU
Tel: 01282 601177
Fax: 01282 619557

NEWARK
The County Court
Crown Building
41 Lombard Street
Newark
Nottingham
NG24 1XB
Tel: 01636 703607

NEWBURY
Kings Road West
Newbury
Berkshire
RG14 5XU
Tel: 01635 40928
Fax: 01635 37704

NEWCASTLE-UPON-TYNE
The Law Courts
Quayside
Newcastle-upon-Tyne
NE1 3LA
Tel: 0191 201 2000
Fax: 0191 201 2001

NEWPORT (GWENT)
3rd Floor
Olympia House
Upper Dock Street
Newport
Gwent
NP20 1PQ
Tel: 01633 227150
Fax: 01633 263820

NEWPORT (I.O.W.)
1 Quay Street
Newport
Isle of Wight
PO30 5YT
Tel: 01983 526821
Fax: 01983 821039

NORTHAMPTON
85–87 Lady's Lane
Northampton
NN1 3HQ
Tel: 01604 470400
Fax: 01604 232398

NORTHAMPTON COUNTY COURT BULK CENTRE
St Katherine's House
21–27 St Katherine's Street
Northampton
NN1 2LH
Tel: 01604 601636
Fax: 01604 601631

221

Addresses of county courts of England and Wales

NORTH SHIELDS
Northumbria House
Norfolk Street
North Shields
NE30 1EX
Tel: 0191 257 5866
Fax: 0191 296 4268

NORTHWICH
25–27 High Street
Northwich
Cheshire
CW9 5DB
Tel: 01606 42554
Fax: 01606 331490

NORWICH COMBINED COURT CENTRE
The Law Courts
Bishopsgate
Norwich
NR3 1UR
Tel: 01603 728200
Fax: 01603 760863

NOTTINGHAM COMBINED COURT CENTRE
60 Canal Street
Nottingham
NG1 7EJ
Tel: 0115 910 3500
Fax: 0115 910 3510

NUNEATON
Heron House
Newdegate Street
Nuneaton
Warwickshire
CV11 4EL
Tel: 02476 386134
Fax: 02476 352769

OLDHAM
New Radcliffe Street
Oldham
Lancashire
OL1 1NL
Tel: 0161 290 4200
Fax: 0161 2904222

OSWESTRY
2nd Floor
Guildhall
Bailey Head
Oswestry
Shropshire
SY11 2EW
Tel: 01691 652127
Fax: 01691 671239

OXFORD COMBINED COURT CENTRE
St Aldates
Oxford
OX1 1TL
Tel: 01865 264200/250800
Fax: 01865 790773

PENRITH
The Court House
Lowther Terrace
Penrith
CA11 7QL
Tel: 01768 62535
Fax: 01768 899700

PENZANCE
Trevear
Alverton
Penzance
Cornwall
TR18 4JH
Tel: 01736 362987
Fax: 01736 330595

PETERBOROUGH COMBINED COURT CENTRE
Crown Buildings
Rivergate
Peterborough
PE1 1EJ
Tel: 01733 349161
Fax: 01733 557348

Addresses of county courts of England and Wales

PLYMOUTH COMBINED COURT CENTRE
The Law Courts
10 Armada Way
Plymouth
Devon
PL1 2ER
Tel: 01752 208284
Fax: 01752 208286

PONTEFRACT
Horsefair Hall
Horsefair
Pontefract
West Yorkshire
WF8 1RJ
Tel: 01977 702357
Fax: 01977 600204

PONTYPOOL
Park Road Riverside
Pontypool
Torfaen
NP4 6NZ
Tel: 01495 762248
Fax: 01495 762467

PONTYPRIDD
Courthouse Street
Pontypridd
CF37 1JR
Tel: 01443 402471
Fax: 01443 480305

POOLE
The Law Courts
Civic Centre
Park Road
Poole
Dorset
BH15 2NS
Tel: 01202 741150
Fax: 01202 747245

PORTSMOUTH COMBINED COURT CENTRE
The Courts of Justice
Winston Churchill Avenue
Portsmouth
PO1 2EB
Tel: 023 9289 3000
Fax: 023 9282 6385

PRESTON COMBINED COURT CENTRE
The Law Courts
Ringway
Preston
Lancashire
PR1 2LL
Tel: 01772 832300
Fax: 01772 832478

RAWTHENSTALL
1 Grange Street
Rawthenstall
Lancashire
BB4 7RT
Tel: 01706 214614
Fax: 01706 219814

READING
160–163 Friar Street
Reading
Berkshire
RG1 1HE
Tel: 0118 9870500
Fax: 0118 9870555

REDDITCH
Court Office
13 Church Road
Redditch
Worcestershire
B97 4AB
Tel: 01527 67822
Fax: 01527 65791

Addresses of county courts of England and Wales

REIGATE
Law Courts
Hatchlands Road
Redhill
Surrey
RH1 6BL
Tel: 01737 763637
Fax: 01737 766917

RHYL
The Courthouse
Clwyd Street
Rhyl
Denbighshire
LL18 3LA
Tel: 01745 330216
Fax: 01745 336726

ROMFORD
2a Oaklands Avenue
Romford
Essex
RM1 4DP
Tel: 01708 750677
Fax: 01708 756653

ROTHERHAM
Portland House
Mansfield Road
Rotherham
South Yorkshire
S60 2BX
Tel: 01709 364786
Fax: 01709 838044

RUGBY
5 Newbold Road
Rugby
Warwickshire
CV21 2RN
Tel: 01788 542543
Fax: 01788 550212

RUNCORN
Halton Lea
Runcorn
Cheshire
WA7 2HA
Tel: 01928 716533
Fax: 01928 701692

ST ALBANS
Victoria House
117 Victoria Street
St Albans
Hertfordshire
AL1 3TJ
Tel: 01727 856925
Fax: 01727 852484

ST HELENS
1st Floor
Rexmore House
Cotham Street
St Helens
Merseyside
WA10 1SE
Tel: 01744 27544
Fax: 01744 20484

SALFORD
Prince William House
Peel Cross Road
(off Eccles New Road)
Salford
M5 2RR
Tel: 0161 745 7511
Fax: 0161 745 7202

SALISBURY COMBINED COURT CENTRE
Alexandra House
St John Street
Salisbury
Wiltshire
SP1 2PN
Tel: 01722 325444
Fax: 01722 412991

SCARBOROUGH
Pavilion House
Valey Bridge Road
Scarborough
North Yorkshire
YO11 2JS
Tel: 01723 366361
Fax: 01723 501992

Addresses of county courts of England and Wales

SCUNTHORPE
Crown Buildings
Comforts Avenue
Scunthorpe
DN15 6PR
Tel: 01724 289111
Fax: 01724 291119

SHEFFIELD COMBINED COURT CENTRE
The Law Courts
50 West Bar
Sheffield
South Yorkshire
S3 8PH
Tel: 0114 281 2400
Fax: 0114 281 2425

SHOREDITCH
19 Leonard Street
London
EC2A 4AL
Tel: 020 7253 0956
Fax: 020 7490 5613

SHREWSBURY
4th Floor
Cambrian Business Centre
Chester Street
Shrewsbury
Shropshire
SY1 1NA
Tel: 01743 289069
Fax: 01743 237954

SKEGNESS
Town Hall Annexe
North Parade
Skegness
Lincs
PE25 1DA
Tel: 01754 762429
Fax: 01754 761165

SKIPTON
The Old Court House
Otley Street
Skipton
North Yorkshire
BD23 1EH
Tel: 01756 793315
Fax: 01756 799989

SLOUGH
The Law Courts
Windsor Road
Slough
Berkshire
SL1 2HE
Tel: 01753 690300
Fax: 01753 575990

SOUTHAMPTON COMBINED COURT CENTRE
The Courts of Justice
London Road
Southampton
Hampshire
SO15 2XQ
Tel: 023 8021 3200
Fax: 023 8021 3222

SOUTHEND
Tylers House
Tylers Avenue
Southend-on-Sea
Essex
SS1 2AW
Tel: 01702 601991
Fax: 01702 603090

SOUTHPORT
Duke's House
34 Hoghton Street
Southport
Merseyside
PR9 0PU
Tel: 01704 531541
Fax: 01704 542487

Addresses of county courts of England and Wales

SOUTH SHIELDS
25–26 Market Place
South Shields
Tyne and Wear
NE33 1AG
Tel: 0191 456 3343
Fax: 0191 427 9503

STAFFORD COMBINED COURT CENTRE
Victoria Square
Stafford
ST16 2QQ
Tel: 01785 610730
Fax: 01785 213250

STAINES
The Law Courts
Knowle Green
Staines
Middlesex
TW18 1XH
Tel: 01784 459175
Fax: 01784 460176

STOCKPORT
5th Floor
Heron House
Wellington Street
Stockport
Cheshire
SK1 3DJ
Tel: 01614 747707
Fax: 01614 763129

STOKE-ON-TRENT COMBINED COURT CENTRE
Bethesda Street
Hanley
Stoke-on-Trent
Staffordshire
ST1 3BP
Tel: 01782 854000
Fax: 01782 854046

STOURBRIDGE
7 Hagley Road
Stourbridge
West Midlands
DY8 1QL
Tel: 01384 394232
Fax: 01384 441736

STRATFORD-UPON-AVON
5 Elm Court
Arden Street
Stratford-upon-Avon
Warwickshire
CV37 6PA
Tel: 01789 293056
Fax: 01789 293056

SUNDERLAND
44 John Street
Sunderland
Tyne and Wear
SR1 1RB
Tel: 0191 568 0750
Fax: 0191 514 3028

SWANSEA
Carvella House
Quay West
Quay Parade
Swansea
SA1 1SP
Tel: 01792 510350
Fax: 01792 473520

SWINDON COMBINED COURT CENTRE
The Law Courts
Islington Street
Swindon
Wiltshire
SN1 2HG
Tel: 01793 690500
Fax: 01793 690502

Addresses of county courts of England and Wales

TAMESIDE
Scotland Street
Ashton-under-Lyne
Lancashire
OL6 6SS
Tel: 0161 339 1711
Fax: 0161 339 1645

TAMWORTH
The Precinct
Lower Gungate
Tamworth
Staffs
B79 7AJ
Tel: 01827 62664
Fax: 01827 65289

TAUNTON COMBINED COURT CENTRE
The Shire Hall
Taunton
Somerset
TA1 4EU
Tel: 01823 335972
Fax: 01823 351337

TEESSIDE COMBINED COURT CENTRE
The Law Courts
Russell Street
Middlesbrough
Cleveland
TS1 2AE
Tel: 01642 340000
Fax: 01642 340002

TELFORD
Telford Square
Malinsgate
Town Centre
Telford
Shropshire
TF3 4JP
Tel: 01952 291045
Fax: 01952 291601

THANET
Capital House
Northdown Road
Cliftonville
Margate
Kent
CT9 1EQ
Tel: 01843 221722/228771
Fax: 01843 224313

TORQUAY & NEWTON ABBOT
Nicholson Road
Torquay
Devon
TQ2 7AZ
Tel: 01803 616791
Fax: 01803 616795

TROWBRIDGE
Ground Floor
Clark's Mill
Stallard Street
Trowbridge
Wiltshire
BA14 8DB
Tel: 01225 752101
Fax: 01225 776638

TRURO COMBINED COURT CENTRE
The Courts of Justice
Edward Street
Truro
Cornwall
TR1 2PB
Tel: 01872 222340
Fax: 01872 222348

TUNBRIDGE WELLS
Merevale House
42–46 London Road
Tunbridge Wells
Kent
TN1 1DP
Tel: 01892 515515
Fax: 01892 513676

Addresses of county courts of England and Wales

UXBRIDGE
501 Uxbridge Road
Hayes
Middlesex
UB4 8HL
Tel: 020 8561 8562
Fax: 020 8561 2020

WAKEFIELD
The Crown House
127 Kirkgate
Wakefield
West Yorkshire
WF1 1JW
Tel: 01924 370268
Fax: 01924 200818

WALSALL
Bridge House
Bridge Street
Walsall
West Midlands
WS1 1JQ
Tel: 01922 432200
Fax: 01922 432212

WANDSWORTH
76–78 Upper Richmond Road
Putney
London
SW15 2SU
Tel: 020 8333 4351
Fax: 020 8877 9854

WARRINGTON COMBINED COURT CENTRE
Leigh Street
Warrington
Cheshire
WA1 1UR
Tel: 01925 256700
Fax: 01925 413335

WARWICK COMBINED COURT CENTRE
Northgate
South Side
Warwick
CV34 4RB
Tel: 01926 492276
Fax: 01926 411855

WATFORD
Cassiobury House
11–19 Station Road
Watford
Hertfordshire
WD1 1EZ
Tel: 01923 249666
Fax: 01923 251317

WELLINGBOROUGH
Lothersdale House
West Villa Road
Wellingborough
Northamptonshire
NN8 4NF
Tel: 01933 226168
Fax: 01933 272977

WELSHPOOL & NEWTOWN
The Mansion House
24 Severn Street
Welshpool
Powys
SY21 7UX
Tel: 01938 552004
Fax: 01938 555395

WEST LONDON
43 Northend Road
West Kensington
London
W14 8SZ
Tel: 020 7602 8444
Fax: 020 7602 1820

WESTON-SUPER-MARE
2nd Floor
Regent House
High Street
Weston-Super-Mare
Avon
BS23 1JF
Tel: 01934 626967
Fax: 01934 643028

Addresses of county courts of England and Wales

WEYMOUTH & DORCHESTER COMBINED COURT CENTRE
Court Centre
2nd Floor
Westwey House
Westwey Road
Weymouth
Dorset
DT4 8TE
Tel: 01305 778684
Fax: 01305 788293

WHITEHAVEN
Old Town Hall
Duke Street
Whitehaven
Cumbria
CA28 7NU
Tel: 01946 67788
Fax: 01946 691219

WIGAN
The Courthouse
Crawford Street
Wigan
Greater Manchester
WN1 1NG
Tel: 01942 246481
Fax: 01942 829164

WILLESDEN
9 Acton Lane
Harlesden
London
NW10 8SB
Tel: 020 8963 8200
Fax: 020 8453 0946

WINCHESTER COMBINED COURT CENTRE
The Law Courts
Winchester
Hampshire
SO23 9EL
Tel: 01962 841212
Fax: 01962 853821

WOLVERHAMPTON COMBINED COURT CENTRE
Pipers Row
Wolverhampton
West Midlands
WV1 3LQ
Tel: 01902 481000
Fax: 01902 481076

WOOLWICH
The Court House
165–167 Powis Street
London
SE18 8JW
Tel: 020 8854 2127
Fax: 020 8316 4842

WORCESTER COMBINED COURT
The Shirehall
Foregate Street
Worcester
WR1 1EQ
Tel: 01905 730800
Fax: 01905 730801

WORKINGTON
Langdale House
Gray Street
Workington
Cumbria
CA14 2PA
Tel: 01900 603967
Fax: 01900 68001

WORKSOP
8 Slack Walk
Worksop
Nottinghamshire
S80 1LN
Tel: 01909 472358
Fax: 01909 530181

Addresses of county courts of England and Wales

WORTHING
The Law Courts
Christchurch Road
Worthing
West Sussex
BN11 1JD
Tel: 01903 206721
Fax: 01903 235559

WREXHAM
2nd Floor
Crown Buildings
31 Chester Street
Wrexham
Clwyd
LL13 8AT
Tel: 01978 351738
Fax: 01978 290677

YEOVIL
20 Hendford
Yeovil
Somerset
BA20 2QD
Tel: 01935 474133
Fax: 01935 410004

YORK
Piccadilly House
55 Piccadilly
York
YO1 9WL
Tel: 01904 629935
Fax: 01904 679963

Appendix 8

HM Land Registry, District Land Registries and Land Charges Department

HM Land Registry

HM Land Registry Headquarters
32 Lincoln's Inn Fields
London
WC2A 3PH
Tel: 020 7917 8888
Fax: 020 7955 0110
DX: 1098 London/Chancery Lane

District Land Registries

Birkenhead District Land Registry
Cheshire, Kensington and Hammersmith:
Rosebrae Court
Woodside Ferry Approach
Birkenhead
CH41 6DU
Tel: 0151 472 6666
Fax: 0151 472 6789
DX: 24270 Birkenhead 4

Merseyside and Staffs:
Old Market House
Hamilton Street
Birkenhead
CH41 5FL
Tel: 0151 473 1110
Fax: 0151 473 0251
DX: 14300 Birkenhead 3

Coventry District Land Registry
Leigh Court
Torrington Avenue
Tile Hill
Coventry
CV4 9XZ
Tel: 02476 860860/860864
Fax: 02476 860021
DX: 18900 Coventry 3

HM Land Registry, District Land Registries, Land Charges Department

Croydon District Land Registry
Sunley House
Bedford Park
Croydon
CR9 3LE
Tel: 020 8781 9103
Fax: 020 87819110
DX: 2699 Croydon 3

District Land Registry for Lancashire
Wrea Brook Court
Lytham Road
Warton
Lancashire
PR4 1TE
Tel: 01772 836700
Fax: 01772 836970
DX: 721560 Lytham St Annes 6

District Land Registry for Wales (Cofrestrfa Tir Ddosbarthol Cymru)
Titles in Wales:
Ty Cwm Tawe
Phoenix Way
Llansamlet
Swansea
SA7 9FQ
Tel: 01792 355000
Fax: 01792 355055
DX: 82800 Swansea 2

Durham (Boldon House) District Land Registry
Boldon House
Wheatlands Way
Pity Me
Durham
DH1 5GJ
Tel: 0191 301 2345
Fax: 0191 301 2300
DX: 60860 Durham 6

Durham (Southfield House) District Land Registry
Southfield House
Southfield Way
Durham
DH1 5TR
Tel: 0191 301 3500
Fax: 0191 301 0020
DX: 60200 Durham 3

Gloucester District Land Registry
Twyver House
Bruton Way
Gloucester
GL1 1DQ
Tel: 01452 511111
Fax: 01452 510050
DX: 7599 Gloucester 3

Harrow District Land Registry
Lyon House
Lyon Road
Harrow
Middlesex
HA1 2EU
Tel: 020 8235 1181
Fax: 020 8862 0176
DX: 4299 Harrow 4

Kingston upon Hull District Land Registry
Earle House
Portland Street
Hull
HU2 8JN
Tel: 01482 223244
Fax: 01482 224278
DX: 26700 Hull 4

Leicester District Land Registry
Westbridge Place
Leicester
LE3 5DR
Tel: 0116 265 4000
Fax: 0116 265 4008
DX: 11900 Leicester 5

HM Land Registry, District Land Registries, Land Charges Department

Lytham District Land Registry
Birkenhead House
East Beach
Lytham St Annes
Lancashire
FY8 5AB
Tel: 01253 849849
Fax: 01253 840001
DX: 14500 Lytham St Annes 3

Nottingham (East) District Land Registry
Robin's Wood Road
Nottingham
NG8 3RQ
Tel: 0115 906 5353
Fax: 0115 936 0036
DX: 716126 Nottingham 26

Nottingham (West) District Land Registry
Chalfont Drive
Nottingham
NG8 3RN
Tel: 0115 935 1166
Fax: 0115 935 0038
DX: 10298 Nottingham 3

Peterborough District Land Registry
Touthill Close
City Road
Peterborough
PE1 1XN
Tel: 01733 288288
Fax: 01733 280022
DX: 12598 Peterborough 4

Plymouth District Land Registry
Plumer House
Tailyour Road
Crownhill
Plymouth
PL6 5HY
Tel: 01752 636000
Fax: 01752 636161
DX: 8299 Plymouth 4

Portsmouth District Land Registry
St Andrew's Court
St Michael's Road
Portsmouth
Hampshire
PO1 2JH
Tel: 023 9276 8888
Fax: 023 9276 8768
DX: 83550 Portsmouth 2

Stevenage District Land Registry
Brickdale House
Swingate
Stevenage
Hertfordshire
SG1 1XG
Tel: 01438 788889
Fax: 01438 785460
DX: 6099 Stevenage 2

Swansea District Land Registry
Ty Bryn Glas
High Street
Swansea
SA1 1PW
Tel: 01792 458877
Fax: 01792 473236
DX: 33700 Swansea 2

Telford District Land Registry
Parkside Court
Hall Park Way
Telford
TF3 4LR
Tel: 01952 290355
Fax: 01952 290356
DX: 28100 Telford 2

Tunbridge Wells District Land Registry
Forest Court
Forest Road
Hawkenbury
Tunbridge Wells
Kent
TN2 5AQ
Tel: 01892 510015
Fax: 01892 510032
DX: 3999 Tunbridge Wells 2

Wales
See **District Land Registry for Wales**

HM Land Registry, District Land Registries, Land Charges Department

Weymouth District Land Registry
Melcombe Court
1 Cumberland Drive
Weymouth
Dorset
DT4 9TT
Tel: 01305 363636
Fax: 01305 363646
DX: 8799 Weymouth 2

York District Land Registry
James House
James Street
York
YO10 3YZ
Tel: 01904 450000
Fax: 01904 450086
DX: 61599 York 2

Scottish Land Registry

Registers of Scotland Executive Agency
The Keeper
Mr Alan Ramage
Keeper of the Registers of Scotland
Registers of Scotland Executive Agency
Meadowbank House
153 London Road
Edinburgh
EH8 7AU
email: alan.ramage@ros.gov.uk

Land Charges

Land Charges Department
Plumer House
Tailyour Road
Crownhill
Plymouth
PL6 5HY
Tel: 01752 636666
Fax: 01752 636699
DX: 8249 Plymouth 3

Appendix 9

Trade association voluntary codes of practice supported by the OFT

At the time of writing the OFT has not published the list of approved consumer codes of practice. The press release that follows was issued in March 2002 and explains the current situation:

'Tougher Approach to Consumer Codes of Practice from OFT

The OFT is forging ahead with its new tougher approach to consumer codes of practice. From the end of last year endorsement of a particular code by the OFT will be contingent on it fulfilling strict criteria, covering such areas as complaint handling and customer service. The fair trading watchdog has identified priority sectors where consumers appear most exposed and where successful codes would be of most benefit.

Areas where consumers are most vulnerable include:

- used cars;
- car repair and servicing;
- credit;
- funerals;
- travel;
- estate agents;
- direct marketing.

The OFT is currently assessing 34 applications received from code sponsors in a number of these sectors. These applications are being assessed under the first part of a two-stage process. The first stage requires code sponsors to submit their proposed codes of practice and to demonstrate how it promises to meet the scheme's challenging new core criteria. To pass the second stage, code sponsors have to prove they are delivering on the promises made in their codes. If they do, the OFT will vigorously promote the code. This will require additional legal powers, which the OFT expect to be included in the Government's forthcoming Enterprise Bill, as well as further resources. The OFT has supported a

Trade association voluntary codes of practice supported by the OFT

number of codes in the past, but that support ended on 31 December 2001 and the new, more rigorous approach ushered in. Paul Burton, head of Self-Regulation Policy at the OFT, said:

> "The applications received have reaffirmed our view that our ambitions and challenging new approach is worth pursuing. If it is successful, the benefits to consumers and to participating businesses will be considerable.'"

The new approach to codes and rigorous enforcement of the law complement each other. Effective codes will help to make it easier for enforcers of legislation to identify the rogue traders and reduce the opportunities for them to operate. Where necessary the OFT and other bodies will confront such traders using all available tools such as the new Stop Now Orders.

The first Stop Now Order was granted by the county court in Manchester to stop the supplying of poorly made kitchens. Essentially, these orders require individuals to stop breaching consumer legislation.

Stop Now Orders apply to: doorstep selling, timeshare, unfair contract terms, consumer credit, distance selling, package travel, holidays and tours, misleading advertising sale of goods, TV broadcasting activities and advertising of medicinal products for humane use.

For more information on consumer codes of practice visit: www.oft.gov.uk; email: enquiries@oft.gov.uk; call 020 7211 8000; or write to OFT, PO Box 366, Hayes UB3 1XB.

Index

page

Access to justice:
   implementation of reports 36, 37
Accident Line 133
Admission of claim:
   claimant, acceptance by 72, 73
   forms 72, 83
   part 74
Advice:
   centres 22, 23, 133
   Citizens Advice Bureaux 23, 24
   county court, from 25
   legal advice centres 23
   money advice or debt counselling centres 28
   obtaining 7, 8, 10, 12
   personal injury claims, concerning 133
   solicitors, from 24, 25, 133
   sources of 22
   trade unions, from 28, 133
   Which? Legal Service 26–28
Allocation of case:
   appropriate track, to 85
   disagreement with 88
   fee 85
   financial value of claim, assessing 87
   personal injury claim 134
   questionnaire 85, 89, 90, 100–104
Alternative Dispute Resolution:
   forms of 168
Appeal:
   arbitration, in 170
   costs 123, 129
   documents to be filed 122
   grounds for 122
   hearing 123
   notice of 121, 122
   permission for 121
   respondent's notice 122, 123
   stay of order on 123

Index

Arbitration:
    appeal 170
    clauses 169
    consumer, dealing as 170
    consumer dispute resolution scheme 175
    statutory provisions 169, 170
    trade association schemes, *see also* Trade association arbitration
        schemes 170–177
Attachment of earnings order:
    amount of 165
    court making 164
    employer, obtaining information from 164
    existing, search for 164
    operation of 163
    request for 163

Bad workmanship:
    complaints 18, 19
Bailiff:
    control of 160
    county court, attached to 34, 160
    functions of 160
    levy procedure 161
    private 34
    service by 62
Bankruptcy:
    enforcement by 166
    party to action, of 45
Barrister:
    representation by 113
Breach of contract:
    actions for 2, 3
Breach of statutory duty 131
Building contractors:
    complaints 19

Charging order 165, 166
Citizens Advice Bureaux 23, 24
Civil proceedings:
    courts in which heard 32
    time limit for bringing 46, 47
Claim form 52–55
    certificate of service 66
    defendant failing to receive 66
    filling in 51, 56
    ignoring, effect of 71
    issue of 50, 51
    money claims online 60, 61
    multiple claims 60
    notice of issue 59, 81, 82
    obtaining 51

238

Index

particulars of claim 56, 57
personal injury claim 134
receiving, action on 67–70
request for information 77
response to 59, 60
service of, *see also* Service 59, 62–66
value 57–60
Claimant:
   meaning 51
Commencement of proceedings:
   claim form 51–57
   court for 49, 50
   value 57–60
Company:
   action against 43, 44
   business names, display of 43, 44
   representation in court 111
   service on 63, 66
Complaining:
   small consumer disputes, in 16–20
   stages in 16
Complaints:
   companies' responses to 20
Conciliation 168, 169
Consumer advice centres 22, 23
Consumer claim:
   advice and information, obtaining 7, 8, 10, 12
   complaining 16–20
   letter before action 30
   resolution of disputes 3
   types of 2
Contract:
   arbitration clauses 169
   breach, action for 39, 40
   exemption clauses 5
   existence of 7
   law of 3
   statutory provisions 3, 4
   stop now orders 4
   terms, certainty of 7
   unfair terms 5, 6
Contribution:
   claiming 95
Costs:
   appeal, of 123, 129
   claiming 125, 126
   definition 125
   enforcement, of 167
   inflating claim to recover 128
   intransigent opponents 128
   judgment, award on 120, 121
   lay representative, fees or charges of 128
   litigant in person, of 128, 129

Index

```
  no costs rule .................................................................. 125
  small personal injury claims, in ............................... 129
  unreasonable conduct, for .......................................... 127
Counterclaim:
  defence to ....................................................................... 95
  filing ................................................................................. 95
  form .................................................................................. 77
  meaning ........................................................................... 77
County court:
  administrative staff ................................................. 33, 34
  advice from ..................................................................... 25
  bailiffs ............................................................................. 34
  changes to procedure ................................................... 32
  commencement of proceedings, for ...................... 49, 50
  district .............................................................................. 33
  hearing, for ..................................................................... 50
  hours of business ........................................................... 49
  judges of .................................................................... 32, 33
  local, finding .................................................................. 49
  office ................................................................................. 32
  official list ....................................................................... 50
  small claims heard in ................................................... 32
  transfer of proceedings ................................................. 79
Court fees ............................................................................. 58
Court structure .................................................................... 32
Courts Charter ............................................................... 37, 38
Credit repair companies ......................................... 154, 155


Damages:
  claiming ........................................................................... 58
  personal injury, for ..................................................... 132
  special ............................................................................ 141
Debt:
  ability of debtor to pay ................................................ 21
  action .................................................................... 2, 39, 40
  letter before action ................................................. 29–31
  recovery, seeking .................................................... 20, 21
  settlement, negotiating ................................................ 21
Debt counselling centres .................................................. 28
Defective products:
  claim ................................................................................. 42
  complaints ................................................................. 16–18
Defendant:
  bankruptcy ....................................................................... 45
  breach of contract action ..................................... 39, 40
  claim form, failing to receive .................................... 66
  companies .................................................................. 43, 44
  corporate bodies ....................................................... 43, 44
  dangerous premises claims .......................................... 42
  death of ........................................................................... 45
  debt claim ................................................................. 39, 40
```

Index

    defective products claims 42
    doubt as to person to sue 46
    employers' liability 41, 42
    meaning 56
    medical negligence claims 41
    motor accidents 41
    negligence, action in 40–42
    nuisance action 42
    partnership 45
    person under disability 44, 45
    special parties 42–46
    trespass action 42
    vexatious litigant 46
Defending claim:
    amendment of defence 94
    change of venue, request for 79
    counterclaim 95
    Defence and Counterclaim form 75, 76
    valid defence, requirement of 75
Directions:
    holiday and wedding claims 107, 108
    landlord and tenant disputes 107
    special 108, 109
    standard 105–107
    types of 90
Discontinuance of action 84, 93
Distance selling:
    regulations 6, 7
Distress:
    meaning 161
    time for levying 161
Documents:
    hearing by 116
    production, request for 77

E–commerce:
    Directive 7
Employers' liability 41, 42, 131
Enforcement of judgment:
    attachment of earnings order 163–165
    charging order 165, 166
    civil enforcement agents 160
    costs of 167
    county court procedure 150
    court order 151
    debt collection 150
    garnishee order 162
    insolvency or bankruptcy 166
    judgment debt 151, 152
    methods of 150, 157
    oral examination process 155–157
    responsibility for 150

Index

```
  rules of court ............................................................................. 151
  third party debt orders ........................................................ 162, 163
  warrant of execution, by, see also Execution ....................... 157–162
Evidence:
  documents and photographs .................................................. 98
  expert ................................................................................ 97, 119
  faulty goods or equipment as ................................................ 98
  hearing, at ................................................................... 95–99, 118
Execution:
  bailiff, by ............................................................................... 160
  exempt goods ........................................................................ 161
  fees ........................................................................................ 160
  goods outside jurisdiction .................................................... 159
  insolvency, effect of ............................................................. 159
  levy procedure ...................................................................... 161
  other creditors, effect on ..................................................... 159
  ownership, disputes as to ..................................................... 158
  procedure .............................................................................. 158
  sale of goods seized ....................................................... 161, 162
  time for levying ................................................................... 161
  warrant, issue of ........................................................... 157, 158
  withdrawal or suspension of process .................................. 159


Fast track:
  allocation to .................................................................... 85, 86
  personal injury claims, disclosure ................................ 143–149


Garnishee order ........................................................................ 162


Hearing:
  attendance ............................................................................ 114
  closing address ...................................................................... 99
  court for ................................................................................. 50
  date, changing ....................................................................... 93
  delay before ........................................................................... 84
  disposal of case without ....................................................... 92
  documents only, by ............................................................. 116
  dress ..................................................................................... 114
  evidence ..................................................................... 95–99, 118
  expert evidence at ............................................................... 119
  judge ..................................................................................... 115
  lawyer, representation by ................................................... 113
  lay representatives ....................................................... 111–113
  length of .............................................................................. 120
  non-attendance by parties .................................................. 119
  non-English speakers, provision for ................................... 117
  oath, parties or witnesses on ............................................. 117
  place of ........................................................................ 115, 116
  preliminary ............................................................... 84, 91, 92
  presentation of case .................................................... 117, 118
  procedure ..................................................................... 115–120
  representation at .......................................................... 110–113
```

site, on 99
Wales, in 116
witnesses 96–98
Holidays:
claims concerning 13

Indemnity:
claiming 95
Insolvency:
enforcement by 166
execution, effect on 159
Insurance:
legal expenses, cover for 25
Interest:
claim, on 59
Interpreters:
hearing, at 117

Judge:
county court 32, 33
hearing, at 115
Judgment:
amount payable by instalments, review of decision 73, 74
announcement of 120
costs and expenses, award of 120
effect of 155
enforcement *see* Enforcement of judgment
entry of 73
form of 124
interest on 120, 121
law, based on 121
order, embodied in 124
payment under 124
registration 152–155
request for 71, 72, 83
setting aside 78, 120
summary, application for 70, 79, 80
Judgment debt:
instalments, payment by 151
payment of 151, 152
register of 67
unpaid, effect of 67
variation of order 152
Judgment in default:
defendant ignoring claim form, on 71
entry of 71, 72
meaning 70
request for 71
time, calculation of 70, 71

Lay representative:
conduct of proceedings 112

243

Index

disqualification 113
fees 113, 128, 129
Practice Direction 111–113
refusal to hear 112
small claims track, representation on 111
Legal action:
   beginning 30
Legal advice centres 23
Legal aid:
   small claims, not available for 125
Legal executive:
   representation by 113
Letter before action 30–31
Litigant:
   claimant 51
   death of 45
   defendant to action *see* Defendant

McKenzie friend 110
Mediation 168, 169
Medical negligence claims 41
Money advice centres 28
Money claims online 60, 61
Motor accidents:
   claims 41
Multi-track:
   allocation to 85, 86

Negligence action:
   dangerous premises 42
   defective products 42
   employers' liability 41, 42
   meaning 40
   medical 41
   motor accidents 41
   personal injury claims 131
   pure economic loss, damages for 40
Nuisance 42

Occupier's liability action 42
Office of Fair Trading reports 2
Oral examination process:
   application 155, 156
   attending 156
   conclusion 157
   hearing 156
   questions to ask 156
   use of 155

Partnership:
   action against 44
   service on 63

Payment of claim:
  instalments, by 72, 73
  means of 75
  posting 75
  receipt of claim form, before 75
Person under disability:
  action against 44, 45
Personal injury claim:
  advice, seeking 133
  allocation of 134
  costs 129
  damages, award of 58, 132, 141
  definition 130
  deliberately inflicted injuries 132
  difficulties with 132, 133
  disclosure of documents 138, 141
  employers' liability 131
  example of 14, 15
  experts, use of 139, 141, 142
  fast track disclosure 143–149
  insurance company, defended by 131
  issue of 134
  letter before action 31
  letter of claim 137, 138, 140, 142, 143
  medical expert, letter of instruction to 149
  mental suffering, for 130
  negligence, in 131
  negotiations and settlement 139
  pre-action protocol 134, 136–142
  road traffic accidents 143, 144
  scope of 130
  small claims procedure, use of 130
  small, financial value 130
  stocktake of issues 139
  valuing 134, 135
  workplace claims 144–148

Request for judgment:
  admission, acceptance of 72, 73
  default 71
  form 83
Right of action 39

Sale of goods:
  consumer sale, meaning 5, 6
  description, not meeting 14
  rejection of goods 14
  stop now orders 4
Service:
  alternative method of 63
  application notice 64, 65

245

Index

   certificate of 66
   company, on 63, 66
   court bailiff, by 62
   meaning 59
   methods of 62
   partnership, on 63
   personal 63
   post, by 62
Services:
   supply of, statutory provisions 6
Setting aside judgment:
   grounds for 78
   non-attendance by party, after 120
Settlement:
   hearing, before 114
   negotiation of 21, 29
   offer 93
Small claim:
   advice, obtaining 7, 8, 10, 12
   amount of 58
   basic principle 1
   burden of proof 11
   claims not being 13
   discontinuance, consideration of 84
   examples of 13–15
   facts, proof of 11
   holidays 13
   housing 9
   interest on 59
   legal arguments 10
   legal case, making 11
   litigants in person 10, 110
   meaning 9
   monetary limit 1
   money claims online 60, 61
   more than £5,000, for 124
   personal injuries 9
   points of law 15
   potential claimants 1
   subject matter of 1
   value 57–60
Small claims court:
   meaning 32
Small claims procedure:
   claims covered by 9, 10
   cost of 12
   forms 36, 48
   initiation of proceedings 48
   post, use of 35
   purpose of 34
   reduction of claim 9
   Rules and Practice Direction 34–36
   simplification 38

```
    sources of rules ............................................................................................... 35
    waiver of rules ............................................................................................... 36
Small claims track:
    allocation to ............................................................................................ 85–89
    cases suitable for ............................................................................ 85, 86, 88
    Civil Procedure Rules not applying to ................................................. 88, 95
    claims for more than £5,000 on .............................................................. 124
    hearing ............................................................................................... 68, 86
    lay representatives ...................................................................... 111–113
    straightforward, cases to be ............................................................ 87, 88
Solicitor:
    advice from ................................................................................ 24, 25, 133
    representation by ................................................................................... 113
Statement of case:
    amendment ............................................................................................. 94
    striking out ............................................................................................. 69
Stop now orders:
    Regulations ............................................................................................... 4
Summary judgment:
    application for ........................................................................... 70, 79, 80

Third party:
    joining, consideration of ......................................................................... 77
Third party debt orders ..................................................................... 162, 163
Trade association arbitration schemes:
    advantages of ........................................................................................ 171
    Chartered Institute of Arbitrators, organised through ........ 172, 173, 175, 176
    codes of practice ................................................................... 170, 174–176
    court, comparison with .................................................................. 171, 172
    operation of .......................................................................................... 173
Trade unions:
    advice from ..................................................................................... 28, 133
    claims, pursuing ..................................................................................... 28
Trading standards departments
    complaints to ........................................................................................... 2
Trespass ............................................................................................... 42

Vexatious litigants ................................................................................. 46

Welsh:
    legal proceedings in ............................................................................. 116
Which? Legal Service ..................................................................... 26–28
Without prejudice:
    use of term ............................................................................................. 29
Witness:
    compelling to attend ............................................................................. 97
    cross–examination ................................................................................. 99
    expenses ................................................................................................. 97
    expert ............................................................................................. 97, 119
    oath, on ................................................................................................ 117
    small claims hearings, in ...................................................................... 96
```